In this book, John B. Davis examines the change and development in Keynes's philosophical thinking, from his earliest work through to *The General Theory*, arguing that Keynes came to believe himself mistaken about a number of early philosophical concepts. The author begins by looking at the unpublished Apostles papers, written under the influence of the philosopher G.E. Moore. These display the tensions in Keynes's early philosophical views, and outline his philosophical concepts of the time, including the concept of intuition. Davis then shows how development and change in Keynes's philosophical thinking affected the development of his later economic thinking, and goes on to demonstrate how Keynes's later philosophy is implicit in the economic argument of *The General Theory*. He argues that Keynes's philosophy had by this time changed radically, that he had adjusted and revised his earlier philosophical thinking, and had abandoned the concept of intuition for the concept of convention. The author sees this as being the central idea in *The General Theory*, and looks at the philosophical nature of this concept of convention in detail.

Keynes's philosophical development

Keynes's philosophical development

John B. Davis

CAMBRIDGE
UNIVERSITY PRESS

CAMBRIDGE UNIVERSITY PRESS
Cambridge, New York, Melbourne, Madrid, Cape Town, Singapore, São Paulo

Cambridge University Press
The Edinburgh Building, Cambridge CB2 8RU, UK

Published in the United States of America by Cambridge University Press, New York

www.cambridge.org
Information on this title: www.cambridge.org/9780521419024

First published 1994
This digitally printed version 2008

A catalogue record for this publication is available from the British Library

Library of Congress Cataloguing in Publication data
Davis, John Bryan.
Keynes's philosophical development/John B. Davis.
    p.   cm.
Includes bibliographical references and index.
ISBN 0 521 41902 6
1. Keynes, John Maynard, 1883–1946 – Views on philosophy.
2. Economics – Philosophy.   I. Title.
HB103.K47D38   1994
330.15′6 – dc20   93–50564 CIP

ISBN 978-0-521-41902-4 hardback
ISBN 978-0-521-06551-1 paperback

For Mary Rickard Davis

Contents

Preface

This work had its origins in my accidental acquaintance in 1987 with a number of J.M. Keynes's early Apostles papers. Because of this, my introduction to Keynes's philosophical thinking was not through the *Treatise on Probability*, but rather the unpublished papers Keynes wrote in the years before he began the *Treatise*. In contrast, most scholars interested in Keynes and philosophy seem to have gone directly to the *Treatise*, Keynes's major philosophical work. This meant that they began with a work that had been polished for publication over many years, and from which Keynes's hesitations and second thoughts had been either eliminated or finessed. The early Apostles papers, on the other hand, show Keynes thinking on his feet, exploring ideas openly, without concern for publication. They immediately suggested a process of early intellectual development in which Keynes entertained his first theoretical commitments and considered their costs. In my view, this more candid Keynes needs to be closer to the center of our image of Keynes and philosophy, both because Keynes himself was accomplished at placing the weak points in an argument in the background when he turned to the public, and because philosophy itself inescapably involves a balancing of competing considerations that leaves every defended position conditional upon questions and principles put aside. To begin with Keynes's Apostles papers, then, made Keynes an essentially dynamic thinker, one constantly adapting his views as he engaged issues, rather than one producing definitive works later to be labeled classics.

A second factor influenced my initial reaction to the topic of Keynes and philosophy. My own training in analytic philosophy in its heyday in the early seventies exposed me to the history of accepted critique of the Cambridge philosophy of the century's first decades. I learned in particular that G.E. Moore's *Principia Ethica*, though it had initiated metaethics and changed the study of ethics, had failed not too long after its publication to be persuasive to most professional philosophers. This told me immediately that Keynes, who was much taken with the *Principia* early on, had begun by attaching himself to an unsuccessful program, and this suggested that it was not unlikely that he would have been driven at some point to struggle with its assumptions. To think otherwise would have meant attributing a conservatism in thinking to Keynes that was clearly not supported by his personal history. But more importantly, to think that Keynes remained committed to the logic of the *Principia* and the reasoning of early Cambridge philosophy would have implied that *The General Theory* ultimately depended in important respects upon controverted philosophical claims. For these reasons, I thought Keynes's philosophical thinking needed to be approached as a philosophical development.

Finally, a third factor contributed to my view of Keynes and philosophy. This was my interest in the history of economic thought of the other two great philosopher-economists, Adam Smith and Karl Marx. Each has for many years been the subject of disputes among scholars over the relative importance of their different works, their different forms of thought, and the different stages in their intellectual careers. Yet while it would be difficult to say consensus has emerged regarding these issues for either individual, no one appears to believe that the early philosophical work of these two thinkers passed relatively unchanged into their later thinking and economics. Strangely enough, however, this seemed to be essentially the conclusion that many of the contributors to the topic of Keynes and philosophy were in danger of adopting. This indicated to me that an argument at least had to be made that Keynes's philosophical thinking underwent important development as his focus shifted to economics. Like Smith and Marx, Keynes was a complex thinker in whom different modes of thought constantly interacted with one another. Thus understanding the development in Keynes's thinking required understanding how philosophy and economics influenced one another in an overall intellectual development.

My friends and colleagues who have generously contributed their time, ideas, and encouragement to my work on Keynes over the last six years deserve to be credited here: Philip Arestis, Brad Bateman, Vicky Chick, Bob Coats, Avi Cohen, Allin Cottrell, Sandy Darity, Amitava Dutt, John Elliott, Zohreh Emami, Donald Gillies, Geoff Harcourt, Suzanne Helburn, Jim Henderson, Hans Jensen, Mike Lawlor, Tony Lawson, Donald Moggridge, Gary Mongiovi, John Pheby, Roy Rotheim, Jochen Runde, Warren Samuels, Claudio Sardoni, Margaret Schabas, and a number of anonymous readers. I am especially grateful to Donald Gillies and Jochen Runde who read the entire work, and did much to help me think about Keynes and philosophy. I am also grateful to Marquette University for financial support for my work on Keynes, Clare Hall for the privilege of visiting and working at Cambridge, King's College at Cambridge for permission to quote from the unpublished Keynes papers, the King's Modern Archivist Jacky Cox for very kind access to the Keynes papers, Milo Keynes for helping with photographs of Keynes, and Patrick McCartan for most professional and considerate assistance as editor at Cambridge University Press. Parts of Chapters 3 and 4 appear in the *Cambridge Journal of Economics* and *History of Political Economy* respectively. Finally I am most indebted to Zohreh Emami for deep support for my work generally. This book is dedicated to the memory of my mother, my first intellectual mentor.

Introduction: Keynes and philosophy

Explanation of John Maynard Keynes's philosophical thinking raises serious problems of interpretation, the neglect of which threatens to jeopardize the entire enterprise of understanding Keynes's overall thought. One important problem derives from the fact that Keynes's philosophical and economic work occurred at different stages of his intellectual career. After an early preoccupation with philosophy, when Keynes thought that his important scholarly contributions were likely to be made in extending the philosophy of logic beyond the foundations only recently laid in Bertrand Russell and Alfred North Whitehead's *Principia Mathematica*, Keynes turned almost exclusively to the study of economics, and seemed to lose interest in or at least the time for serious work in philosophy. Indeed after the beginning of the First World War, by which time his *Treatise on Probability* was largely complete, he never again attempted to produce the sort of systematic and complete discussion of philosophical ideas he had achieved in his undergraduate and postgraduate years at Cambridge. The result is that philosophical ideas are either altogether absent from the language and thought of Keynes's economics, which adopts from the beginning the categories and modes of reasoning of Alfred Marshall, or such philosophical themes as do appear in Keynes's economics are at such a significant remove from the contexts in which they originally functioned at Cambridge that we must wonder whether their meanings and roles have been subtly changed by their re-location to economics.

The first problem confronting interpreters of the role of philosophy in Keynes's thought, then, is to determine how far one ought to go in reading Keynes's early philosophical ideas into his economics. Since Keynes developed his first philosophical ideas almost entirely before he had begun to think seriously about economics, it is by no means clear that those ideas were apt or relevant to his subsequent abstract thinking in economics. Of course were Keynes to have troubled himself over abstract economic questions at an earlier date, or at least by the time he began to think about philosophy, it could then be argued that his early philosophical

1

commitments were in some degree motivated by his theoretical concerns in economics. But this did not occur. Thus, that Keynes made relatively little connection between these two spheres of ideas after he turned to economics rather suggests that he found his early philosophical views marginally valuable for the deeper theoretical issues of economics. This would not necessarily imply that none of Keynes's early philosophical ideas found application to economic topics. Indeed one would hardly expect any philosophically accomplished thinker to engage in wholesale abandonment of hard-won ideas upon turning to another field. Rather the idea is that since Keynes's first thinking in economics shows no systematic imprint of his previous philosophical thinking, what incorporation of his early ideas as did occur was arguably more in the nature of an incidental addition to an economic thinking that possessed its own theoretical integrity.

A second, independent problem involved in interpreting the place of philosophy in Keynes's economics stems from the fact that Keynes's economic thinking itself changed substantially over his career, particularly in his own estimation. Though scholars dispute the manner and degree to which Keynes departed from his early economic thinking in *The General Theory*, none deny that there were important changes in his later theoretical commitments, nor dispute that Keynes himself believed these later commitments involved a change in his thinking at the most profound level. While abstract commitments in economic reasoning are not to be confused with traditional philosophical themes and ideas, there is no doubting the fact that change in one sphere is often linked to change in the other. Thus it would be a mistake to assume uncritically that the changes in Keynes's theoretical commitments in economics were likely to have occurred without concomitant changes or adjustments in his philosophical thinking, and indeed a more natural presumption would be to suppose that the changes in Keynes's economic thinking were actually accompanied by changes in his philosophical thinking. Keynes, it must be remembered, made his theoretical revolution in economics, not in philosophy, and consequently one would want to be especially cautious about advancing an interpretation of Keynes and philosophy that ultimately had it that a philosophical tail wagged the dog that Keynes was most genuinely concerned about.

This second problem and complication, it should be emphasized, can hardly offer a very welcome prospect to interpreters of the place of philosophy in Keynes's economics, given that our first problem noted above already suggests we should be prepared to find that the functioning of philosophical ideas in the non-philosophical context of economic theorizing may well have the effect of transforming the significance and meaning of these ideas relative to their original meaning and significance in pure philosophy. Should, that is, the interpreter of philosophy in Keynes's economics already be working with philosophical materials in somewhat transformed guise, because embedded in the logic of economic discourse, then a change in economic paradigms requires that we further attempt to identify philosophical ideas not easily discernible as *per se* philosophical in a language of economics that has itself evolved since this initial embedding of philosophical ideas. The second problem of interpretation, then, compounds the difficulties associated with the first, leaving us, as it were, to locate Keynes's philosophy in his later economics at two removes from its original elaboration – removed from its original location in pure philosophical discourse and removed from its original point of entry into Keynes's economics. Twice so removed, such philosophical thinking would lack the clear outlines of Keynes's pre-economics philosophy, and also raise unavoidable questions concerning the path of development of Keynes's philosophical thinking.

Because of these problems, it is assumed here that interpreters of Keynes's philosophical thinking as it operates in his economics must employ some theory of reading or strategy of interpretation regarding how ideas which were developed in one discursive framework should be thought to function in another, where the modes of inference, conceptual contents, and goals of analysis of the two frameworks are characteristically different. Such a theory, whether it be consciously or unconsciously, provides the ultimate foundation for claims about the meaning and role of philosophy in Keynes's economics, since clearly all an analysis's substantive claims must themselves ultimately depend upon the system of translation adopted between different conceptual frameworks. In effect, interpreters of Keynes's philosophical thinking must respond to what has been explained in more linguistic terms as a fundamental indeterminacy of translation across languages (Quine, 1969), that is, the inherent difficulty involved in explaining notions from different equally viable, self-contained languages or conceptual frameworks in terms of one another, when there exists no third medium or base language into which each might be adequately translated. From this perspective, a theory of reading or strategy of interpretation regarding Keynes and philosophy, like a theory of translation between any two languages, must be prescriptive in nature in that just as there cannot be definitive translations from one language into another, so there cannot be any last word on how Keynes's early philosophical concepts are to be seen at work in the very different world of his economics. This is not to say, it should be emphasized, that all theories of reading are equally adequate and acceptable, so that all opinions about Keynes and philosophy are equally acceptable. Rather, theories of reading must themselves be evaluated according to how well they appear to address the essential problems of interpretation involved in the literature in question, so that on the view here a theory of reading for Keynes and philosophy must be evaluated according to how well it addresses the two chief problems noted above.[1]

From this perspective, a naive theory of reading of Keynes on philosophy and economics (whether conscious or unconscious) would claim that Keynes's early philosophical ideas slipped unchanged and unaffected into his subsequent economics, and that his economics was thereby more surely constituted upon the foundation of these added notions. On this Panglossian view, not only is the fit between these two different systems of ideas essentially smooth and frictionless, but the incorporation of philosophical concepts in economics is also assumed to be conducive to straightforward progress in economic thought. Such a view, it needs to be emphasized, has as a central assumption the notion that philosophical ideas are relatively uncontroversial and convincing once grasped and appreciated, so that the chief question facing the interpreter is to see whether, and perhaps how, such ideas can be seen to find a foothold in non- philosophical disciplines. Philosophers, however, are more inclined to believe that philosophical ideas are complex and often problematical, in that they typically amount to shorthand for entire philosophical theories which themselves possess strengths and weaknesses relative to competing theories and the philosophical ideas that summarize them. But if philosophical ideas are inherently complex and problematical, then the view that they can easily constitute secure foundations for economic theory is mistaken. Moreover, since their incorporation in non-philosophical disciplines is likely to bring to light different dimensions of these ideas, or, better, theories, clearly their manner of incorporation and the different disciplines themselves into which they are incorporated are likely to affect their very meaning and interpretation. Thus, the incorporation of philosophical ideas in economic theory almost certainly transforms those ideas while at the same time injecting complex philosophical agendas into economics.

In an effort to avoid the errors of a naive reading of Keynes and philosophy, the present work takes as its guiding methodological principle the idea that Keynes's philosophical and economic thinking each had important effects upon one another. A first implication of this is that Keynes's philosophical thinking as it can be found in Keynes's early, pre-economics work was transformed in important respects by the development of his economic thinking, especially as it later developed in *The General Theory*, partly on account of the problematical character of a number of Keynes's early philosophical ideas, and partly on account of Keynes's stronger commitment to the logic of economic explanation to which his philosophical ideas increasingly adjusted. Most importantly, the central philosophical concept of Keynes's early thinking in both his early Apostles papers and his *Treatise on Probability*, namely, the concept of intuition, was altered with the development of Keynes's later economic thinking in such a manner that it ceased to have the meaning and role it possessed in these early works, becoming in *The General Theory* the very different concept of expectation. Significantly, this change in meaning was accompanied by a change in Keynes's view of the very nature of individual judgment in social life, whereby Keynes's early view of judgment as an individual's autonomous insight into the underlying nature of reality was supplanted by one of judgment as socially embedded and contingent.

The second chief implication of the view here that both Keynes's philosophy and economics had important effects upon one another is that the development of Keynes's later economics also depended upon developments in Keynes's philosophical thinking. An important dimension of *The General Theory* is its emphasis upon conventions and the dispositional nature of behavior. Keynes speaks of his independent variables achieving states or levels of activity, and explains this in terms of the role conventions play in structuring the varying degrees to which psychological propensities and attitudes are manifest in different individuals. But this vision of interdependent individual judgment did not achieve prominence in Keynes's thinking until Keynes was struggling with the 1930s drafts of *The General Theory* and shortly after he had published an account of how Frank Ramsey's questions about his early philosophy had caused him doubts about his original concept of intuition. Thus Keynes's later philosophical understanding of individual judgment represented both a response to difficulties he had encountered in attempting to use his old view of intuition in economics, and at the same time a means to the development of his new economic thinking with its emphasis upon the concept of convention. In this way, an overall intellectual development having transformative effects on concepts in both economics and philosophy ended up creating a conceptual structure with reciprocal and mutual influences across its different theoretical domains.

In this work, attention is principally focused upon Keynes's philosophical development. Keynes's economics has long been a subject of intense discussion, and it is reasonable to suppose that most of the difficult problems involved in the interpretation of Keynes's intellectual development in economics have been at least investigated if not resolved. However, because interest in the role Keynes's philosophical thinking plays in his economics is comparatively recent, the methodological issues involved in this sphere have yet to be carefully worked out. It is a concern with these issues that has given this work its particular focus and orientation. Thus, in order to emphasize the transformative effects the development of Keynes's economic thinking had upon his philosophical ideas – the theme underrepresented in the existing literature – this work takes as its chief task the explanation of Keynes's new philosophical ideas in their appearance in the non-philosophical discourse of his later economics. The view here is not that Keynes's involvement with economic reasoning caused him to re-select among preferred, traditional philosophical concepts and theories, and that this arose from an intention to alter his traditional philosophical affiliations. Rather the view here is more radical in supposing that Keynes's changing concerns and increasing allegiance to economic thinking *per se* disrupted the integrity of philosophical reasoning itself for Keynes, so that his philosophical concepts, as they operated in transformed guise in the language of his economics, came to possess different roles from those which were customary for philosophical concepts in pure philosophy.

On this view, traditional philosophical questions appropriate to the early philosophical Keynes, such as whether judgment is objective or subjective, or what rational belief might amount to, can be posed for the later Keynes only by interpreters intent upon disregarding the philosophical commitments implicit in Keynes's later economic reasoning. There, as will be argued at length below, Keynes operated with a view of individual judgment more properly characterized as intersubjective, and though it can indeed be argued by philosophers that elements of both objectivity and subjectivity inhabit such a notion, or that it is possible to regard individual judgments so understood as being consistent with rational belief, the view here is that a preoccupation with sorting out the balance between these pre-eminently traditional philosophical notions - paradigmatically the project of philosophers – chiefly serves to obscure the original philosophical issues at work in Keynes's later economics from the point of view of economics. That is, on the view here, a proper philosophy of economics arises more out of issues and questions internal to the abstract concerns of economics, and less out of effort to apply standard philosophical positions to economics. This distinctive view of the philosophy of economics is relatively recent, emerging – as did a similarly distinctive view of the philosophy of social science – with the discipline's recent maturity, and signaled most recently by methodologists' realization that the philosophy of economics is more than the philosophy of science applied to economics.

The concrete task pursued here, then, is to distill the philosophical views from Keynes's later economics, where the traditional philosophical apparatus of concepts and principles of Keynes's early work is an imperfect guide for the analysis, where non-philosophical reasoning is the chief source of material for analysis, and where the result must be set forth as philosophy! Unavoidably this requires an effort that is at times speculative in nature, so that it will not be surprising should many interpreters of Keynes and philosophy, who prefer to take the ready-made, well-formed philosophical materials of Keynes's early years as their chief resource, dismiss the approach here. They do so at the risk of ignoring the two principal problems involved in the interpretation of Keynes and philosophy described above, and, it should be emphasized, of making *The General Theory* the logical descendant of the *Treatise on Probability* by fitting the arguments of *The General Theory* into the pre-given conceptual layout of the *Treatise*. Indeed put this way, the matter is analogous to the problems of interpretation or reading associated with explaining Keynes's development from the *Treatise on Money* to *The General Theory*, where different interpretations emerge according to whether one sees the latter work as essentially the final step in a generally continuous development of Keynes's ideas on monetary theory, or rather sees *The General Theory* as a significant departure from earlier ideas and a step forward in a discontinuous development of thinking.

Ironically, though the principal interest of the recent literature on the subject of Keynes and philosophy is to explain the contribution of Keynes's philosophical thinking to his later economics, most scholars have begun their research with the *Treatise on Probability*, as if Keynes's chronological intellectual development betokened a parallel conceptual or logical development, that is, as if later ideas depend upon earlier ones just as they follow earlier ones. Rather, then, than make *The General Theory* the starting point of their philosophical investigation, that book becomes the investigation's last step in a search to determine how the earlier book's themes came to be represented in the latter. This all implies, however, that the ideas of *The General Theory* tend to end up being evaluated according to conceptual requirements of the *Treatise*, a work largely completed before Keynes even began serious study of economics, and even longer before he began to revise his economic thinking. Ruled out is the notion that the *Treatise* might itself be evaluated by the standard of *The General Theory*, or, in the extreme, be regarded as an immature, fundamentally flawed conceptual structure that Keynes later found to be of little use as a whole upon turning to the problems of the social world. Of course, to represent the issue of the relationship between the *Treatise* and *The General Theory* dichotomously as a choice between only two approaches is to over-simplify the matter. The work here presses the idea that it is necessary to explore how the *Treatise* measures up to *The General Theory*, in part because scholars have so much favored the *Treatise*, and in part to find what is philosophically distinctive in *The General Theory*.

Practically speaking, then, what does this alternative emphasis imply? To argue that *The General Theory* should in important respects be taken as the measure of the *Treatise* is not to see the former as the teleological end-point in a march of progress toward some right economic philosophy. It is rather to show that Keynes's early philosophical thinking bore various contradictions and deficiencies, some of which he attempted to resolve while also working upon a number of relatively independent problems in economic theory. The philosophy of *The General Theory*, from this perspective, represents something of a temporary equilibrium in this process – one not necessarily free of its own difficulties, but nonetheless a comparatively settled state of affairs for a mature Keynes given the degree of accomplishment in the book. As an active thinker who was famously willing to change his mind, Keynes thus continually reconstituted the structure of philosophical ideas that backed up his practical- theoretical affairs outside of philosophy, ever in search for what would assist him in accomplishing his goals. To tell the story of this process one must necessarily involve oneself in producing a rational reconstruction of what may be termed Keynes's philosophical development. Keynes, unfortunately, was too absorbed in economics and policy to be as aware himself of the path of development of his philosophical commitments as he was of his economic ones.

In this respect, Keynes was little different from the other two great philosopher-economists, Adam Smith and Karl Marx. All three developed philosophical views first, and then turned almost exclusively to economics and political economy. All three gave comparatively little indication of their later philosophical views, and especially how these corresponded to their earlier ones. And all three, arguably, were less concerned with the philosophical implications of their later work than with its more immediate significance. Scholars, of course, have for some time disputed the relationships between the Smith of the *Moral Sentiments* and the Smith of the *Wealth of Nations*, and between the Marx of the *1844 Economic and Philosophical Manuscripts* and the Marx of *Capital*. But few have been persuaded to think that the earlier works of these authors contained the essence of the latter works. Indeed few have been persuaded to think that the conceptual structure of those earlier works carried over unaffected into the frameworks of the latter works. This work takes it that the same views will ultimately be established in regard to Keynes's intellectual career, and that the *Treatise* will be then seen as a work distinct in purpose and much removed from the goals and ambitions of *The General Theory*.

1   Keynes's early intuitionism

Historians of philosophy generally agree that the initially influential early Cambridge philosophy of Moore, Russell, and the young Ludwig Wittgenstein had by the 1930s been subjected to a decisive and quite far-reaching criticism since accepted by most philosophers (e.g., Passmore, 1966; Weitz, 1967). Indeed to recount this critique in detail would require a review of much of the development of modern Anglo-American philosophy, so pervasive and varied have been the changes and adjustments in contemporary philosophical thinking upon the early Cambridge project. This chapter only attempts to explain the critical reception of one important strand of this philosophy that Keynes inherited in his undergraduate years at Cambridge. Its objective is to elucidate a number of Keynes's early philosophical commitments, both because they have not received careful attention from previous scholars, and because understanding these commitments is central to the task of understanding Keynes's departure from them in his later philosophical thought.

In one respect, the discussion here builds upon recent efforts originating in Cambridge to explain Keynes's philosophy of probability in his *Treatise on Probability* (Lawson, 1985, 1988; Carabelli, 1988; Carvalho, 1988; O'Donnell, 1989; Runde, 1990, 1991). It holds to the view that Keynes developed and remained committed throughout his lifetime to a view of logic that premised non-deductive, non-conclusive, rational argument, and that a number of key themes from the *Treatise* concerning such matters as the different classes of probability judgments, inductive inference, and weight play a role in Keynes's later thought. Where the argument here begins to differ from this line of interpretation is in its attention to an issue that lies outside of the principal ambit of the *Treatise*, namely, the philosophical meaning of probability. As emphasized by other scholars (Bateman, 1987, 1990; Gillies, 1988; Davis, 1991; Gillies and Ietto-Gillies, 1991; Cottrell, 1993), Keynes had doubts about this aspect of the *Treatise* almost immediately after its publication. The chapter here tries to get at the source of Keynes's difficulties in this regard by detailing the nature and early history of Keynes's attachment to the single philosophical concept that underlies his own view of the philosophical meaning of probability, the concept of intuition.

The concept of intuition was central to the theory of judgment advanced by Moore and Russell in their attack upon the idealist neo-Hegelian philosophy dominant at Cambridge at the beginning of the twentieth century. Later Anglo-American philosophers by and large came to share this rejection of idealism, but they also found the concept of intuition advanced by these first Analytic philosophers problematic. Indeed Moore, Russell, and Wittgenstein themselves each in different ways departed from their early views in this regard, and thus participated in the subsequent evolution of Analytic philosophy in Britain (cf. Urmson, 1956; Hylton, 1992). My argument is that Keynes also changed his thinking about the concept of intuition, and that this was the chief force involved in the development of his own later philosophical views. In Chapter 3, I explain how the obscurity and intractability of that notion led Keynes to adopt new foundations for his later theory of judgment. But to understand Keynes's later views, it is important to first explicate Keynes's original conception of intuition.

Keynes's early views, it is now clear (Harrod, 1951; Skidelsky, 1983, 1992; Moggridge, 1992), were in large part formed under the influence of Moore, especially in connection with Keynes's study of the *Principia Ethica*. Indeed not only did Keynes write a number of unpublished papers on Moore's ideas in which he worked out the elements of his own early philosophy, but the key doctrine of the *Treatise* concerning the indefinability of the probability relation is a direct extension of Moore's view that the concept of good is indefinable and knowable only through intuition. Given philosophers' subsequent critique and rejection of Moore's views on intuition and indefinability, the present discussion begins with the analysis of Moore's thinking on the subject in the *Principia*. This serves as an introduction to Keynes's own like views, especially in light of the fact that, having had Moore's arguments to rely upon, Keynes naturally needed to devote little time to discussing foundational doctrines.

Moore on indefinability and intuition

In Moore's view, his principal discovery was that "that object or idea" which the word "good" is used to stand for is indefinable. Definitions, he believed, "describe the real nature of the object or notion denoted by a word" (Moore, 1903a, p. 7), and do not merely capture the ways words are used in everyday communication. Definitions, he went on to explain, "are only possible when the object or notion in question is something complex" (*Ibid.*). In giving a definition of something one enumerates all the properties and qualities that are true of that thing, so that upon achieving this enumeration that item is reduced to its simplest terms, each of which is no longer definable, but which in each case one merely thinks of or perceives. Indeed, "to anyone who cannot think of or perceive them, you can never, by any definition, make their nature known" (*Ibid.*).

'Good' then, if we mean by it that quality which we assert to belong to a thing, when we say that the thing is good, is incapable of any definition, in the most important sense of that word. The most important sense of 'definition' is that in which a definition states what are the parts which invariably compose a certain whole; and in this sense 'good' has no definition, because it is simple and has no parts. It is one of those innumerable objects of thought which are themselves incapable of definition, because they are the ultimate terms by reference to which whatever is capable of definition must be defined. (pp. 9–10)

Moore offered "yellow" as a further example of a simple notion which was indefinable. Though one can say that yellow things produce a certain vibration in light, just as one can say that good things produce pleasure, it remains the case that "yellow" does not mean productive of a certain vibration in light, just as "good" does not mean productive of pleasure. In the final analysis, then, "good" and "yellow" are indefinable, because they are the fundamentally simple elements of our reality.

Moore believed there were only two conceivable objections to characterizing "good" as indefinable. In the first place, it might be thought that "good" does not denote a single, simple quality, but rather denotes "a complex, a given whole, about the correct analysis of which there may be disagreement" (p. 15). On this view, "good" is to be defined and explained in terms of something else, say, pleasure or happiness, and one's understanding of what is good then becomes a matter of one's understanding of pleasure or happiness. In a response that has since come to be known by philosophers as the open-question argument, Moore argued that "whatever definition be offered, it may be always asked, with significance, of the complex so defined, whether it is itself good" (*Ibid.*). Thus, were good defined by a hedonist as whatever produces pleasure, then because on the hedonist's own admission such an assertion is not tautological, there must be two distinct notions involved, good and pleasure, and it cannot be the case that good can be reduced to or defined in terms of pleasure. That is, because it is always informative to say that pleasure is good, there must be two distinct, simple qualities present, each of which is itself indefinable.

Moore thought that this reasoning could be applied to any "complex" definition of "good" in that it always makes sense to ask whether what a proposed definition of "good" defines as "good" is indeed "good." He termed the failure to appreciate this the naturalistic fallacy, and argued at length in the *Principia* against a variety of moral philosophers he believed had committed this simple error in reasoning. Indeed, though Moore termed the error the naturalistic fallacy (because in his view its most common offenders had thought "good" could be defined in terms of some natural property of the world such as pleasure or happiness), he clearly believed that the fallacy was equally committed by those moral philosophers who sought to define "good" in metaphysical or theological terms. Quite simply, then, because "good" was indefinable, it could not be explained in terms of anything else.

Yet it might still be the case, Moore allowed, that though "good" is a distinct term in our language, there is the possibility that it really "means nothing at all, and there is no such subject as Ethics" (p. 15). Against this second conceivable alternative to his view that "good" is indefinable, Moore appealed to introspection to demonstrate that "good" did indeed denote some "unique object."

But whoever will attentively consider with himself what is actually before his mind when he asks the question 'Is pleasure (or whatever it may be) after all good?' can easily satisfy himself that he is not merely wondering whether pleasure is pleasant. And if he will try this experiment with each suggested definition in succession, he may become expert enough to recognise that in every case he has before his mind a unique object, with regard to the connection of which with any other object, a distinct question may be asked. (p. 16)

Ethics thus concerns a genuinely independent subject of investigation, because introspection reveals that any given characterization of "good" always presupposes there to be some unique object in our minds that lies behind our use of the term "good." With this conclusion, Moore felt he had successfully addressed the only possible objections to his conception of "good" as indefinable, and thus successfully established "the fundamental principles of ethical reasoning" (p. ix).

It should be emphasized, however, that in arguing that there were but two conceivable objections to the view that "good" is indefinable, Moore implicitly adopted a particular theory of the nature of language and meaning that required that the meaning of a term be identified with that object or thing to which it refers. Termed the referential theory of meaning by later philosophers (e.g., Schwartz, 1977), and developed by Moore, Russell, and the young Wittgenstein in the first decades of the century, the theory's assumption that the meaning of a term is that thing which it names or that to which it refers meant for Moore that "good" referred either to a simple quality, a complex, or nothing at all: "My business is solely with that object or idea, which . . . the word is generally used to stand for" (Moore, 1903a, p. 6). Accordingly, though he might dispose of two conceivable alternatives to his own view through his open-question argument and introspective claims respectively, unless the referential theory was correct, it still did not follow that "good" denoted a simple, unique object, and was thus indefinable.

In fact, the referential theory was later subjected to a serious and now widely accepted critique, especially as ultimately emerged in the elaboration of an alternative philosophical account of language and meaning in terms of the use of ordinary language, as developed by Wittgenstein (1953) in his later years at Cambridge and J.L. Austin (1962) at Oxford. Though it was indeed a number of years before this critique became well established, elements of it began to appear in the very first responses to Moore's arguments in the *Principia*. C.D. Broad (1934), in particular, drew attention to the presuppositions of Moore's indefinability view in arguing that it was far from clear that terms such as "good" actually stand for anything at all, that it was accordingly not clear that "good" denotes something that is simple and unanalyzable, and that this all meant that the sort of property Moore suggested "good" had to denote was virtually impossible to understand. This last point brought out the fact that since Moore had assumed "good" must refer to something not definable in terms of the natural properties of things, it followed that "good" denoted a non-natural or super-sensible property of the world, that is, one which could not be detected by the senses. Indeed, Moore reinforced this conclusion by insisting that while a natural property can, a non-natural property such as that denoted by "good" cannot be thought to exist in time (Moore, 1903a, pp. 40–1). Goodness, it followed, was a non-natural property of the world which could not be said to exist, which could be identified only with itself, and which was simple and unanalyzable.

More importantly, however, that "good" had to stand for some non-natural quality also implied that individuals had to possess some special cognitive faculty which would enable them to apprehend it as such. Since non-natural properties were super-sensible, individuals thus had to possess a specifically non-sensory sort of insight into the essential nature of the world to be able to recognize such things as goodness. Indeed, Moore saw this as one of the important conclusions of his particular approach to ethics. In his view, ethics required a clear distinction between two questions: "What kinds of things ought to exist for their own sakes," that is, what was good in and of itself, and "What kind of actions ought we to perform," or what was involved in right action or duty (p. viii). Moreover, since things that "ought to exist for their own sakes" clearly had intrinsic value – in contrast to the instrumental value associated with achieving good things through the "actions [we] ought . . .

to perform" – propositions about what had intrinsic value possessed an entirely different status compared to those that concerned right action or duty. Specifically, propositions about what had intrinsic value were in their very nature "incapable of proof or disproof," and had consequently to be merely labeled "Intuitions" (p. x). For Moore, then, that "good" denoted an unique, non-natural property of the world – as reflected in its having intrinsic value – meant that goodness had to be known intuitively.

The intuition of intrinsic value, as being incapable of proof or disproof, had an additional, important role in Moore's ethics. Specifically, were one confronted with a multitude of competing claims concerning what was good, each of which seemed to possess some apparent plausibility, one might be tempted to conclude that "good" denotes "a complex, a given whole, about the correct analysis of which there may be disagreement" sufficiently endless to cast doubt on the very enterprise of Ethics. However, were "good" to denote an unique, non-natural property of the world that could be recognized only in an act of intuition incapable of proof or disproof, then disagreement in Ethics, Moore thought, would not be interminable. Special attention to this argument is given in the summary to his discussion of "What kinds of things ought to exist for their own sakes?"

We cannot tell what is possible, by way of proof, in favour of one judgment that 'This or that is good,' or against another judgment 'That this or that is bad,' until we have recognised what the nature of such propositions must always be. In fact, it follows from the meaning of good and bad, that such propositions are all of them, in Kant's phrase, 'synthetic': they all must rest in the end upon some proposition which must be simply accepted or rejected, which cannot be logically deduced from any other proposition. This result, which follows from our first investigation, may be otherwise expressed by saying that the fundamental principles of Ethics must be self-evident. (p. 143)

Intuition, therefore, possesses the crucial function of telling us what indeed is the case, since that which is self-evident must be true in and of itself, irrespective of any argument or proof of its being true. Intuition, it might even be said, is merely the unmediated recognition of truth, and, as such, is necessarily incorrigible. Yet, as Moore was at pains to emphasize, this does not imply that intuition is some sort of intellectual state of mind. Rather intuition is simply the individual's direct connection with reality itself. Thus he continued:

But I am anxious that this expression should not be misunderstood. The expression 'self-evident' means properly that the proposition so called is evident or true, *by itself* alone; that it is not an inference from some proposition other than *itself*. The expression does *not* mean that the proposition is true, because it is evident to you or me or all mankind, because in other words it appears to us to be true. That a proposition appears to be true can never be a valid argument that true it really is. By saying that a proposition is self-evident, we mean emphatically that its appearing so to us, is *not* the reason why it is true: for we mean that it has absolutely no reason. (p. 143)

For Moore, that is, having a sure conviction that something is true not only has nothing to do with whether or not the proposition in question is true, but indeed there are no arguments or grounds whatsoever for the truth of things that are in fact true. Put differently, things that are true simply are the case as a matter of fact, and the sheer fact of their being true neither needs a rationale, nor can it have one. Thus, the certainty we have about true propositions flows from their truth, and not the reverse. We can be certain about something that is true only when it is already self-evident. Moral debate about what is good, consequently, need not be interminable, because there exist truths about what is good or has intrinsic value, and because these truths can be self-evident to us.

Self-evidence, Moore thus insisted, is not something that can be described in any psychological terms whatsoever. Indeed, though it would not have been inappropriate in Moore's view to term intuition a purely cognitive insight (as many have done for him), even this notion requires careful interpretation in light of modern thinking about intellectual processes. Specifically, when Moore asserted that there is "absolutely no reason" for a proposition's self-evidence, he meant to deny the necessity of any intellectual mediation of recognized truth. In a key respect, that is, Moore rejected the very essence of the modern philosophical problem of intentionality, namely, the problem of determining how our representations of reality correspond to that reality (cf. e.g. Stalnaker, 1987, pp. 6–7), by characterizing self-evidence in terms of pure access to that which is truly the case. Put differently, in seeing directly that which is self-evident, one goes altogether beyond mental representation to direct contact with the world itself. And though difficult as this doctrine is to explain and defend, in effect Moore reasoned that it simply had to be correct. One otherwise would never be able to confidently say what was in favour of one judgment that "This or that is good" or another, unless one assumed that some things possessed intrinsic value, that is, were objectively good, and that this could be self-evident to us.

This view, it should be added, presupposed a particular view of the nature of truth, developed and defended by Moore, Russell, and the young Wittgenstein in reaction to the neo-Hegelian understanding of truth that had dominated British philosophy at the turn of the century. The idealists, as represented most notably by F.H. Bradley, Bernard Bosanquet, T.H. Green, and J.M.E. McTaggart, believed the world to be a single, indivisible whole – the Absolute – and argued that any attempt to isolate particular self-contained facts involved distortion and partial falsehood. Their key doctrine was that all relations between things in the world were internal, meaning that any two things related to one another shared as part of their respective identities characteristics of the other. Their criterion for the truth of a given proposition was accordingly that proposition's coherence with the whole of all true propositions. Moore, Russell, and Wittgenstein, in developing what was later to be termed the New Realism (Strong, 1905; Mackenzie, 1906; also cf. Passmore, 1966), argued that relations between things were rather external, and that truth thus involved a correspondence between individual propositions and independent facts about the world. Their conviction that the facts of the world were autonomous and self-contained, and that the truth of true propositions about the world could be established in relation to their correspondence to those facts alone, formed the conceptual foundations of the Analytic movement in philosophy that still influences contemporary Anglo-American philosophy.

Moore's understanding of truth and self-evidence in *Principia Ethica* derived from this larger project, so that his positions regarding goodness as a simple element of reality and "good" as indefinable ultimately had their justification in the New Realists' alternative view of the nature of the relation between thought and the world. Indeed, in the same year that Moore published the *Principia* he also published a paper which was probably more influential and significant both immediately and in the long run. In "Refutation of Idealism" (1903b) Moore claimed that the idealists had confused the independent object of sensation with the act of sensation itself. He thus insisted against the idealists that one could speak meaningfully about the world apart from our cognition of it, and thus imposed upon himself the necessity of arguing that some unmediated access or direct contact with the world was both intelligible and possible. Without entering into an evaluation of this crucial premise of modern philosophical realism, the general implications of Moore's thinking can be seen. First, in reasoning in this way, Moore set as his standard of objectivity the independent existence of the world upon which conception was thought to be grounded. That is, unlike the idealists who essentially made the coherence of reason and thought in and of itself the standard of objectivity, and for whom the idea of a genuinely external world was self-contradictory, Moore believed the fundamental results of philosophy depended upon a conceptualization of the relationship between thought and that which was outside of thought.

Secondly, in his adherence to the doctrine of external relations and correlative view that truth is atomistic (or made up of a collection of fully independent true propositions), Moore insisted on the essential determinacy and definiteness of truth. On the thinking of the idealists, since truth could be established only at the level of the whole, and since the whole could never be grasped in its entirety, particular truths were always subject to revision as one attempted to establish their place in the whole of truth. Moore, apparently, found this unsettled state of knowledge and reality something next to appalling, and argued with conviction throughout his lifetime that some things could be known with certainty to be true, despite our considerable ignorance concerning so much else about the world (cf. esp. Moore, 1925, 1939). Indeed, the very motto of the *Principia*, drawn from the philosopher-theologian Bishop Butler, signaled this conviction and critical view of idealism: "Everything is what it is, and not another thing" (Moore, 1903a, p. ii). Put slightly differently, certain things were the case for once and for all – were determinately so – and some of these things, perhaps many, were knowable as such.

This latter doctrine received one its most important statements in Moore's discussion of the principle of organic unities. Organicism, that "self-contradictory doctrine . . . which shews the influence of Hegel upon modern philosophy," and holds that "a part can have 'no meaning or significance apart from its whole'" (p. 34), was for Moore a key element in the idealists' defense of internal relations. Because the nature of each seemingly individual thing was in part tied up with the nature of every other seemingly individual thing, the idealists believed one always had to talk about the whole of conceivable reality in order to be able to talk about its parts. Moore, however, in an extension of his argument from "Refutation of Idealism," denied that this view was coherent.

It is supposed that just as the whole would not be what it is but for the existence of the parts, so the parts would not be what they are but for the existence of the whole; and this is understood to mean not merely that any particular part could not exist unless the others existed too . . . but actually that the part is no distinct object of thought . . . That this supposition is self-contradictory a very little reflection should be sufficient to shew. We may admit, indeed, that when a particular thing is a part of a whole, it does possess a predicate which it would not otherwise possess – namely that it is a part of that whole. But what cannot be admitted is that this predicate alters the nature or enters into the definition of the thing which has it. When we think of the part *itself*, we mean just *that which* we assert, in this case, to *have* the predicate that it is part of the whole; and the mere assertion that *it* is a part of the whole involves that it should itself be distinct from that which we assert of it. (p. 33)

He went on to conclude, not surprisingly, that it was of the utmost importance that this "self-contradictory" doctrine be "utterly rejected" (p. 34). Interestingly enough, Moore allowed that a thoroughly reformulated principle of organic unities still did have a legitimate place in philosophy, as long as it was clearly distinguished from the understanding of organicism in Hegel's writings. Specifically, in "our ethical investigations" it is necessary to recognize that "[t]he value of a whole must not be assumed to be the same as the sum of the values of its parts" (p. 28). For example, it was clear that the value of one's consciousness of a beautiful object was superior to the sum of the value of that beautiful object and the value of consciousness. Given this, Moore still insisted that the parts of an organic whole retained their existence and value as independent parts, and that it is never the case that a part of something had "no meaning or significance apart from its whole" (p. 34).

Moore's views regarding good and intuition in *Principia Ethica*, then, were part of the larger project of the New Realists Moore, Russell, and the young Wittgenstein. In particular, Moore's indefinability doctrine regarding the analysis of a term such as "good," just as with terms such as "yellow," presupposed the idea that the definition and conceptualization of any notion was ultimately a matter of discovering some set of simple notions which themselves corresponded to the simple elements or atoms of reality. This view, based upon the referential theory of meaning, was far removed from the sort of thinking about language and meaning that emerged in the later work of Wittgenstein and Austin, in which a term's meaning might be objectively (or intersubjectively) determined through attention to the social and linguistic practices associated with the term's use. From this latter standpoint, though Moore clearly felt his account consistent with common sense (p. 224), his argument really turned on a notion that shared little with common sense, namely, the idea of a non-social private intuition (the reliance upon which was most evident in his recourse to introspection to answer the objection that "good" might correspond to nothing at all). As will be seen below, this crucial reliance on an introspective mind's eye to establish an objective link between reality and conception was not persuasive to later philosophers. Though later philosophers were to retain the realist convictions of the Cambridge New Realists, they were almost universally to abandon the atomist model of a correspondence between indefinable terms and a world of simple elements. Understanding the breakdown of this atomist project is important for understanding the development of Keynes's early thinking, since his early views about definition and intuition did not differ significantly from Moore's.

Keynes on indefinability and intuition

As early as his unpublished "Ethics in Relation to Conduct" paper and his first thinking about the meaning of probability, Keynes had already begun to give expression to Moore's indefinability view in simultaneously asserting "I do not claim to have put forward any precise definition of probability" and doubting that it was possible to do so (Keynes, 1904, UA/19).[1] By the time of his successful fellowship dissertation of 1908, Keynes was prepared to assert unequivocally that the probability notion was indefinable. He maintained this view when he came to publish his much-reworked dissertation as the *Treatise on Probability* in 1921. Indeed not only did he take the occasion to demonstrate in the *Treatise* that he had become entirely convinced of the applicability of Moore's indefinability thesis to the concept of probability – "A *definition* of probability is not possible," since "We cannot analyse the probability-relation in terms of simpler ideas" (Keynes, VIII, p. 8)[2] – but he was also ready to make use of the maneuver Moore employed in defense against the second objection Moore thought might be advanced against the claim that "good" was indefinable.

This opinion is, from the nature of the case, incapable of positive proof. The presumption in its favour must arise partly out of our failure to find a definition, and partly because the notion presents itself to the mind as something new and independent . . . The attempts at definition, which have been made hitherto, will be criticised in later chapters. I do not believe that any of them accurately represent that particular logical relation which we have in our minds when we speak of the probability of an argument. (pp. 8–9)

That is, just as Moore, in regard to the claim that "good" might mean nothing at all, had thought introspection demonstrated to whomever would "attentively consider with himself what is actually before his mind" that "good" referred to an "unique object" (Moore, 1903a, p. 16), so Keynes agreed that introspection revealed that the probability "notion presents itself to the mind as something new and independent." Keynes did not, it might be noted, echo Moore's open-question argument, nor did he charge other writers on probability with something akin to the naturalistic fallacy in their proposed definitions of probability. His conviction that probability was indefinable, however, flowed from the same view of definition Moore had employed in pursuing complex notions until arriving at sets of irreducible simples. "Probability," just as "good," then, was just such a simple notion.

Consequently, Keynes was also, like Moore, committed to the idea that an indefinable referred to some unique object which was not characterizable in terms of any known properties of the world, natural or otherwise. While Moore, in an effort to distinguish his view from those that characterized goodness in terms of some natural property, had found himself effectively arguing that "good" denoted some non-natural property or quality of things, Keynes, in reasoning that probability statements concerned relationships between sets of propositions (Keynes, VIII, p. 9), concluded that "the subject-matter of the logic of probability" was that simple "relation" between propositions "in virtue of which, if we know the first, we can attach to the latter some degree of rational belief" (pp. 6–7). This was particularly clear in his continual emphasis on the objective character of probabilities. Thus Keynes asserted that, "When we argue that Darwin gives us valid grounds for our accepting his theory of natural selection, we do not simply mean that we are psychologically inclined to agree with him . . . We believe that there is some real objective relation between Darwin's evidence and his conclusions, which is independent of the mere fact of our belief, and which is just as real and objective . . ." (pp. 5–6). Probability statements, that is, just as claims about what might be good, possessed their meaning in virtue of something real and objective referred to by the term "probable," namely, the probability relation itself. Keynes, therefore, also presupposed the referential theory of meaning, as developed by Moore, Russell, and Wittgenstein, and in this important regard could equally be termed a member of what was to become the New Realist movement in philosophy.

Perhaps more importantly, however, the fact that Keynes thought there was some unique object denoted by "probable" – a relation objectively existing in the world apart from and foundational to our inclinations concerning what was "probable" – meant that he also had to suppose individuals possessed some special non-sensory, cognitive faculty for apprehending this relation. This faculty, following Moore, Keynes variously labeled intuition or a capacity for direct knowledge (e.g., pp. 56, 69, 75, 76, 94, 121, 139, 284). Intuition or direct knowledge, moreover, itself arose out of or emerged from an additional cognitive capacity, altogether distinct from direct knowledge, that Keynes termed direct acquaintance. Individuals, Keynes asserted, were capable of being directly acquainted with their "own sensations, which we may be said to *experience*, the ideas or meanings, about which we have thoughts and which we may be said to *understand*, and facts or characteristics or relations of sense-data or meanings, which we may be said to *perceive*; – experience, understanding, and perception being three forms of direct acquaintance" (p. 12). In contrast to the objects of direct acquaintance, Keynes went on, the objects of knowledge, whether direct or indirect, were propositions. Consequently, an important component of Keynes's epistemology in the *Treatise* concerned the intellectual movement he understood individuals to make from those objects with which we were acquainted to the objects of knowledge proper. Moreover, since within the realm of knowledge itself, Keynes distinguished direct and indirect knowledge, he also supposed the epistemic process involved a movement from the objects of direct knowledge to those of indirect knowledge.

In this analysis, Keynes expanded upon the key features of Moore's account of the indubitability of certain first cognitions by elaborating successive stages of self-evidence where the things apprehended or known were subject to neither proof nor disproof. First, at the level of direct acquaintance, since individuals could not be mistaken about their own sensations, meanings, and perceptions, these were necessarily self-evident. At the same time, however, since this level of certitude lacked the character of knowledge – on account of the fact that the content of such experiences had yet to be formulated propositionally or in terms of statements that could be said to be true or false – that there be such a thing as direct knowledge (Keynes's intuition) required that the certitude available in experience be transferable to the realm of knowledge. Secondly, then, individuals also made the transition from direct acquaintance to direct knowledge "by some mental process of which," Keynes admitted, "it is difficult to give an account."

From acquaintance with a sensation of yellow I can pass directly to a knowledge of the proposition 'I have a sensation of yellow'. From acquaintance with a sensation of yellow and with the meanings of 'yellow', 'colour', 'existence', I may be able to pass to a direct knowledge of the propositions 'I understand the meaning of yellow', 'my sensation of yellow exists', 'yellow is a colour'. Thus, by some mental process of which it is difficult to give an account, we are able to pass from direct acquaintance with things to a knowledge of propositions about the things of which we have sensations or understand the meaning. (p. 13)

That, in his view, the quality of self-evidence at the stage of direct acquaintance should be thought sustained at the stage of direct knowledge likely contributed the rationale in Keynes's mind for his opinion that the mental process which permitted that transition was essentially opaque. If indeed direct knowledge was fully intuitive in the sense of being subject to neither proof nor disproof, then that mental process could not be subject to any essential analysis, or else direct knowledge would lose its self-evident character. Like Moore – and indeed in the very use of Moore's own example of "yellow" – Keynes thus employed intuition or direct knowledge to establish the foundations for knowledge in self-evidence.

This permitted Keynes, as it had Moore, to distinguish that further part of the analysis which was specifically inferential in nature or, as Keynes put it, was a matter of indirect knowledge and argument. Moore, recall, distinguished between two questions, "What kinds of things ought to exist for their own sakes?" and "What kind of actions ought we to perform?" (Moore, 1903a, p. viii), and then insisted that the first was properly a matter for intuition, and thus incapable of proof or disproof, while the second, precisely in virtue of there being an answer to the first question, was then subject to argument and accordingly capable of proof or disproof. Keynes, similarly, distinguished between knowledge obtained "directly, as the result of contemplating the objects of acquaintance; and indirectly, *by argument* through perceiving the probability-relation of the proposition, about which we seek knowledge, to other propositions" (Keynes, VIII, p. 12). Keynes's view of "argument," however, itself made important use of the same mechanism of direct acquaintance involved in obtaining direct knowledge.

Next, by the contemplation of propositions of which we have direct knowledge, we are able to pass indirectly to knowledge of or about other propositions. The mental process by which we pass from direct knowledge to indirect knowledge is in some cases and in some degree capable of analysis. We pass from a knowledge of the proposition *a* to a knowledge about the proposition by perceiving a logical relation between them. With this logical relation we have direct acquaintance. The logic of knowledge is mainly occupied with a study of logical relations, direct acquaintance with which permits direct knowledge of the secondary proposition asserting the probability-relation, and so to indirect knowledge about, and in some cases of, the primary proposition. (p. 13)

Indirect knowledge, then, involved a knowledge of propositions about propositions, rather than a knowledge of propositions about things (such as sensations, meanings, and perceptions), or, as Keynes put it, indirect knowledge was a knowledge of primary propositions via a direct knowledge of secondary propositions about primary propositions. Thus, though indirect knowledge is, in effect, at one remove from the subject matter with which we are directly acquainted in primary propositions, for Keynes the fact that we have a direct knowledge of secondary propositions, via the act of perceiving the logical relations between the primary propositions we contemplate and the secondary propositions we formulate about them, guarantees that even indirect knowledge is direct and intuitive.

Keynes followed Moore, then, in distinguishing between things known intuitively and things known inferentially. Yet at the same time, by elaborating a distinction between two stages of self-evidence, direct acquaintance and direct knowledge, Keynes is also able to explain inference as well as intuitive knowledge in terms of self-evidence, since the movement between those propositions of which we have direct knowledge becomes itself a matter of direct knowledge when direct acquaintance (with the logical relations between propositions) comes into play. In short, intuition provides us with both the items of knowledge and ultimately the connections between them. This was crucial to Keynes's account of probable knowledge. Indeed, Keynes went on to comment, because our perception of the logical relations between propositions may not always possess perfect clarity, it is necessary to distinguish between "knowledge proper," "which results from a distinct apprehension of the relevant logical relations" (p. 14), and "vague knowledge" (p. 17), where there is some indistinctness in this perception. In the latter case, the requisite certitude normally afforded us in direct acquaintance with logical relations is insufficient, and consequently Keynes insists that, though it may well seem that a knowledge of some sort is involved in such instances, such knowledge is not "susceptible of strict logical treatment," and would not accordingly figure in the arguments of the *Treatise* (p. 17).

Keynes goes on to explain the nature of self-evidence and certainty in terms reminiscent of Moore's discussion. Moore, recall, was at pains to emphasize that he was concerned with genuine cognitive insight, and that he accordingly did not associate a state of something being self-evident with a particular mental conviction. For Keynes, this is a matter of what he called rational belief.

It must be added that the term *certainty* is sometimes used in a merely psychological sense to describe a state of mind without reference to the logical grounds of belief. With this sense I am not concerned. It is also used to describe the highest degree of rational belief; and this is the sense relevant to our present purpose. (p. 15)

That is, something is certain not because we have a conviction that it is so, but rather because we have rational grounds for thinking it so. As with Moore, then, self-evidence is a matter of the correct apprehension of things as they are in and of themselves. When we are directly acquainted with some logical relation through its perception, we have pure cognitive insight into the nature of that logical relation. In essence, therefore, Keynes grounded intuition in realism, as did Moore and Russell, since for him, as them, the very basis for intuition or direct knowledge was the possibility of reality being self-evident to us.

Given this, the probability relation is an indefinable, because it, like goodness, is a real feature of our world. In effect, there is no reason for saying that particular propositions are more or less probable beyond the simple fact that we are directly acquainted with the underlying logical relations that reveal this to be so. Keynes's reliance on direct acquaintance for the detection of probability relations is especially important here. Because one cannot be mistaken about that with which one is directly acquainted, the fact that we are directly acquainted in Keynes's view with logical relations implies that we have a direct, unmediated access to the reality of what is more or less probable. That, moreover, this reality presents itself to us on distinct occasions in particular episodes of direct acquaintance, when our concern is focused on the likelihood of particular propositions relative to particular bodies of evidence, further implies that that reality is atomic in nature, and thus externally rather than internally related.

Here, it should also be noted, Keynes agreed with Moore that the idealists had misconceived organicism and the principle of organic unities. In two successive and connected papers Keynes wrote in 1905, "Miscellanea Ethica" (Keynes, 1905b, UA/21) and "A Theory of Beauty" (Keynes, 1905a, UA/23),[3] Keynes adopted the formulation of organic connection Moore had set forth in the *Principia* in connection with things of value, to the effect that the parts of an organic whole retained their distinctness as separate parts of a whole, though indeed the value of such a whole did not equal the sum of the values of its parts. Keynes did desist, as we will see in the next chapter, from Moore's extension of the principle of organic unities to the goodness of the entire Universe, arguing in both the early papers and later in the *Treatise* (Keynes, VIII, p. 343) that the proper application of the principle was to the goodness of individual minds and not to the goodness of groups of individuals.

Keynes departed from Moore's thinking in one further respect that deserves special comment. Moore had argued in his *Principia Ethica* discussion of right conduct that, though right action depends upon recognizing the full range of consequences of one's actions, because we are in "utter ignorance of the far future," we often have "no justification for saying that it is even probably right to choose the greater good within the region over which a probable forecast may extend" (Moore, 1903a, p. 153). As a result, we are entitled – indeed obliged, Moore insisted – to rely on various well-established rules of conduct to assist us in determining appropriate right actions, though it may well be the case that from time to time such rules actually produce undesirable results. Now, it is fair to say that as a matter of personal temperament Keynes in his early years at Cambridge was not inclined to accept a domination of rules in matters where individual judgment might be brought to bear. However, there was more to Keynes's early critique of Moore's thinking in this regard. Indeed, it is now reasonably clear that it was precisely at this point in his career that Keynes initiated his first original thoughts concerning probability theory, and determined upon his first major intellectual project, namely, what was to emerge after two fellowship dissertations and many additional years of revision as the *Treatise on Probability*.

More specifically, what Keynes detected in Moore's position on rules and conduct was a commitment on the latter's part to the frequency theory of probability. Keynes recognized this in his first written comment on Moore's *Principia*, his "Ethics in Relation to Conduct," and reiterated the point seventeen years later in the *Treatise* (Keynes, VIII, p. 342). The problem with this commitment, Keynes argued, was that an "utter ignorance of the far future" did not preclude the possibility of rational judgments about actions and require passive recourse to general rules of conduct. One in fact could be driven to such a conclusion only if it should be thought that one had to be certain about the exact balance of consequences, good and bad, of actions taken in the present. This sort of determination was precisely what the frequency theory of probability claimed to offer, since its judgments regarding what was more or less likely depended upon comprehensive past information about those events from which one could calculate, with certainty, future probabilities. However, Keynes reasoned, since this sort of information is quite often unavailable, adherence to the frequency theory made certainty an improper standard for predictions about the future consequences of our actions. It thus had a paralyzing effect on our use of individual judgment, which Keynes thought could be defended on the grounds that we possessed a genuine capacity of intuition.

Thus, Keynes argued in "Ethics in Relation to Conduct," in terms that were to foreshadow his thinking in the *Treatise*, that when he made a probability claim he meant, "I mean something of the nature 'I have more evidence in favour of A than in favour of B'; I am making some statement concerning the bearing of the evidence at my disposal; I am not stating that in the long-run A will happen more often than B for certain" (Keynes, 1904, UA/19). Probability statements, that is, do not register probabilities that we hold with certainty. Rather probability statements capture the rational grounds relating the evidence at hand to propositions that concern us. Accordingly, when

we have evidence to show that an action will produce more good than not in the next year and have no reason for supposing either that it will produce more good than evil or the reverse after the end of that period, if, in fact, we are in complete ignorance as to all events subsequent to the end of the year, – in that case we have, in my opinion, more evidence to support the view that x is right than to support the contrary and hence we are justified in saying 'x is probably right'. (*Ibid.*)

In the later thinking of the *Treatise*, because one can be directly acquainted with the logical relations between particular (primary) propositions and other (secondary) propositions about them, one can arrive at a direct or intuitive knowledge about probabilities that itself possesses the character of self-evidence Moore sought in his demand that we know whether "in the long-run A will happen more often than B for certain."

In Keynes's view, then, Moore had abandoned the faculty of intuition at a critical juncture. While his account of goodness as an indefinable made it clear that one could be certain about what was intrinsically good without recourse to any further inferences about good (whether it was pleasurable, brought happiness, etc.), his account of right action required that he attribute an additional property to the foreseen good and bad consequences of an action, in order to be certain the balance was good or bad. Keynes, seeing that Moore's analysis of things known by inference or argument could not support a reasonable characterization of right action and duty, re-formulated his own theory of things known by inference or argument, so as to bring direct acquaintance, and thus direct or intuitive judgment, into play in the characterization of probabilities. Because, that is, one could be directly acquainted with the probability relations that obtained between secondary and primary propositions, one could establish a direct knowledge of secondary propositions without any need to survey some future (or past) range of events.

In this way, of course, Keynes did not abandon Moore, but rather improved on Moore's approach by handling conduct in terms of a probability theory more consistent with Moore's original assumptions. Moore, it is fair to say, was indeed unable to discuss conduct in an adequate manner, since, excepting those rare cases when complete information about past events that might establish relative frequencies was available, probability judgments concerning the likely consequences of action would generally be unavailable. In Keynes's words, "Moore's reasoning endeavours to show that there is not even a *probability* by showing that there is not a *certainty*" (Keynes, VIII, p. 342). Yet for Keynes, the matter transcended the issue of a proper analysis of right conduct, since in his view the domain of demonstrative reasoning and certain knowledge was quite small, and most of our epistemological concerns rather involved some conception of rational belief.

He consequently believed his work on probability theory to be an important contribution to the development of the New Realist philosophy emerging at Cambridge, and regarded his emendation of Moore's system as principally an advance on that philosophy's theory of knowledge and self-evidence. Thus, whereas Moore had been driven to explaining the future consequences of action in *ad hoc* conventional terms, that is, according to general rules drawn empirically from past experience, Keynes sought to extend Moore's account by emphasizing probability reasoning as a form of rational belief (pp. 3, 10). While he allowed that "The highest degree of rational belief, which is termed *certain* rational belief, corresponds to *knowledge*" (p. 3), that part of our reasoning concerning that which is only probable and is the subject of rational belief bears an intimate relation to knowledge. As Keynes explained it,

The proposition (*say*, *q*) that we know in this case is not the same as the proposition (*say*, *p*) in which we have a probable degree (*say*, α) of rational belief. If the evidence upon which we base our belief is *h*, then what we *know*, namely *q*, is that the proposition *p* bears the probability-relation of degree α in the proposition *p*. (p. 11)

Keynes, we have seen, went on (following the Cambridge logician W.E. Johnson) to term propositions such as p primary propositions and propositions such as q secondary propositions. Yet since a probable degree of rational belief in a particular primary proposition arises out of knowledge of an appropriate secondary proposition, that rational belief necessarily arises out of knowledge. Indeed, this was a direct knowledge which itself had its own origins in an acquaintance with probability relations.

In the case of every argument, it is only directly that we can know the secondary proposition which makes the argument itself valid and rational. When we know something by argument this must be through direct acquaintance with some logical relation between the conclusion and the premiss. In *all* knowledge, therefore, there is some direct element; and logic can never be made purely mechanical. All it can do is so to arrange the reasoning that the logical relations, which have to be perceived directly, are made explicit and are of a simple kind. (p. 15)

Accordingly, though Keynes reserved the term certainty for knowledge involving the highest degree of rational belief, knowledge of secondary propositions involving degrees of probability less than certainty still amounted to knowledge, though a knowledge, as Keynes put it, *about* some primary proposition rather than *of* it. In this way, then, Keynes was able to treat probability in stronger cognitive terms than had Moore. At the same time, Keynes accomplished this by extending the direct knowledge framework (through the distinction between primary and secondary propositions) in a manner that justified speaking of rational belief, whether of certain or merely probable propositions.

Both Moore and Keynes, thus, operated within a philosophical framework that was generated largely in response to inadequacies perceived to lie in the idealist systems of thought that pervaded philosophy at the beginning of the century. Central to this framework, we have seen, was a realist reliance on the referential theory of meaning. This in turn implied a particular emphasis upon direct knowledge or intuition, which then functioned as the basis or foundation for inferential knowledge and the rational justification of things known through argument. Put simply, the underlying epistemological structure that Moore and Keynes imagined was that of a hierarchical ordering of epistemic claims grounded incontrovertibly in self-evident intuitions. It was their understanding of intuition, of course, which carried the weight of this conception of knowledge as hierarchical, since it was in the nature of the view that the traditionally more tenuous epistemological claims concerning rational conduct and probabilities were ultimately to be accounted for in terms of the incorrigibility of intuition.

This general philosophical conception, often known as logical atomism, came in for serious and now widely accepted criticism in subsequent years. Much of this critique is associated with the later work of Wittgenstein (1953) who, because he himself had originally propounded many of the views that he later criticized, was driven to advance especially effective and persuasive arguments against the view (Monk, 1990). In particular, Wittgenstein contested the referential theory of meaning that he, Moore, and Russell had earlier defended, putting forth in its stead an understanding of meaning in terms of use. More generally, the critique of the referential theory brought into question the idea that knowledge was a hierarchically organized structure ultimately depending on self-evident intuition, whether it was in the manner of Moore and Keynes's explanation of inferential knowledge, or in the manner of Russell and Whitehead's paradigmatic *Principia Mathematica* grounding of all mathematical knowledge upon but a handful of self-evident logical axioms.

The philosophical critique of the views of Moore and Keynes

The referential theory of meaning – the view that the meaning of a term is that to which it refers – achieves what plausibility it possesses chiefly in connection with the names of objects or persons, since the meaning of a name might well be thought to be learned through a practice of associating names and things. Yet even in instances such as these there is something peculiar about saying that the object or person referred to is a meaning. Thus, were we to say of someone, "N has gone away," it would follow on the referential theory that we could equally say, "The meaning of the name 'N' has gone away," though this would be nonsensical (Waismann, 1965, pp. 312–13). An additional difficulty arises from the fact that two different terms in a language could have the same referent yet have different meanings; alternatively, two terms might have the same meaning but different referents (Alston, 1964, p. 13).

It is true that the referential theory can be re-stated to avoid some of its most obvious difficulties, so that the meaning of a term is not simply identical with its referent, but somehow presupposes our being acquainted with the things to which it refers. Still, serious difficulties remain. In particular a great variety of non-name terms in language seem patently not to acquire their meanings by referring to things in the world. Prepositions, conjunctions, and the modal auxiliaries of verbs are clear examples. This alone suggests that the conception of language that the referential theory offers is too simplistic. The basic assumption of the referential theory is that meaning is essentially explained by saying what language is about. Yet it might be better to say that this is at best only a part of what is involved in explaining meaning, since in addition to saying what terms are about, meaning fundamentally involves the business of saying *how* language comes to be about the things it concerns.

Wittgenstein's *Philosophical Investigations* (1953) emphasized the importance of this in its critical examination of a number of Wittgenstein's own early views. Language, he came to believe, does not possess meaning simply in virtue of having a relation to the world, since the terms of our language refer to things in the world only at our instigation. People *use* language to refer to things in the world, and there are also, casual inspection demonstrates, a multiplicity of different ways in which language can be used by people. Indeed, many meaningful expressions are clearly not used in a referential manner, a good example being the sentence itself. Sentences can be used to make statements, but also ask questions, express feelings, issue commands, etc. Wittgenstein urged, "Look at the sentence as an instrument, and at its sense as its employment" (pt. I, sect. 421). Then one will not be tempted to search for meanings as some peculiar set of entities existing in a metaphysical realm beyond ordinary experience.

This preoccupation with a metaphysical realm beyond ordinary experience of course was precisely what Moore and Keynes were all about in their efforts to characterize goodness and probability as indefinables. Specifically, on the assumption that language is meaningful precisely to the extent that it refers to things in the world, they reasoned that a process of definition that reduced complex notions to their simplest elements had to have thereby picked out basic elements of reality. Further, because these simples were clearly distinct from the meaning complexes of ordinary experience from which they were abstracted, it followed that these simple indefinables had to designate a unique collection of entities occupying a distinct realm of reality. For Wittgenstein, these conclusions were the result of a confusion that arose from uncritical adherence to the referential view. That is, since names seem to refer to their bearers, it was tempting to think that all terms got their meanings from the things to which they would refer, so that general terms such as "good" and "probable" then referred to some special set of abstract entities characterizable as the bearers of these terms. But, Wittgenstein argued, it was hardly necessary to postulate a special realm of reality populated by universals such as goodness and the probable to account for such terms as "good" and "probable." One only had to attend to the ways in which such terms were used to acquire insight into how their meanings came to be what they were.

As it turned out, Moore and Keynes's view that there was a special realm of reality which served as an anchor for judgments about what was good or probable was to become a source of considerable philosophical controversy. Wittgenstein, even in his earlier thinking when he had been a proponent of the referential theory, had refused to regard ethical terms as meaningful, since he thought that a meaningful language had to reflect what is in fact the case in terms of what exists in the world, while ethics concerned what ought to be the case, and thus could not refer to things that exist (Wittgenstein, 1921, sect. 6.41; 1958, pp. 11–12). Broad, as we have seen, argued influentially that it was doubtful that "good" actually stands for anything, while suggesting that "good" had an emotive rather than descriptive meaning. Indeed, the central component of Moore's indefinability view of "good," namely, the distinction between natural and non-natural objects, struck Broad as unsustainable, precisely because Moore had thought the latter inhabited their own special domain of reality. C.L. Stevenson (1937), in a line of reasoning that will be explored at more length in the next chapter, also criticized Moore for assuming that terms such as "good" had descriptive rather than emotive meaning, with the result that Moore finally allowed that he might indeed have been mistaken in thinking that "good" referred to some object. It "simply had not occurred" to him, he admitted, that "good" might possess its meaning in virtue of its being used in emotive fashion (Moore, 1942, p. 546).

Keynes's own view came in for like criticism, in this case from those concerned with his understanding of the meaning of probability and account of probability relations. In 1922, Ramsey, who had been attracted to the study of the problems of induction and probability by Keynes's *Treatise on Probability*, published a critical review of Keynes's *Treatise* in *The Cambridge Review*, which was to go unanswered by Keynes until 1930 after Ramsey's death. Going directly to the heart of Keynes's philosophical position, Ramsey asserted that

a . . . fundamental criticism of Mr. Keynes' views, is the obvious one that there really do not seem to be any such things as the probability relations he describes. He supposes that, at any rate in certain cases, they can be perceived; but speaking for myself I feel confident that this is not true. I do not perceive them, and if I am to be persuaded that they exist it must be by argument; moreover I shrewdly suspect that others do not perceive them either, because they are able to come to so very little agreement as to which of them relates any two given propositions. (Ramsey, 1978, p. 63)

Two other notable students of probability theory much influenced by Keynes later came to have similar doubts about Keynes's fundamental assumptions. R.B. Braithwaite, with Ramsey another of Keynes's early students, questioned whether it made sense to say that probability relations were somehow there to be perceived (Braithwaite, 1975). Walter Kneale, though in agreement that probability could not be defined in terms of the logic of implication, denied that this meant the concept of probability was unanalyzable and indefinable. Indeed, Kneale took Keynes's view that probability was about some set of "ultimate entities" to be a vestige of an early, outmoded Cambridge metaphysics that he termed a "jungle of subsistence" (Kneale, 1949, pp. 11–13).

Given the critical response to the referential theory of meaning and its associated doctrines of indefinables and unanalyzability, then, it will be helpful to recount how the view had been advanced and defended in the first place. Recall that Moore and Keynes had both made the introspection an individual might exercise central to their respective accounts. Moore, perhaps in anticipating Wittgenstein's early doubts about the meaningfulness of terms such as "good," had said that introspection always reveals an unique object in our minds that lies behind our use of the term "good" (Moore, 1903a, p. 16). Keynes, in rejecting past attempts at defining probability, had similarly insisted that these efforts failed to apprehend "that particular logical relation which we have in our minds when we speak of the probability of an argument" (Keynes, VIII, p. 9). Yet that Moore and Keynes made use of introspection, it was argued above, followed from their original supposition that goodness as a quality and the relation of probability were simple and unanalyzable, and as such occupied an unique super-sensible or non-natural domain of reality to which we nonetheless possessed intuitive access. Introspection, that is, essentially involved an intellectual process of exhibiting our mental contents that rendered transparent to us the collection of simples that made up the world. Accordingly, whatever plausibility Moore and Keynes's approach possessed in the final analysis came down to their shared view that this super-sensible, non-natural domain of reality was directly accessible to us through intuition.

Such a view, we have seen, required treating the domain of super-sensible reality as atomistic, since those indefinables referred to by such terms as "good" and "probable" were judged to be simple in virtue of their analytical method of definition. Accordingly, since grasping these simples in acts of intuition was necessary to a proper understanding of the meaning complexes from which they were abstracted, the epistemology that Moore and Keynes adopted and developed necessarily also assumed a hierarchical ordering of epistemic claims grounded in a collection of incorrigible, original intuitions. This conception of knowledge as depending upon and built up from secure foundations – or as foundational in nature – has been the object of extensive critical analysis by contemporary philosophers going back to Karl Popper (1934).[4] Here, only two aspects of this epistemological view will be touched upon: first, the idea that there exists a set of original intuitions thought to be immediate and incorrigible, and second, the idea that knowledge constitutes a structure progressively built up from original intuitions, so as to validate more complex epistemic claims that are not self-evident in themselves.

The idea that we possess a sort of original intuition, immediate and incorrigible, functions for Moore and Keynes as a means of direct access to the real. As noted earlier, to reason in this way is tantamount to denying the significance of the modern problem of intentionality, that is, the problem of explaining how our representations of the world reflect or correspond to the world. That there is such a problem derives from the assumption that our representation of the world and the world itself are not identical. The idealists, of course, believed that it did not make sense to speak of the world apart from its conceptualization, and thus circumvented the problem from the outset. However, for the New Realists at Cambridge at the beginning of the century, especially after Moore's "Refutation of Idealism" (1903b) argument that the object of perception and perception itself were distinct, the question of the relationship between the world and thought was inescapable. Moreover, the problem was a particularly difficult one for realist philosophers, since the idealist legacy of seeing one's characterization of the world as somehow mind-dependent was still fresh and familiar. The strategy of Moore, then, was to set apart a particular category of mental acts, namely, intuitions, and argue that these produced an intellectually unmediated, direct access to reality, while the balance of our epistemic claims involving inferential knowledge reflected an intellectually constituted architecture of knowledge grounded in original intuition.

The view of intuition as foundational to all our knowledge, however, was paradoxical in the formulation given it by Moore. In essence, in representing intuition as that insight any individual might possess were he or she to consider carefully what lay before his or her mind on a given occasion, Moore's characterization of intuition as immediate and incorrigible undermined the very confidence he had hoped to invest in intuition as a means to inferential knowledge. Specifically, since the self-evident character of intuition precluded any verification or legitimation of an individual's intuitive claims, those claims had to be taken on faith alone, as Moore effectively concluded in insisting that there was "absolutely no reason" that something self-evident be taken as self-evident. Yet were the claims of intuition to be taken on faith alone, then it would be impossible to distinguish genuine intuition from misapprehension. The doctrine of immediate and incorrigible intuition, it might thus be said, precluded a theory of error concerning our original intuitions, though being able to explain error (and its possible correction) is arguably essential to having the confidence we ultimately rest in our various epistemic claims, intuitive or otherwise.

Such difficulties are compounded when one turns to the question of grounding or legitimating inferential knowledge. There of course the issue is whether or not our non-intuitive epistemic claims can be justified by reference to immediate, direct knowledge. Yet if the latter is in principle "incapable of proof or disproof," then an additional dilemma confronts Moore's analysis, since it follows that indirect or inferential knowledge is then ultimately justified in terms of that which must be taken on faith or is in principle unjustifiable. Moreover, because the objective of attaining a hierarchically structured epistemology is to ground our more complex, non-intuitive epistemic claims in our more elementary simple ones, the epistemological project is generally taken to involve a process of validating and legitimating claims of the former sort in terms of the latter. However, the deliverances of intuition, though classified as a direct knowledge, fail to qualify as epistemic claims in and of themselves by the standard required of those more complex claims whose explanation is central to the epistemological project. Perhaps the underlying difficulties in this regard were signaled most obviously in the indecision the New Realists felt about the concept of intuitive acquaintance, with, for example, Russell (1910–11, 1912) believing acquaintance a form of direct knowledge and Keynes thinking direct knowledge was derived from acquaintance.

Why was it, then, that the early-twentieth-century Cambridge school made intuition and the hierarchical conception of knowledge central to their realist response to late-nineteenth-century idealism? The answer to this question lies in the fundamental appeal possessed by the notion that knowledge constitutes a hierarchical structure progressively built up from immediate and incorrigible intuitions. Two arguments about the nature of knowledge appear to require that one adopt the hierarchical conception, even when objections to the view appear significant. First, in line with the idea that intuition must be direct and immediate, there is an important infinite regress argument. If, as in idealist philosophy, all beliefs somehow depend upon all other beliefs, then no belief is capable of justification as knowledge, because this would always require the justification of an infinite series of beliefs. For knowledge to be thought possible at all, there must thus exist some set of basic, non-inferential beliefs from which we infer and justify all other beliefs. Second, it seems that if there are basic, non-inferential beliefs, then these must be incorrigible. A belief that is basic, clearly, is one that cannot be subject to revision or correction in light of subsequent justification of other beliefs. Otherwise these original beliefs would certainly cease to be basic and non-inferential.

Both arguments, it turns out, also underlay the New Realists' attachment to the referential theory of meaning. Specifically, just as there had to exist some set of elementary, intuitive beliefs, were knowledge generally to be well founded, so also there might be said to exist some set of basic, simple statements whose meanings underlay more complex meanings. Since the meanings of these simple statements – sometimes termed observation statements in accordance with the Vienna Circle's emphasis on empirical science – were not to be explained in terms of the meanings of other statements, there necessarily existed a set of statements understood solely in terms of their correlation with the world outside language.[5] Observation statements precluded the possibility of an infinite regress of meanings, and possessed the characteristic of being incorrigible in that they could be learned only by observing their correlation with the things to which they corresponded. Wittgenstein in his early *Tractatus Logico-Philosophicus* (1921) seemed to have encouraged this conception, arguing in terms of his picture theory of meaning that more complex, molecular statements were compounded through logical connectives (conjunction, disjunction, and conditionals) from atomic or elementary statements in virtue of the composition of their terms exactly picturing facts about the world. On this view, the meaning of a term (in the context of a statement) was just that to which it referred.[6]

However, just as the referential theory and its associated hierarchical conception of knowledge came in for serious criticism in succeeding decades, so the arguments that motivated these positions were also subjected to re-examination and critique. In the case of the infinite regress argument that there had to exist some set of basic beliefs or statements that functioned as foundations for other epistemic claims, critics took advantage of the fact that the argument only suggested the existence of some independent set of basic beliefs or statements without actually demonstrating that such basic beliefs or statements existed. Otto Neurath from the Vienna Circle (1921, 1932–3), following Pierre Duhem (1906), cast doubt on the idea that it was possible to isolate any set of statements, beliefs, or concepts in a fashion that would permit their functioning as independent grounds for other epistemic claims. Using a provocative and often-quoted metaphor, Neurath commented that

Duhem has demonstrated most forcefully that every assertion concerning any event whatsoever is steeped with hypotheses of all sorts which in the final analysis derive from our whole world view. We are like sailors who must rebuild their ship on the open sea, without ever being able to begin anew from the bottom. When a beam is removed, a new one must at once be put in its place, with the remaining ship being employed as a support. Thus, with the help of the old beams and drifting timbers, the ship can be completely refashioned – but only through gradual reconstruction. (quoted in Will, 1974, p. 165)

Knowledge, that is, is like a ship at sea, in that its structure always makes all its elements depend upon all others in a manner that precludes its rational reconstruction upon any one set of foundations. W.V. Quine, in his influential 1951 paper, "Two Dogmas of Empiricism" (Quine, 1961), repeated this critique, targeting the idea that individual epistemic claims about material objects could be grounded in appropriate sets of statements reporting the sense experience associated with those objects. Quine argued that were we to examine our statements about material objects, we would discover that they "face the tribunal of sense experience not individually but only as a corporate body" (p. 41), and that our statements about material objects are thus judged in terms of the whole of sense experience. As he went on to explain,

science is like a field of force whose boundary conditions are experience. A conflict with experience at the periphery occasions readjustments in the interior of the field. Truth values have to be redistributed over some of our statements. Reevaluation of some statements entails reevaluation of others . . . But the total field is so underdetermined by its boundary conditions, experience, that there is much latitude of choice as to what statements to reevaluate in the light of any single contrary experience. No particular experiences are linked with any particular statements in the interior of the field, except indirectly through considerations of equilibrium affecting the field as a whole. (pp. 42–3)

Later, Popper (1963), also addressing the view that knowledge must possess empirical foundations, argued that observation always depends upon the theory that suggests it, so that it cannot be the case that theories are derived inductively from an observation of facts. Theories, he suggested, are put forward as conjectures or hypotheses, and from these we derive predictions which guide our empirical investigation. Observation statements are thus already theory-laden, and theories accordingly cannot be said to possess the sort of foundations that can be built up out of some sort of immediate and incorrigible intuition.

Contrary to those who have argued that knowledge must be built up upon secure and certain foundations, philosophers such as Neurath, Popper, Quine, and others have argued that such foundations simply do not exist. No set of beliefs, statements, or concepts can be said to be any more basic than any others, and all function in various different ways to support the architecture of knowledge. Moreover, since there are not any special beliefs, statements, or concepts foundational to all our other epistemic claims, neither are there beliefs, statements, or concepts immune to revision or correction, or that count as the products of an incorrigible intuition. Wittgenstein had argued this latter thesis in a particularly convincing manner in his *Investigations*. Noting that the idea of a genuinely incorrigible intuition implied that individuals each possessed a mental experience about which they could not be mistaken, he concluded that this implied each individual possessed a fully private language in which they articulated the meanings of these experiences. Yet, Wittgenstein insisted, the idea of a fully private language is self-contradictory, since language is by nature an intersubjective, public affair. Individuals represent even their private, mental experiences in a common, shared language, and thus also in terms that are ever revisable in the light of changing linguistic conventions. The notion of a truly incorrigible intuition is thus itself impossible, since an individual often has the occasion to revise or correct a characterization of a given mental experience, though he or she is alone in a position to report that experience. Reasoning in related terms, Austin (1962) noted that though a given sentence will sometimes be used to give a direct report of individual observation, the fact that that sentence can on other occasions be used in an entirely different manner demonstrates that language possesses a versatility to which we adjust, rather than the reverse. Intuition, then, to the extent that we imagine it as central to knowledge, nonetheless rests on a system of communication which makes speaking of incorrigible intuition obscure and misleading.

Intuition, accordingly, is presumably neither immediate nor incorrigible. Nonetheless, it might still be argued that a suitably re-formulated conception of intuition could occupy a significant role in the theory of knowledge. On such a view, the intuitive quality of certain claims might depend upon some prior explanation of intuition within a system of knowledge constituted in part around linguistic conventions. On this basis, the objectivity of our intuitional claims would be explained in terms of their place within the social practices involved in those sciences or epistemologies which make use of intuition. Of course this defense of intuitive knowledge in terms of a role accorded intuition in a particular sort of theory essentially requires that the results of intuition be interpretable in terms of the objectives and nature of the theory in question. This would then entail some theory of error in intuition and its correction, and would be incompatible with the early, Cambridge realist characterization of intuition as immediate, incorrigible, and foundational for derived knowledge generally. Perhaps most interestingly it would also put a non-individualistic or social cast on intuitive knowledge. In this respect, it would not be correct to suppose, as did Moore and Keynes, that any individual can simply consult what lies within his or her mind to determine what must be the case. What is the case, and what each of us may know intuitively, depends largely upon those conventions we abide by in each instance in which intuition is thought justified. We will return to these ideas below.

Keynes again

Keynes, it should be noted, emphasized at the outset of his *Treatise on Probability* that it was necessary to "pass from problems of ultimate analysis and definition . . . to the logical theory and superstructure" of probability and induction, and that in this task both Moore's *Principia Ethica* and Russell and Whitehead's *Principia Mathematica* were stylistic exemplars on which he intended to model his own presentation (Keynes, VIII, pp. 19–20). He thus adopted the essential distinction of the early Cambridge realists between a set of basic statements or propositions which constituted the axioms of his system and a set of derived or non-basic statements or propositions which presented the key results of that system. Indeed, Keynes believed that he had made an important advance within this overall framework upon the efforts of his predecessors, since of the two possible classes of derived statements, namely, those which are equivalent to some closed or finite set of basic statements and are established by deductive inference, and those as general statements which are equivalent to an open set of basic statements and are established by inductive inference, Russell and Whitehead had attempted an analysis only of the former, while Moore's right conduct account of the latter was patently unacceptable. Keynes, then, believed that he was extending and completing the analysis of his philosophical mentors in connection with that part of "logic [which] investigates the general principles of valid thought, the study of arguments, to which it is rational to attach *some* weight," but which are not demonstrative in nature (Keynes, VIII, p. 3).

However, in presupposing a set of basic statements or propositions, which for Russell, Moore, and Keynes had to embody an intuitive knowledge, Keynes's account was vulnerable to the standard critiques of intuition as a form of direct insight that were to cast doubt on the possibility of direct knowledge among most later philosophers. Indeed, this was particularly a problem for Keynes, since his own account of the intuition of probability relationships most pointedly lay open to the critiques of later philosophers in light of his insistence – in one of the most important philosophical doctrines of the *Treatise* – that the availability of new evidence regarding a given probability relation produced, not the revision of a past intuition of the probability relation in question, but rather the occasion for an altogether new intuition of the underlying probability relation (Keynes, VIII, p. 4). Clearly, Keynes could not both allow that new evidence regarding a probability relation forced a revision of a past intuition about that relation and that intuition was always immediate and incorrigible. Yet there was nothing in the *Treatise* that gave reason to think that Keynes could distinguish a new intuition and the revision of a past intuition, though his entire philosophy of the meaning of probability relationships depended upon being able to make this distinction.

On the arguments of later critics of the idea of a foundations epistemology, of course, any attempt to make this distinction was misguided. First, for Neurath, Popper, and Quine, since it cannot be said that any of our beliefs, statements, or concepts can be independently known or justified, what Keynes's insistence on the intuition of entirely new probabilities through new evidence represented was an unpersuasive attempt to claim that one set of statements or propositions were basic – in virtue of their purportedly singular origin in independent acts of intuition – in the face of the obvious dependence of these propositions upon a variety of processes of reasoning that presumably incorporated that sort of knowledge Keynes would have termed derived or non-basic. Second, for Wittgenstein and Austin, Keynes's claim that we always intuit entirely new probabilities when the relevant evidence changes would have appeared an effort to deny the corrigibility of our intuitions, since the idea that we revise and correct our estimation of given probabilities in the light of new evidence makes the notion of an immediate and incorrigible intuition meaningless.

Keynes, interestingly, was not insensitive to the great weight that he had placed on intuition in his analysis, and made a special point of emphasizing that though the relativity of probabilities to evidence introduced subjective considerations into this account, nonetheless "once the facts are given which determine our knowledge, what is probable or improbable in these circumstances has been fixed objectively, and is independent of our opinion" (Keynes, VIII, p. 4). However, in light of later criticisms of foundations epistemology, whether probabilities were to be thought arbitrary and subjective was less at issue than what constituted the proper standards for objectivity in probabilities. None of the critics considered above were proponents of relativism, nor thought that an epistemology without foundations implied knowledge was irretrievably subjective. All did question the individualistic characterization of intuition that the early Cambridge thinkers had employed, though all still allowed some distinction between more intuitive and more inferential forms of knowledge.

The crucial problem with Keynes's early thinking, then, was in his adherence to an understanding of intuition that, as privately available to each and every one of us, purportedly provided certain and objective foundations for the great bulk of knowledge. Indeed, the vulnerability of Keynes's early account is revealed by its combination of ambiguity concerning the nature and process of intuition – "some mental process of which it is difficult to give an account" and a "process" that is "unanalysable" (Keynes, VIII, pp. 13, 14) – and its continual reliance on intuition virtually throughout the argument of the *Treatise*. Ramsey, Braithwaite, and Kneale, three early, sympathetic critics of Keynes, also judged this focus to be the peculiar weakness of an otherwise sophisticated analysis of probability. Keynes, however, was unable to imagine that the orientation he learned from Moore and Russell was misconceived, and accordingly turned quickly in his scholarship to the body and "super-structure" of probability theory. As will be argued below, earlier doubts he had hesitatingly entertained about the concept of intuition and then put aside in the writing of the *Treatise* were not to be resurrected until his work turned to intellectual matters less abstract than logic and more closely linked to the topic of individuals' behavior in economic and political life. Before turning to that later reconsideration of intuition, however, a closer look at the dilemmas Keynes implicitly faced in his thinking about ethics in light of philosophers' subsequent critical evaluation of Moore's intuitionist ethics deserves special attention.

2   The dilemmas of Moore's *Principia* for ethics and economics

To better understand the dilemmas that adherence to Moore's doctrines imposed on Keynes's early philosophical thinking, it will be helpful to first examine the effects that Moore's *Principia Ethica* had on thinking in ethics and economics among professional moral philosophers and economists in the several decades succeeding its publication. Moore's influence was clear and significant in the subsequent development of modern moral philosophy in that the emotivist ethical views that shortly supplanted Moore's *Principia* approach typically made a critique of the book their starting point. In contrast, the effect of Moore's thinking in economics was indirect and subtle, since the methodological thinking that was to have a lasting influence on the economics of price theory, namely, Lionel Robbins's views in *An Essay on the Nature and Significance of Economic Science* (1935), drew implicitly upon these same emotivist ideas advanced in critique of Moore in their popular formulation. The points of convergence between these two different lines of intellectual development have been little explored.[1] Even less well appreciated is Moore's original role in this history, especially in light of the fact that while Moore had meant to provide objectivist foundations for ethics, it was rather the subjectivist, or, as the emotivists had it, non-cognitivist critique of Moore's thinking that counted as the lasting if unintended influence of his work in both ethics and economics. Ironically too, though in philosophy, where Moore's influence was the most tangible, emotivist views have been all but universally abandoned,[2] in economics where Moore's indirect influence is difficult to recognize emotivist views today retain widespread acceptance among economists in their reflections upon policy and normative economics.

In the discussion here, the influence of Moore's *Principia* is first examined in ethics and metaethics as it emerged from Moore's work and then in economics. The treatment of the emotivist moral philosophers – Moore's first successful critics – focuses upon how the inadequacies of Moore's epistemological and ontological thinking led these latter thinkers to produce a view of ethics that was, if less attractive than that set forth in the *Principia*, nonetheless quite persuasive for a time to many philosophers on account of its critical extension of an important part of Moore's argument. The analysis of Robbins's influential methodological position then focuses upon how Robbins's acceptance of key elements of the emotivists' critique of Moore reproduced in economics the same subjectivist, non-cognitivist view of ethical thinking that the emotivists had popularized. Robbins's methodological opinion that economics was natural science, of course, was the target of remarks Keynes made in the late 1930s regarding the nature of economics as a moral science. Thus my argument is that Robbins's implicit adoption of the emotivist critique of Moore was a factor in Keynes's determination to re-appraise Moore's ideas. Below in Chapter 4 I will link the argument to Ramsey's subjectivist probability critique of Keynes.[3] To motivate this argument, this chapter concludes with a critical evaluation of the philosophical thinking shared by the emotivists and Robbins, tying the failings of these two sets of views to the same untenable assumptions adopted in response to Moore. It should be emphasized that my view is that Keynes became especially sensitive to the difficulties in Moore's thinking when he recognized the distortions it imposed on its critics. Their re-channeling of Moore's ideas exposed problems in the *Principia* framework that Keynes had been unable to appreciate when inside the circle of the New Realists. As we will see in the following chapter, this recognition of what Moore's thinking might produce interacted with Keynes's own early hesitations over the concept of intuition.

The reaction to Moore in ethics

Moore's *Principia Ethica* underwent serious and damaging criticism relatively soon after its publication. Moreover, the controversy that surrounded it was ultimately sufficiently momentous that in later decades moral philosophers by and large came to regard the *Principia* as the pivotal work of the century in ethics and metaethics in light of the train of developments it generated in the thinking of its critics (Warnock, 1960; Hudson, 1970; Mayo, 1986). On this view, Moore's thinking contained an unstable combination of appealing and unappealing elements, selection among which imposed difficult and unsatisfactory choices upon its critics. On the one hand, there were Moore's arguments concerning the uniqueness and indefinability of the good. Ethics did indeed seem to be a subject matter fully distinct from non-normative disciplines, and this might well be represented in terms of this special doctrine. On the other hand, Moore's intuitionist view of the objective character of the good seemed entirely implausible. Few disagreed with Broad that this part of

Moore's thinking was unlikely to stand up. The upshot was that Moore's immediate critics retained his view of good (and other moral terms) as unique and indefinable, as well as of ethics as fully set off from all science, while abandoning his objectivist grounding of good and ethics on the grounds that there was no reason to think that the contents of an individual's intuitions corresponded to some objective, non-natural property of the world. Ethics was thus subjective, principally because the contents of individual consciousness taken by themselves were an insufficient epistemological foundation for Moore's conception of the good. Oddly then, once Moore's premise concerning the uniqueness of the ethical was accepted, his foundationalist epistemology with its reliance on the reports of individual consciousness undermined his very efforts to set up an objectivist account of ethics.

Moore's highly philosophical approach to ethics in the *Principia*, it should be noted, was also largely responsible for a substantial change in the way moral philosophers pursued their subject matter, since it effectively made questions in ethics turn on issues in metaethics. Ethics concerns normative claims and reasoning. Metaethics is the study of the epistemological and ontological problems associated with the justification of normative claims. It is not concerned with making or defending any particular set of normative claims or moral judgments, nor does it attempt to provide answers to questions about what is good, right, or obligatory. Metaethics, it might be said, is a second-order discipline devoted to philosophical appraisal of the various claims about what is good, right, or obligatory made by moral agents themselves. Indeed in the view of many contemporary philosophers, what distinguishes the thinking of moral philosophers from that of moralists is that the former are primarily interested in metaethical questions, while the latter are primarily interested in particular normative claims. Metaethics, it might thus be said, has supplanted ethics as moral philosophy proper.

That Moore – in light of his conviction (expressed most emphatically in the Preface to the *Principia*) that a proper understanding of ethics depends upon careful delineation of the philosophical issues surrounding ethical questions – is generally thought to be almost solely responsible for initiating the modern twentieth-century tradition of thinking in metaethics is a particularly important fact behind the reception of the *Principia* and the subsequent evolution of twentieth-century metaethics. Because Moore was especially original in making general philosophical questions central to ethics, he exposed ethics to new issues which in virtue of their novelty were then to become the subject of an extensive debate in following decades. Indeed this development made this period something of a laboratory in ethics that was later to generate many a strong statement about the nature of ethics from commentators outside philosophy. At the same time, however, because Moore was committed to philosophical positions that he, Russell, and Wittgenstein had developed in reaction to nineteenth-century British idealism, which were later subjected to considerable critique, and because the full range of specifically metaethical issues that were to emerge in the following decades were only barely appreciated by Moore, the metaethical views of Moore's *Principia* were not surprisingly vulnerable to the insights and fresh enthusiasm of later philosophers attracted to approaching ethics through metaethics. Thus it might be said that Moore's views were as important for the reaction they inspired as for their own content.

What were Moore's most important metaethical views? As seen in the preceding chapter, what characterized Moore's thinking more than anything else was his conviction that the term "good," by which "we mean . . . that quality which we assert to belong to a thing, when we say that the thing is good," is indefinable (Moore, 1903a, p. 9). By this Moore meant to emphasize that "good" stood for some unique quality which was the referent of the term, and that philosophers who thought "good" could be explained in terms of other properties or qualities of the world committed what he called the naturalistic fallacy. Behind this view, however, was a fundamental metaethical assumption, later to be contested by other philosophers. In insisting that "good" referred to a quality belonging to some things and not others, Moore also adopted the view that moral judgments were either true or false in precisely the same way that descriptive statements are either true or false. That is, if indeed something could be said to be morally wrong, then it was also a fact that this was the case. Later labeled the cognitivist view of moral judgments, the subsequent five decades of metaethical thinking among moral philosophers were to debate this as one of the central propositions of ethics. In particular, thinkers later deemed non-cognitivists denied that correct moral judgments stated truths, and insisted that moral judgments expressed such things as attitudes and prescriptions. In direct opposition to Moore, the most important corollary of this latter view was that there was no such thing as a moral fact.

Moore, it is fair to say, exposed his own thinking to this sort of response, because of his particular view of intuition in the *Principia*. Since intuition was immediate and direct, that is, something that by nature could not be corroborated, it was also incorrigible in that what one successfully intuited was also necessarily true. In effect, it made no sense to suppose that there was even a possibility of false intuition, since false intuition, as equally a matter of pure insight, would be indistinguishable from true intuition, and this would render intuition meaningless as a source of knowledge. Things known intuitively, then, were necessarily true. But, Moore's critics were to ask, if in regard to those things we claim to intuit there exists no possibility of our being wrong, does it really make sense to say that these things are true? That something is true implies that it is not false. Yet that this latter possibility is necessarily excluded makes it unclear that the category of truth is even at issue. Put differently, that intuition for Moore had a necessity to it, or that it was compelling in the manner of a revelation, in no way required that intuition also be about what is true. Truth and falsity are inescapably linked, but truth and necessity are not. Necessary truths, it might better be said, are a limiting case derivative of contingent truths which may be false.

In effect, then, Moore's insistence on intuition as a form of incorrigible insight undermined his view that correct moral judgments stated truths. His first non-cognitivist critics accordingly agreed that moral judgment had its origin in an individual's direct revelation of what might be said to be good, right, etc., but reasoned that, since there was no clear reason to think that this was also a matter of what might truly be thought the case (and some good reason to think it was not), this sort of moral revelation was but an expression of emotion and personal attitude. This way of looking at the matter seemed to possess a special advantage over Moore's view. For Moore, it was all but impossible to reconcile individuals' conflicting intuitions. When two individuals disagreed in their apprehension of what was good, though one necessarily had to be mistaken (since moral judgments stated truths), there was no way of saying with any confidence which had failed to correctly intuit the good. That is, in linking truth and intuition as he did, Moore was unable to produce a theory of error in intuition, and consequently was constrained to place the greater part of his emphasis on the persuasive capacities of those presumably gifted with the ability to see the good as it truly was. This clearly questionable strategy, however, was rendered superfluous by the non-cognitivists' view that moral judgment simply expressed individuals' personal attitudes and emotions. Were moral judgments only to express attitudes and emotions, then individuals might disagree in their apprehension of what they thought good or right without contradicting one another. Though their feelings and views might conflict, this did not imply one or the other was actually wrong in judgment. The non-cognitivists, then, made explanation of error irrelevant to an account of the intuitive apprehension underlying moral judgment. At the same time, they also removed ethics from the domain of objective investigation, as reflected in their conclusion that moral judgments did not target moral facts.

This particular development in thinking about ethics, it should be emphasized, followed directly from Moore's original arguments and assumptions. Moore, recall, had insisted that good was an unique and indefinable quality, and that attempts to characterize what was good in terms of sensible qualities committed what he termed the naturalistic fallacy. For him there was a special "class of objects or properties of objects, which certainly do not exist in time . . . which, in fact, do not *exist* at all . . . [to which] belongs what we mean by the adjective 'good'" (Moore, 1903a, p. 110). Indeed Moore had specifically considered and rejected the possibility that "good" might not mean (or refer to) anything at all. But a view as elusive as this one was hardly likely to recommend itself to many as a means to getting at what was distinctive about moral goodness. C.K. Ogden and I.A. Richards, for example, in their widely read *The Meaning of Meaning* (parts of which are said in the preface to have been written as early as 1910) early on rejected Moore's claim that "good" refers to a common characteristic of things, and did not hesitate to reject the idea that it stood for anything whatsoever. This simple denial of Moore's fundamental assumption (later influentially repeated by Broad in 1934) left them the space to conclude that "good" effectively "serves only as an emotive sign expressing our attitude . . . and perhaps evoking similar attitudes in other persons" (Ogden and Richards, 1923, p. 125). Yet, were there no special quality denoted by "good," it also followed that there was no necessity (as Moore had believed) that individuals possess some special intuitive faculty whose deliverances made this quality self-evident to more or less every one of us. Individuals, it seemed reasonable to say following the thinking of Ogden and Richards, simply made moral discriminations through the use of natural capacities such as perception and emotional response. Moore, it turned out, was little prepared to explain why this should not be so. Thus, as the general philosophical climate of the 1920s and thirties became increasingly empiricist, the idea that individuals possessed special cognitive powers that permitted them unmistakable insight into a metaphysical realm of non-natural qualities became increasingly suspect.

Not surprisingly, those who were to do the most to advance the brand of non-cognitivist metaethics that was to dominate metaethical thinking in the succeeding three decades, that is, emotivism, were the logical positivists, especially A.J. Ayer. Ayer, in his influential *Language, Truth and Logic*, took advantage of the considerable interest that the work of Ogden and Richards had generated in the idea of emotive meaning of language to distil an emotivist critique of Moore that was to popularize more subjectivist thinking about ethics. The logical positivists, of course, first and foremost hoped to combat what they regarded as unscientific, metaphysical thinking, and to this end advanced their famous Verification Principle that asserted "a statement is held to be literally meaningful," that is, not metaphysical, "if and only if it is either analytic or empirically verifiable" (Ayer, 1936, p. 9). This in turn suggested the stance that should be adopted toward ethics. Since moral judgments or ethical statements of any variety were clearly neither analytic nor empirically verifiable, they had to be metaphysical in nature. As such, they failed to achieve the standard scientific statements possessed, and were consequently denied to be objective.[4]

Ayer, in fact, had from the beginning accepted the essential thrust of Moore's naturalistic fallacy argument, agreeing that good could not be defined in naturalistic or empirically meaningful terms. At the same time, he also appreciated that this might well suggest to some that good was therefore a unique and indefinable quality that might be known only through intuition. In admitting that normative ethical concepts cannot be reduced to empirical concepts, he reasoned, we are in danger of leaving the way clear for an "absolutist" view of ethics – that is, the sort of view whereby statements of value, in contrast to ordinary empirical propositions, are established through the agency of a mysterious "intellectual intuition" (p. 106). This, however, was hardly in keeping with the general spirit of the logical positivist project, and thus Ayer saw early on that confronting Moore's view was by no means of secondary importance in the elaboration of a new scientific philosophy.

Considering the use which we have made of the principle that a synthetic proposition is significant only if it is empirically verifiable, it is clear that the acceptance of an "absolutist theory" of ethics would undermine the whole of our main argument. And as we have already rejected the "naturalistic" theories which are commonly supposed to provide the only alternative to "absolutism" in ethics, we seem to have reached a difficult position. We shall meet the difficulty by showing that the correct treatment of ethical statements is afforded by a third theory, which is wholly compatible with our radical empiricism. (pp. 106–7)

What, then, was Ayer's new strategy, and just how did it produce a metaethics alternative to Moore's?

Quite simply, Ayer saw that he could embrace Moore's premise that good was indefinable and unanalyzable, and yet deny the referential theory of meaning premise that the meaning of the term was that to which it referred. On the Verification Principle a term's meaning is coextensive with its conditions of verification, and this made it unnecessary to posit entities underlying the use of terms such as "good." The early Cambridge metaphysics of unobservable entities functioning as the referents of terms was thus abandoned together with the view that ethical statements or moral judgments, because metaphysical, were in any way meaningful. Ayer thus reasoned:

We begin by admitting that the fundamental ethical concepts are unanalyzable, inasmuch as there is no criterion by which one can test the validity of the judgements in which they occur. So far we are in agreement with the absolutists. But, unlike the absolutists, we are able to give an explanation of this fact about ethical concepts. We say that the reason why they are unanalyzable is that they are mere pseudo-concepts. (p. 107)

But, that terms such as "good" are "pseudo-concepts" implies that those ethical statements in which they occur themselves possess only the appearance of being genuine statements. Accordingly, Ayer went on to conclude,

We can see now why it is impossible to find a criterion for determining the validity of ethical judgements. It is not because they have an "absolute" validity which is mysteriously independent of ordinary sense-experience, but because they have no objective validity whatsoever. If a sentence makes no statement at all, there is obviously no sense in asking whether what it says is true or false. And we have seen that sentences which simply express moral judgements do not say anything. They are pure expressions of feeling and as such do not come under the category of truth and falsehood. They are unverifiable for the same reason as a cry of pain or a word of command is unverifiable – because they do not express genuine propositions. (pp. 108–9)

Ethical statements or moral judgments, because they could not be explained in terms of a scientific, non-metaphysical theory of meaning, were not to be thought meaningful. Though they indeed resembled meaningful statements in virtue of their verbalization and sentence form, in fact they were no more than expressions of feeling or attitude, functioning in essentially the same way in human experience as gestures and emotional reactions.

Interestingly, Moore later admitted that it had never occurred to him when he was writing *Principia Ethica* that terms such as "good" might principally have an emotive rather than descriptive function (Moore, 1942, p. 546). When he did come to give consideration to the idea, moreover, he felt that it had to be mistaken, since its being true would imply that moral discourse and debate were meaningless (Moore, 1912, Chapter 3). On such a view, he argued, were one individual to assert something was right and another to assert that same thing was wrong – both presumably on the basis of their respective feelings or attitudes about the matter – then it would follow that this thing would be both right and wrong at the same time. Or, if a single individual asserted something to be right on one occasion but wrong on another, say, in light of changing feelings (though in the absence of any change in the circumstances surrounding the matter at hand), this same thing would again be both right and wrong at the same time. This all made nonsense of the idea that at issue in differences in moral opinion were objective differences between right and wrong or good and bad. Feelings and attitudes might be contrary to one another, but they could never be strictly in contradiction with one another. Moral judgments, Moore believed, concerned truths and moral facts, or otherwise moral discourse and indeed morality itself would be a sham and an illusion.

Ayer, however, found not the least difficulty in responding to Moore's concerns. Addressing Moore's position and argument directly, he denied that moral debate was about objective distinctions between right and wrong or between good and bad, and rather insisted that the only thing objectively at issue in moral debate were the facts relevant to the matter at hand.

For we certainly do engage in disputes which are ordinarily regarded as disputes about questions of value. But, in all such cases, we find, if we consider the matter closely, that the dispute is not really about a question of value, but about questions of fact. When someone disagrees with us about the moral value of a certain action or type of action, we do admittedly resort to argument in order to win him over to our way of thinking. But we do not attempt to show by our arguments that he has the "wrong" ethical feeling towards a situation whose nature he has correctly apprehended. What we attempt to show is that he is mistaken about the facts of the case. (Ayer, 1936, pp. 110–11)

And, when individuals continue to disagree with one another having agreed upon the relevant facts, debate may go on without end.

We pursue such debate in the hope that we have only to get our opponent to agree with us about the nature of the empirical facts for him to adopt the same moral attitude towards them as we do. And as the people with whom we argue have generally received the same moral education as ourselves, and live in the same social order, our expectation is usually justified. But if our opponent happens to have undergone a different process of moral "conditioning" from ourselves, so that, even when he acknowledges all the facts, he still disagrees with us about the moral value of the actions under discussion, then we abandon the attempt to convince him by argument. We say that it is impossible to argue with him because he has a distorted or undeveloped moral sense; which signifies merely that he employs a different set of values from our own. We feel that our own system of values is superior, and therefore speak in such derogatory terms of his. But we cannot bring forward any arguments to show that our system is superior. (p. 111)

In the final analysis, then, moral debate, despite an appearance as rational exchange, is nothing but an exchange of feeling and opinion. No individual's moral judgments are in any sense objectively better or any worse than any other's for the simple reason that differences in moral opinion ultimately depend upon differences in individuals' feelings and attitudes.

Ayer, then, had grasped an essential weakness in Moore's position. Moore, having cut off the ordinary, natural world from the domain of the ethical by means of his unanalyzability doctrine, had little remaining with which to defend his view of moral discourse as objective, other than the presumed existence of moral facts. Moral facts were presumed to exist only because, on the referential theory of meaning, "good" could be said to pick out some real quality of the world, such that things having this quality were then said to be truly good. On the Verification Principle, in contrast, because "good" and other such terms lacked conditions of empirical verification, they therefore lacked meaningfulness altogether. However, while such a view was no doubt persuasive to many logical positivists preoccupied with the language of science and the topics of truth and fact, a stronger response to Moore entailed explaining how moral terms and assertions actually functioned in our language. Such a theory was advanced by the most influential contributor to emotivist metaethics, C.L. Stevenson, who was a student of Moore's and also took Moore's work as his starting point.

Stevenson recognized that the emotivist view required some theory of emotive meaning specifically appropriate to ethical discourse, and advanced what has since come to be known as the causal or psychological theory of meaning of ethical terms. On this theory, the emotive meaning of a word is just that set of psychological causes and effects that tend to be associated with its utterance. "The emotive meaning of a word is the tendency of a word, arising through the history of its usage, to produce (result from) affective responses in people" (Stevenson, 1937, p. 14). The usage of terms such as "good," then, simply reflects the psychological conditions associated with speakers' and hearers' communication of their favorable interests, and does not in the least signal anything distinctively normative in the world. Perhaps the most important reason for thinking this, Stevenson believed, was that while it could be empirically verified (and thus be true or false) that individuals had certain interests, favorable and unfavorable, that they might reflect in their use of moral language, the purported normative content of their claims, for example, that something was thought good or right, could never be empirically verified (nor ever be true or false). That is, in contrast to those matters that could be treated in descriptive or scientific terms, moral discourse as it was traditionally understood was best characterized as non-cognitive, and one could therefore talk about moral discourse scientifically only if one were to concentrate on examining the causal relations between psychological states of individuals. Traditional moral discourse itself on Stevenson's view, then, lacked any identifiable cognitive content in and of itself.

Stevenson's psychological or causal theory of the meaning of ethical terms, consequently, both reinforced Ayer's claim that ethical terms were "pure expressions of feeling," and provided further theoretical support for the logical positivist–emotivist distinction between the cognitive (or logical) and non-cognitive (or psychological) properties of language. For our purposes here, it is important to note that the addition of a causal theory of meaning of evaluative terms to the verificationist theory of meaning of descriptive terms, and the associated logical positivist–emotivist demarcation of science and non-science, was, subsequent to Robbins's methodological arguments in his *Essay*, to play an important role in economics in encouraging the view that positive economic analysis was objective while values, ethics, and policy were subjective. Ironically, then, philosophers were soon by and large to agree with one of Stevenson's principal critics, R.B. Brandt, that, though ethical terms and evaluative language did indeed possess an emotive dimension, this hardly implied that moral discourse was non-cognitive or irremediably subjective (Brandt, 1950). Separately but no less significantly, when growth of knowledge considerations and the distinction between the context of discovery and the context of justification became central to epistemology and the philosophy of science in the late 1960s (e.g., Lakatos and Musgrave, 1970), many philosophers also became persuaded that science was not demonstrably more objective than ethics. Together, these developments arguably thus meant that logical positivist–emotivist efforts to demarcate science and non-science were not just a more complicated enterprise than originally believed, but were rather for most philosophers simply misconceived in intent.

This reversal and transformation of philosophers' thinking about the relationship between the objectives and nature of science and ethics is unfamiliar to most economists. Thus it seems fair to say that while economists who reflect on economic methodology increasingly believe logical positivist verificationist views to be exaggerated and unsound, they nonetheless still remain attached to the emotivist counterpart of these views in their thinking about value judgments, ethics, and policy statement. This is not just of interest for understanding contemporary economics, however. It is central to an account of the development of Keynes's own understanding of economics, since, as will be argued in the next chapter, the hesitations Keynes had felt about the concept of intuition in a number of his early Apostles papers offered elements of a rudimentary response to the emotivist critique of Moore. Not unrelated also are Keynes's later critical remarks on Robbins's view of economics. Before turning to all of this, then, how was Robbins's characterization of economics linked to emotivism?

Robbins's *Essay* and the development of emotivist thinking in economics

Robbins's *An Essay on the Nature and Significance of Economic Science* (1935), and later exchange with R.F. Harrod in the *Economic Journal* concerning the feasibility of interpersonal comparisons of utility (Harrod, 1938; Robbins, 1938), was by most accounts of central importance in establishing both the view of economics as a science held by the great majority of modern economists, as well as their view of its normative or policy component.[5] In both the *Essay* and in his later response to Harrod, Robbins argued against the use of interpersonal utility comparisons in economics, upon which many had relied in making utilitarian welfare recommendations, and then went on to define economics as the "science which studies human behaviour as a relationship between ends and scarce means which have alternative uses" (Robbins, 1935, pp. 16–17). This means–ends conception depended upon distinguishing "economic science," which was positive and value-free, and concerned how best to allocate scarce resources between alternative ends, and "political economy," which explicitly concerned values and the normative selection and evaluation of the ends of economic activity. More importantly for purposes here, however, was the position that Robbins took regarding the relative standing of economics and ethics. In his view, economics as science of resource allocation constituted a fully rational form of analysis pursued entirely separately from our choices over alternative ends. Ethics was about individuals' "logically incompatible" alternative goals or ends, which as such were not themselves susceptible to rational treatment, but which could nonetheless be rationally elucidated using economic analysis (pp. 154–5).

Robbins, it should be noted, was not actually a logical positivist himself. Indeed Robbins's means–ends definition of economics was not so much derived from the empiricist tradition of the Vienna Circle Austrians, but more so from the Austrian economics deductivist tradition that had F.A. von Hayek as an important representative at the London School of Economics where Robbins was located.[6] However, that Robbins made use of an axiomatic, *a priorist* form of reasoning in a spirit foreign to the practices of the Vienna Circle did not preclude his adopting a position on the status of ethics that was entirely conformable to the logical positivist–emotivist conception. Whether he himself was directly influenced by the more general programmatic claims of the logical positivists of the 1930s regarding the distinctiveness of science, then, is less at issue than whether the position he did assume regarding the status of ethics well suited the logical positivist–emotivist view that economists were to pursue after absorbing the message of the *Essay* in succeeding decades.[7]

Robbins's arguments concerning ethics appeared chiefly in the sixth and last chapter of his *Essay*. Responding to the views of Ralph Hawtrey and J.A. Hobson who had maintained that economics and ethics could not be dissociated, Robbins insisted that there was "a logical gulf" between economics and ethics, because, as he put it, the "two fields of inquiry are not on the same plane of discourse" (p. 148). This followed, Robbins explained, from the simple fact that economics, or more accurately economic science, is composed of propositions that involve the verb "is," while ethics is composed of propositions that involve the verb "ought." Because of this difference in propositional forms, economics can be seen to concern facts and ethics values. This implied, Robbins went on to argue, that economics and ethics are ultimately fundamentally different in that we are able, at least in principle, to verify the propositions of economics, while the idea of verifying the propositions of ethics is altogether inconceivable.

That Robbins thus made verifiability the touchstone of his distinction between the propositions of economics and those of ethics accorded nicely with the thrust of Ayer's thinking about the differences between science and non-science. Indeed Ayer's expression of the famous Verification Principle of meaning similarly focused on propositional forms and language in that it used the distinction between "ought" propositions and "is" propositions to distinguish what was a matter of fact (or analytically the case) from what was a matter of value. Ayer's expression of the demarcation criterion, nonetheless, was only a first step toward the emotivist view of ethical statements, since many earlier thinkers had believed ethics and science fundamentally different and yet had not judged ethics an intrinsically less objective enterprise. The decisive step toward emotivism, rather, involved Ayer's further claim that because (non-analytic) "is" propositions, unlike "ought" propositions, were verifiable, they alone were scientific and objective. That is, because the former could be put to the test of experience through our observation of the world, they alone could be guaranteed to be free of the sort of incoherence and confusion that Ayer and the logical positivists thought metaphysical and ethical thinking typically brought to science.

We saw above that Ayer effectively brought this emphasis on experience and observation to bear against the idea that moral dispute and debate might be a rational exchange. Moore had been particularly vulnerable on the subject in that while he was persuasive in arguing that good was unique and indefinable, he was thoroughly unpersuasive in arguing that intuition gave us access to good as an objective, non-natural – and therefore unobservable – property of the world. Ayer, following Broad and others who had simply denied that there was any reason to believe in the existence of such non-natural properties, reasoned that moral dispute without an anchor in a transcendent, metaphysical realm was inherently irresolvable. At best, one could reach agreement on the facts at hand, but after this there was nothing objective left to establish. Whereas factual propositions could be adjudicated relative to the test of experience, ethical statements lacked comparable means of examination and evaluation. They therefore appeared subjective in comparison with factual statements, making ethics subjective in comparison with science.

This, essentially, was just the sort of view that Robbins had adopted, with the result he also took the same, decisive step toward the emotivist position that Ayer took by adding to the business of demarcation of science and ethics a comparative judgment of economics and ethics that left ethics an essentially subjective enterprise. Reasoning in terms of his Austrian means–ends characterization of economics, Robbins not only insisted that economic science was entirely neutral with respect to ends, in that it concerned an analysis of the allocation of scarce resources that was entirely free of all considerations of value, but he also asserted, in terms reminiscent of Ayer's position, that this truly "scientific analysis" alone permitted the sort of dispute resolution that made objective distinctions in thought possible.

In the rough-and-tumble of political struggle, differences of opinion may arise either as a result of differences about ends or as result of differences about the means of attaining ends. Now, as regards the first type of difference, neither Economics nor any other science can provide any solvent. If we disagree about ends it is a case of thy blood or mine – or live and let live, according to the importance of the difference, or the relative strength of our opponents. But, if we disagree about means, then scientific analysis can often help us resolve our differences. If we disagree about the morality of the taking of interest . . . then there is no room for argument. But if we disagree about the objective implications of fluctuations in the rate of interest, then economic analysis should enable us to settle our dispute. (Robbins, 1935, pp. 150–1)

Thus, like Ayer in his reference to differences in "moral 'conditioning'," intellectual dispute for Robbins was susceptible of only as much resolution as could be achieved in establishing the facts at issue. In economics this involved a form of analysis that had earlier been argued in the *Essay* to depend upon an examination of facts about individual preferences, which Robbins noted one was able to verify through introspection and observation (pp. 78–9, 148). Beyond this, however, no resolution of differences concerning competing ends was to be hoped for or expected. It was simply "a case of thy blood or mine," or at best "live and let live," since there simply were no "objective implications" about the morality of one view compared to another.

This conception of ethics as a subjective, even irrational realm of human thought perfectly captured the spirit and intent of the logical positivist–emotivist non-cognitivism. Robbins's espousal of the position, moreover, was particularly important in economics, in that it underlay his re-definition of the discipline along means–ends lines in a manner that was to have special appeal to economists concerned to emphasize the scientific character of their field. The ways in which this occurred have been the subject of extensive controversy. Robbins argued that though the welfare economics dominant at the time had relied on interpersonal comparisons of utility for important policy recommendations, because interpersonal utility comparisons were at best conventional judgments and "essentially normative," they necessarily fell outside the scope of positive science. To state that some individual A's preference stands above some other individual B's preference in order of importance is an entirely different thing from stating that individual A prefers n to m and individual B prefers m to n. Doing the former involves an element of conventional valuation. Hence it is "essentially normative," and can have no place in pure science (p. 139). Doing the latter involves making a claim subject to empirical examination. In the final analysis, then, value judgments had no place in economics, because in cases such as these *"There is no means of testing the magnitude of A's satisfaction as compared with B's"* (pp. 139–40; original emphasis).

Robbins's thinking thus resembled that of the logical positivists in important respects. This may in part have derived from the influence on his thinking of Philip Wicksteed, who himself had strong positivist inclinations. Yet it would be wrong to suggest that Robbins's thinking was entirely consistent with the logical positivists' program. With his Austrian deductivist methodological convictions, Robbins basically restricted verification to the practice of determining the applicability rather than the validity of principles and concepts. Further, his emphasis on introspection as a means of verifying individuals' ranking of their preferences was hardly in keeping with the logical positivists' treatment of testing and observation as a characteristically public form of verification. These differences, nonetheless, suggest something important about the nature of the affinities between Robbins and the logical positivists. In particular, they suggest that the strongest affinities between Robbins and the logical positivists had principally to do with their shared emotivist view of ethics as irremediably subjective. That Robbins seems to have adopted strong verificationist language only in connection with his critique of ethics argues that prior convictions about the nature of ethics shared with the logical positivists–emotivists made verificationism in the name of science a ready theoretical tool. Robbins was thus in effect predisposed to accept the emotivist critique of the sort of ideas Moore had advanced, and apparently felt that an emphasis on verification was compatible with his existing methodological and theoretical views about economics. In support of this interpretation of a chain of influence from

Moore to Robbins through the logical positivist–emotivists is the continued success of Robbins's critique of interpersonal utility comparisons among contemporary economists. Though contemporary economists remain methodologically empiricist, they no longer espouse simple-minded verificationism.[8] They do, however, continue to regard value judgments as subjective, while by and large agreeing with Robbins that interpersonal utility comparisons have no place in economics. This would argue that what had the strongest appeal in Robbins's *Essay* was his critique of ethics and vision of economics as a science. What, then, precisely was it in Robbins's characterization of interpersonal utility comparisons as conventional and "essentially normative" that was so appealing to economists?

In light of his assertion about being unable to test the magnitude of one person's satisfaction compared to another's, Robbins's chief emphasis rested on the non-comparability of different individuals' preferences. While earlier in the *Essay* Robbins had said that it was "an essential constituent of our conception of conduct with an economic aspect" and "an elementary fact of experience" that each individual is able to rank his or her preferences (pp. 75, 76), it was an "entirely different" matter – and something that can be treated only in conventional and therefore subjective terms – to say that one individual's satisfaction is of greater magnitude than another's. In terms of the thinking that has come to represent this distinction for most contemporary economists, this is of course to say that preferences are the sort of thing that can be evaluated ordinally but not cardinally. However, in terms of the psychology of individuals this was also to say that preferences are essentially private in nature in the sense that it is never possible to say why an individual prefers one thing to another, merely that such a ranking obtains. Ordinal comparisons of taste, that is, require only that an individual's preferences be discriminated one from another in terms of their relative desirability. This registered, these preference rankings are then obscure in all other respects. Indeed, were it possible to attribute additional meaning to individuals' preferences beyond their simple ranking, then there would exist a rudimentary basis for assessing and comparing one individual's preferences with those of another, and thus a potential basis for making cardinal comparisons of taste across different individuals. Non-comparable preferences, accordingly, had the simple virtue for Robbins and subsequent ordinalist thinkers of allowing preference and taste to play a role in economics without yet allowing any substantive discussion of the social nature of taste.

This understanding, as is well known, was instrumental in re-shaping economists' conception of the proper boundaries of economic policy in the years subsequent to the publication of the *Essay*. In contrast to the potentially far-reaching scope of traditional utilitarian policy recommendations that had made important use of interpersonal utility comparisons, economists accepting Robbins's arguments now adopted the less ambitious Pareto efficiency framework which allowed only ordinal welfare comparisons. Perhaps more importantly, however, for some time many economists wondered whether economics possessed any justifiable normative component whatsoever. Harrod, for example, argued in his Presidential Address to Section F of the British Association that were economists to accept Robbins's view of interpersonal utility comparisons, then policy recommendation would ultimately cease to be a part of economics (Harrod, 1938). Indeed, according to Robbins ethics was entirely conventional, and thus did not merit scientists' involvement. Ends were given from outside of economic science, and economists were restricted to explaining their analytical implications (Robbins, 1935, p. 149). In short, policy recommendation could never flow from positive economic analysis itself, since "ought" and "is" were on two separate, incommunicable planes of discourse, and (following David Hume) one could never argue from "is" to "ought."

Pareto efficiency judgments, moreover, possessed a unique advantage in being grounded in what Robbins had designated the "main postulate of the theory of value," namely, "that individuals can arrange their preferences in an order" (pp. 78–9), since a given Pareto improvement might be recommended if it could be shown that but one individual preferred the result and no others thought themselves worse off. Surely, many economists must have then reasoned, to demonstrate that a given change was Pareto efficient was not to argue in normative terms at all, but only to show what (at least) one person preferred. Were it the case as Robbins had said that it was "an elementary fact of experience" that "individuals can arrange their preferences in an order," then Pareto efficiency judgments primarily possessed descriptive rather than prescriptive significance. Indeed, the economist as scientist need not even prescribe possible Pareto improvements, since it was sufficient to simply explain what in fact constituted an unequivocally greater satisfaction of preferences, and then allow society to make what determination of the matter it chose (cf. e.g. Archibald, 1959).

Robbins's privacy view of individuals' preferences, then, had a very significant impact upon economists' conception of their discipline. Indeed, the logic in Robbins's position was strong. Were the contents of an individual's preferences fully private to that individual, then either interpersonal utility comparisons were meaningless or they were conventional and subjective. Moreover, since ethics made interpersonal comparisons of utility when it weighed one person's ends against another's, ethics was thus concerned with the content and nature of intrinsically private preferences, and was thus either meaningless or simply conventional. Robbins's privacy doctrine, then, corresponded in a precise way to the emotivists' understanding of ethical statements. Whereas for the emotivists ethical statements were expressions of feeling and attitude, and thus private by nature, for Robbins and the ordinalists preference rankings were fully private, and thus not different in nature from expressions of feeling and attitude. Ordinalism, consequently, replicated in economics the principal doctrine of logical positivism concerning ethics, leaving economists in effect in the same camp as Moore's more immediate critics in philosophy.

These developments in ethics and economics in the 1930s sprang from a single critique of Moore's thinking about intuition in the *Principia*, namely, that intuition as a form of immediate judgment was necessarily subjective. Yet there were other ways to address Moore's views and the reliance upon intuitive judgment in epistemology alternative to that adopted by the emotivists and ordinalists. To understand one of the most important of these alternative paths of development, the general critique of Moore and early Cambridge philosophy initiated at the end of the last chapter will now be extended in the discussion of a critique of subjectivism launched by important figures in economics and philosophy contemporary to Ayer and Robbins. Then, in the chapter to follow, Keynes's own early critique of Moore's thinking will be examined with an eye to determining its later development as well as linkages to this alternative response to Moore on intuition. On the argument to be developed, Keynes was ultimately to remove himself philosophically from his early commitment to Moore, not by following the subjectivist critique of Moore by thinkers like Ayer and Robbins, but by pursuing a line of thought not unlike that of the later Wittgenstein.

Fundamental difficulties in the emotivist and ordinalist frameworks

The principal difficulties inherent in emotivism were evident to most philosophers by the late 1940s. In the first place, it became clear that although moral or ethical statements can be and are often used in a persuasive and expressive manner, this does not imply that they either lack other significance or are necessarily subjective. Indeed, the suppressed premise in the emotivist argument concerning the nature of moral discourse is that ethical statements can be fully reduced in meaning to something non-cognitive in character, or expressions of attitude or feeling. This reductionist strategy, however, achieves what apparent plausibility it possesses only in virtue of the ostensibly inadequate theory of the meaning of moral language provided by Moore, namely, the referential theory. Indeed, the emotivists never themselves gave independent arguments for limiting the meaning of ethical statements to emotive meaning. Accordingly, moral philosophers were ultimately to reason that, given the diverse variety of uses of moral language, there must arguably be a whole number of ways of explaining meaning in moral discourse, the existence of which precludes treating moral statements as nothing more than expressions of attitude and feeling (cf. e.g. Hare, 1981).

This emphasis on greater attention to the various uses and functions of moral language led philosophers to reconsider the emotivists' important arguments concerning the nature of moral dispute and disagreement. Ayer, it was seen, claimed that moral dispute and disagreement were a fundamentally non-cognitive exchange of opinion. As Brandt argued, however, attention to the nature of moral discourse demonstrates that at the very least there exists a distinction between the expression of sentiments peculiar to particular individuals and the expression of sentiments approved by individuals generally (Brandt, 1950). Moral judgments, on this view, are typically made with the expectation that they will withstand some degree of rational scrutiny, and this expectation signals the functioning of a standard and measure of objectivity we attribute to moral discourse. Moreover, Brandt went on to argue, moral judgments, like positive propositions, seem subject to two kinds of truth criteria, namely, ethical consistency and that such judgments involve something more substantive than temporary attachment to what one expresses (pp. 315–16). From this perspective, "is" and "ought" propositions are not so nearly different in nature as many might suppose. More strongly, ethics is not obviously less objective as intellectual enterprise than is science.

Given the acceptance of these arguments by philosophers, it might have been thought that economists would also have begun to question the conclusions of Robbins's arguments regarding ethics, especially the proposition that value judgments were best thought merely conventional. A re-evaluation of ethics might then have led to a reconsideration of Robbins's definition of economics, which cast economics as a positive science. However, Robbins's more general view, we have just seen, possessed an additional conceptual foundation in his implicit understanding of preferences as essentially private. Thus, though Robbins's view of the normative employed essentially the same ideas as had the emotivists, the fact that Robbins made the psychology of the economic agent central to his own critique of interpersonal utility comparisons and re-definition of economics meant that philosophers' subsequent re-evaluation of ethics did not directly address what was of central importance to economists in the *Essay*. For economists, the privacy of individual preference accorded especially well with their prior commitment to individualism since Jevons. Robbins's implicit commitment to the privacy of preferences, then, drew upon this in a way that gave the emotivists' view of ethics a natural place in economic methodology, irrespective of its merits or lack thereof as doctrine or critique of earlier philosophy. For these reasons, the alternative path of critique of Moore influenced in important respects by Wittgenstein (1953) was to be lost upon most economists, who were to remain subjectivist in regard to agent psychology and non-cognitivist in regard to policy and ethics.

Interestingly enough, one economist, T.W. Hutchison, anticipated a number of important arguments Wittgenstein later advanced in a perceptive, early evaluation of Robbins's argument against interpersonal utility comparisons (Hutchison, 1938). For Hutchison, if interpersonal utility comparisons made no sense, it was not clear that one had grounds for saying that intrapersonal utility comparisons made any sense either. That is, were it not possible to say how one person's satisfactions compared with those of another, it seemed equally unlikely, Hutchison thought, that a single individual was able to say that one thing produced more satisfaction than some other thing. Economists in the ordinalist tradition, of course, were not impressed with this suggestion, and indeed their reasoning is not difficult to appreciate. Cardinal utility comparisons across individuals were doubly demanding in that not only was it necessary that a single individual be able to say precisely how much more satisfaction one thing yielded than another, but at the same time different individuals had to possess commensurate scales of measure were the magnitude of their satisfactions to be interpersonally comparable. Thus, that single individuals could only rank their satisfactions and that these rankings were not interpersonally comparable seemed to be the most conservative assumption compatible with any analysis of individuals' preferences whatsoever.

The logic of this retreat from the undeniable difficulties inherent in making interpersonal utility comparisons, however, does not take into consideration the underlying dilemma Hutchison's suggestion raised for Robbins's view. If it can indeed be said that we cannot make cardinal utility comparisons, then we must presumably have some specific reason for saying that we can make ordinal utility comparisons. Robbins, however, never offered a reason *per se* for saying that ordinal comparisons were possible. Indeed, he specifically disclaimed the need to produce such a reason, insisting both that it was merely a fact that this was so, as well as a fundamental, *a priori* postulate of the theory of value that individuals "can arrange their preferences in an order" (Robbins, 1935, pp. 78–9). Thus, as Hutchison recognized, nothing commands us to think that the critique of cardinal utility comparisons does not also extend to ordinal utility comparisons. More formally speaking, absent from Robbins's critique are the criteria necessary for an identification and comparison of preferences to rule out cardinal comparisons yet permit ordinal ones. This, of course, is as one would expect with Robbins's view of taste as intrinsically private in nature, since criteria as a conceptual tool are public by nature, and Robbins, if anything in his critique of interpersonal utility comparisons, was intent upon denying the appropriateness of any social review of taste.

However, that neither Robbins nor subsequent ordinalists enunciated criteria for the identification and comparison of preferences does not mean that some philosophical defense of the privacy of taste is not possible. Indeed, in the absence of some such defense, it seems Robbins's view would have ultimately been rejected, so that consequently its having remained plausible to many economists for so long indicates that the opposite is the case, that is, that there is indeed an underlying philosophical rationale for the view. The position taken here, then, is that this implicit philosophical defense needs to be elaborated, in order to determine whether there exist reasonable criteria for utility comparisons of any sort. What, then, precisely are the central assumptions underlying Robbins's view that ordinal utility comparisons alone are possible? Further, what philosophical conception supports these assumptions?

To say that the content of an individual's preferences are meaningful only to the individual experiencing them, or at least that their meaning and significance is so limited for others that they are unable to find any way of evaluating or understanding a given individual's preferences relative to their own or others', is central to the idea of a privacy of tastes. This conception of privacy, on the surface, is a seemingly problematic one, however, since it both requires preferences be highly opaque, in that even the individual to whom preferences belong cannot articulate to others anything more than that one preference ranks above another, yet also requires that preferences be sufficiently intelligible to the individual having them that they can somehow be ranked. How is it, it might be asked then, that an individual can rank his or her own preferences, but cannot give his or reasons for doing so? How is it, that is, that an individual can differentiate his or her own tastes to the extent of placing a greater or lesser value upon them, but still cannot say anything about the basis for these distinctions?

The answer to these questions, it can be argued, lies in the suitability of the emotivists' reformulation of Moore's *Principia* theory of intuition to Robbins's view of the privacy of preferences. The emotivists, recall, denied that "good" referred to a simple, non-natural property of the world which Moore believed objectively anchored ethical statements. However, they retained his view that an individual's ethical pronouncements were a matter of some sort of intuitive grasp, transforming this to mean an individual's expression of attitude or feelings. Just as Moore had thought intuition immediate and incorrigible, so too the emotivists agreed that an individual could not be mistaken in his or her moral opinions, since the individual was always the final arbiter over his or her own attitudes and feelings. Indeed, the essence of the non-cognitivism, as reflected in the emotivists' view of moral dispute, was that the intuitional quality of different persons' moral opinions gave ethics its fundamentally unsettlable nature. The emotivists, therefore, captured the crucial element in Moore's understanding of intuition as incorrigible and immediate, yet, in their commitment to a rationality driven by scientific concern with publicly replicable observation and experiment, concluded that the sort of intuition one found in ethical statements was non-cognitive in nature.

This re-formulation of Moore's understanding of intuition provided the essential framework for Robbins's conception of the privacy of preferences, since it postulated a realm of mental experience that produced determinate distinctions, in that intuition was certain and incorrigible, and yet also one whose results could not be communicated to others, in that on the emotivist understanding intuition involved a characteristically non-cognitive expression of individual attitude and feeling. On this view, Robbins could say that an individual was able to differentiate his or her preferences to the extent of placing a greater or lesser value upon them without at the same time finding it necessary to say anything about the meaning of these distinctions to others, simply because individuals apparently possessed a non-intellectual or emotive faculty of intuition that enabled them to do so. Whether or not, then, Robbins actually believed he was making use of the ideas developed by his philosophical counterparts of the 1930s, his own view ultimately depended for its creditability upon a philosophical psychology and epistemology of mental experience that shared the emotivists' principal conclusions. On this conception, an individual could effectively name his or her preferences or private mental experiences (in feeling one thing, n, preferred to another, m), and communicate these names and preference to others (in actually saying "n is preferred to m"), though the logic and rationale inherent in using this language as it was used was necessarily unintelligible to others. Indeed since on this understanding why an individual might name or designate his or her preferences in one manner or another is unintelligible to others, individuals are free to identify their preferences simply by naming the experience he or she associates with a preferred item "more preferred" and the experience associated with a less preferred item "less preferred." Robbins himself makes use of this simplifying strategy in his own characterization of individual preferences in terms of n's and m's. It does not matter, he thus assumes, just how individual preferences are named and labeled, because their naming involves an individual's essentially private mental association between something felt to be preferred over something else and the labels this individual alone afixes to these things so experienced. The individual, that is, is in a privileged position relative to his or her private mental experience, and is thus able to generate an intrinsically private language about this mental experience. Indeed, since all individuals are in this same position, there are as many private languages concerning mental experience as there are individuals.

Yet while this account of Robbins's thinking provides a philosophical rationale for the privacy of tastes missing in (but true to) Robbins's thinking in the *Essay*, it still fails to provide an answer to the question Hutchison raised about ordinal utility comparisons, namely, whether they should be thought possible when cardinal comparisons are said to be impossible. In fact, the philosophical psychology or epistemology of mental experience provided above, by making explicit the philosophical assumptions inherent in the privacy view, actually makes clear in a way Robbins's own account does not what the fundamental dilemmas are facing those who wish to allow ordinal utility comparisons but rule out cardinal ones. To see this, it is necessary to see how this particular brand of philosophical psychology itself came in for criticism from philosophers, most importantly in Wittgenstein's later arguments in his *Philosophical Investigations* (1953) concerning the impossibility of private languages.

Wittgenstein's critique

Wittgenstein, who had earlier in his own *Tractatus Logico-Philosophicus* (1921) held a view that in important respects resembled the one described above, came to believe that this sort of philosophical psychology suffered from a fundamental dilemmas, the solution to which revealed important requirements any language necessarily had to fulfill.[9] A language, Wittgenstein noted, involved rules for the usage of terms and expressions that language-users employ, such that once one had learned a rule governing the usage of a particular term or expression, one's past intentions in using this language would seem to determine uniquely how this bit of language would be put to use in similar contexts in the future.

Yet, Wittgenstein noted, when one examines an individual's past intentions in using a particular term or expression, it is never quite possible to discover any single fact about that individual's intentions that conclusively demonstrates just how the term or expression in question is to be used on future occasions. Language, like scientific generalization, that is, faces a seemingly insoluble problem of induction in that while one might attempt to distill from past intention various principles for the use of a given term or expression in the future, nonetheless because of the innumerably different contexts in which language might later be applied which may add to its sense and meaning from past occasions, it seems impossible to employ past intentions governing language's use as a guide to establishing principles that conclusively distinguish appropriate from inappropriate language use. As Wittgenstein paradoxically put it: "no course of action could be determined by a rule, because every course of action can be made out to accord with the rule" (1953, sect. 201).

Moreover, Wittgenstein reasoned, private languages of the sort described above compound the general inductive difficulty involved in explaining language, since private languages concern an intrinsically inaccessible form of human experience, namely, that which might be said to be internal to the individual. Thus, for it to be possible to say that an individual consistently gives the same names to the same mental experiences over time, it must be possible to say that that individual is able to employ some rule in a private language concerning his or her past intentions in using certain expressions to designate certain mental experiences to similarly name those same mental experiences on future occasions. For Wittgenstein, however, not only does it seem that no single fact nor indeed anything that one could describe in one's past intentions in using language would ever explain the future use of that same language, but, moreover, it also seems altogether inconceivable that an individual could ever conclusively establish facts of any sort whatsoever concerning his or her mental life for those necessarily external to it. This follows from the fact that the only evidence concerning an individual's mental experience others could ever acquire would derive from that individual's own reports concerning his or her mental experience. However, no one could ever establish the veracity of these reports, since they would never be in a position to examine their connection to the inner mental experience of the individual reporting them. Consequently, it is inconceivable that a private language-user could ever demonstrate that there were any facts about past intentions in using language to describe his or her mental experience that figured in a rule for the future use of that same language.

One cannot agree with Robbins, then, that it is a simple matter of fact that individuals are able to arrange their preferences in an order, since facts about preferences are impossible to establish when reported in a private language, as Robbins's critique of cardinal utility comparisons and defense of ordinal comparisons requires. Hutchison was thus correct to suspect that intrapersonal utility comparisons are put in jeopardy when interpersonal ones are brought into question in the manner of Robbins. However, that Wittgenstein's critique of the idea of a private language is a species of his more general skeptical paradox about language suggests that were it possible to somehow explain how language rules generally operate, then it might also be possible to somehow explain how language about an individual's internal mental experience operates. Indeed, Wittgenstein himself neither believed that it was impossible to explain the rule-governed character of language, nor thought that it was impossible for individuals to use language to characterize their own internal mental experiences in terms understandable by others. He offered what might be said to amount to a "skeptical solution" to his paradox about language, requiring a significant re-conceptualization of what language involves, and, most importantly for the discussion here, a rejection of the philosophical psychology that had its origins in Moore's theory of intuition (Kripke, 1982, pp. 66–9).

For Wittgenstein, the difficulties involved in explaining language described above were closely linked to a model of language too narrowly focused upon truth conditions in fact-stating declarative sentences. People, Wittgenstein realized, use language in a variety of ways that do not always require reference to facts or truth conditions, and that language can accordingly best be understood in terms of the different social practices associated with these different uses of language. An understanding of the rules governing the use of language, moreover, is first and foremost concerned with establishing just what is involved in the successful use of language. This means that the circumstances in which language is used together with the function a given language practice possesses in people's lives are our primary objects of concern, and that determining whether a sentence fulfills truth conditions is often irrelevant to determining that sentence's significance. Accordingly one did not ask what facts had to be true to explain an individual's past intention in using a given term or expression properly on a future occasion, but rather asked what justified an individual's assertion in particular circumstances in a particular "language-game" (Wittgenstein, 1953, sect. 23). This depended in important degree upon the on-going judgments of language-users themselves regarding whether the new use of a given term or expression was appropriate in the circumstances at hand relative to language-users' past intentions in using that term or expression in similar but different circumstances. It was thus – contrary to the spirit of his paradox about language rules – not a collection of facts that explained the use of new language so much as individuals' commitment to play a "language-game" with one another that was central to the explanation of language use.

With this emphasis upon the dynamic character of judgment in a community of language-users, however, it no longer makes sense to speak of private languages, since an individual's meaning always depends upon the nature of the "language-game" in which he or she participates and interacts with others. Language, it might simply be said, is by nature a public affair, so that even the use of that set of terms and expressions used to characterize an individual's private experiences must still be governed by intersubjective assertability conditions. Thus, while individuals of course always have their own individual preferences regarding the items of their experience, the language in which they understand and interpret these preferences cannot be private. Just how an individual sees him or herself preferring one thing to another, then, is inseparable from the way language-users generally employ commonly recognized distinctions in language to characterize the relative desirability of the various things they experience.

All of this, clearly, is quite inconsistent with the philosophical psychology and epistemology of mental experience which made its way, albeit with some changes, from Moore to the emotivists. For Moore, each individual in isolation is supposed to be able to determine what a term such as "good" applies to in virtue of possessing a special faculty of intuition affording immediate and incorrigible insight into the underlying nature of reality. Similarly for the emotivists, each individual is supposed to be able to grasp without being in interaction with others that the meaning of "good" is tied to the feelings or attitudes of approval each individual detects in him or herself toward his or her environment and others. For Wittgenstein, however, since meanings depend upon the language-games in which they are employed, meanings can never be explained solely in terms of a single individual's private apprehensions of his or her mental experience. An individual's apprehension of a particular meaning, rather, is always conditional upon the social determination of meaning, and the idea that individuals possess an autonomous and unchallengeable intuitive grasp of meanings – whether this apprehension is a matter of cognitive insight or affective response – is simply mistaken. Preferences, accordingly, are neither private in Robbins's sense, because of their interpretation in an intrinsically public language, nor indeed immediate and unmistakable, on account of the fact that an individual's very apprehension of his or her own tastes and preferences involves an element of evaluation involved in that individual's integration of a social meaning and an inner experience. It is not just, that is, the fact that the language we use to describe our preferences is social by nature that is significant for Wittgenstein. It is also significant that the very process of our making use of language in connection with our personal experience requires we emphasize the social nature of language.

Most importantly, however, because for Wittgenstein our tastes and preferences always possess an element of social interpretation and understanding, as determined by the "language-game" in which they are described, language also possesses an undeniably normative dimension. After his statement of the paradox he had discovered involved in following language rules, Wittgenstein went on to say that "to *think* one is obeying a rule is not to obey a rule . . . it is not possible to obey a rule 'privately': otherwise thinking one was obeying a rule would be the same thing as obeying it" (1953, sect. 202). A language rule, it might alternatively be said, possesses its public dimension precisely in virtue of the fact that it is something that binds or obliges individuals to use language in certain ways if they are to be said to obey it. That is, whether one has correctly or incorrectly followed a rule cannot be determined solely on the authority of the individual language-user or privately, but depends fundamentally upon how the language community believes the rule ought to be observed. In this respect, the rules governing language prescribe rather than describe what is involved in the successful use of language, and thus the reason why there is paradoxically never any single fact about a language-user's intentions in using some term or expression that would explain how that term or expression is to be used on future occasions is that an individual's successful following of the rules that govern a particular language practice involves discovering what generally ought to be done to secure the role and utility of that practice in the language community.

In contrast to the emotivist–ordinalist view of the normative as non-cognitive, then, Wittgenstein's reasoning about rules makes the normative dimension of language the objective – not subjective – element in thought and communication. Indeed on his understanding, an individual cannot begin to use language characterizing his or her preferences or tastes without bringing into play the standards and norms for its use that are embodied in an appropriate practice or "language-game," since even to begin to say that one thing is preferred to another, an individual must employ a system of distinctions involving the social concept of desirability already operative in the "language-game" employed to address the subject of desirability. It follows from this that interpersonal comparisons of taste and preference objectively underlie intrapersonal ones in that it is only the existence of a shared language about taste and preference that enables us to describe our own inner tastes. Contrary to Robbins, then, intrapersonal comparisons of taste and preference are possible only because interpersonal ones are possible, while the latter are possible precisely because they are normative and embody value-judgments.

A final, related point deserves brief attention preparatory to examining Keynes's own thinking in connection with the matters discussed here. Robbins's privacy of preferences view was central to his methodological individualism, since private preferences can be acted upon only by those individuals to whom they belong. Put differently, that an individual can only have his or her own preferences implies that an individual's self-identity is determined by the collection of preferences which that individual alone possesses. Note that when we say that an individual possesses a distinct identity, we assume that we are able to identify and re-identify that individual through any series of changes that affect that individual.[10] However, if it cannot be said that preferences are private in the sense intended by Robbins, then it is no longer clear how one individual is to be distinguished from another. On Wittgenstein's reasoning about language and mental experience, it does not make sense to speak about preferences as intrinsically private, since an individual's distinctions in taste and preference depend on distinctions in desirability embedded in the appropriate public "language-game". From this perspective, a significant component of an individual's self-identity is also in some sense social, and a methodological individualist conception of the economic agent is inappropriate. Keynes, we will see below, arrived at a similar conclusion in his later thinking.

Looking ahead to Keynes

Moore's influence on ethics and economics, then, led to views that were questionable in important respects. On the one hand, the emotivists construed the arguments of the *Principia* in such a way as to reverse Moore's view of the objective character of ethics. Yet their view of value judgments as non-cognitive, and comparative elevation of science was, and is, indefensible. On the other hand, this same positivist spirit in economics was embodied in Robbins's conclusions regarding the private nature of taste and the status of interpersonal comparisons of utility. Despite the immense influence of the *Essay*, it is arguable that the basic underlying conceptions of Robbins's arguments are mistaken. It is this latter development, of course, which is ultimately of chief interest here, since it represented a theoretical path alternative to the one Keynes adopted as he progressively freed himself from important elements of Moore's thought. Keynes was to signal his fundamental differences with Robbins after the completion of *The General Theory* in his comments on the nature of economics as a moral, rather than, as Robbins had it, natural science. Keynes, we will see, did not believe value judgments were non-cognitive, did not believe that interpersonal comparisons were meaningless, and did believe that one could speak coherently about individuals as social beings. These beliefs, moreover, are central to his understanding of economics and the economy. To see how they came to underlie *The General Theory* it will be necessary to first consider Keynes's own critique of his early ideas as inherited from Moore.

3   Keynes's self-critique

Though Keynes's philosophical thinking was originally thought to derive principally from his single published philosophical work, the *Treatise on Probability* (Harrod, 1951; Braithwaite, 1975), there has always been good reason to doubt that Keynes adhered unhesitatingly to his early views after he had turned from philosophy to economics. Indeed on two occasions in the 1930s when his thinking about economics was undergoing significant change, Keynes explicitly said that he thought he had been mistaken about key positions he had earlier taken on philosophical subjects. First, in 1930 he allowed that Ramsey had in an important respect been correct in his criticism of Keynes's intuitionism in the *Treatise* (Keynes, X, pp. 338–9). Second, he granted in his 1938 "My Early Beliefs" memoir that he and the others who had enthusiastically espoused Moore's *Principia* views in Keynes's first years at Cambridge had seriously underestimated the importance of rules in moral life (Keynes, X). Unfortunately, on neither of these occasions was Keynes particularly clear regarding just what these admissions implied concerning what he still accepted and what he had then come to reject among his former positions. Indeed, his response to Ramsey's criticism was so brief that scholars have been unable to agree whether it represented a major reversal or minor modification in Keynes's thinking about probability (cf., e.g., Bateman, 1987 and O'Donnell, 1989). At the same time, Keynes's critical comments on his early reading of Moore have never been shown to be clearly linked to the central philosophical issues of the *Treatise* in a way that would expand upon the meaning of Keynes's admission to Ramsey. This is important, because the close links between Keynes's early thinking about Moore's ideas and the *Treatise* would make "My Early Beliefs" an important source of understanding for Keynes's later view of his work in the *Treatise*. Despite real questions about the path of Keynes's subsequent philosophical development, then, scholars have had little success in accounting for just how that development might have occurred, though the evidence indicates that it almost certainly did occur in some fashion.

The recent availability of Keynes's early unpublished Apostles papers, many of which were written principally on themes from Moore's *Principia*, stands to change this situation.[1] The papers constitute an excellent opportunity for analyzing Keynes's philosophical development, in that in them Keynes both advances for the first time the central philosophical idea of the *Treatise*, namely, that probability relationships are known through intuition rather than through a knowledge of relative frequencies, and also a number of additional ideas concerning the philosophical character of intuition that – hesitantly – suggest intuition might possess some social dimension. These latter ideas did not re-appear in any significant manner in Keynes's later treatment of intuition in the *Treatise*, his chief philosophical work, and have arguably for this reason gone largely unappreciated in the recent literature on Keynes's philosophical thinking. However, they were to re-appear – though transformed in important respects – in Keynes's "My Early Beliefs" recantation and commentary upon his early views about Moore's *Principia*. This re-surfacing of Keynes's early concerns about the philosophical credentials of an immediate and incorrigible intuition came soon after Keynes's often quoted remark in the Preface to *The General Theory* regarding the difficulties he experienced in his struggle to escape the underlying assumptions of what he termed "the classical theory" (VII, p. v). Keynes's early Apostle papers are important, then, because, read in conjunction with "My Early Beliefs," they provide the philosophical end-points for an intellectual development which began on the epistemological terrain of the *Treatise*, and then abandoned that terrain for the very different one of *The General Theory*.

Keynes's philosophical development beyond the framework of the *Treatise*, as reflected in his critical revisiting of his most important early philosophical commitments in "My Early Beliefs," is the subject of the chapter here. Its argument is that Keynes came to believe that a number of his early ideas about intuition, which were not entirely in keeping with Moore's vision, and which he had first tentatively explored in his early papers but then put aside in the writing of the *Treatise*, were in fact indispensable to his later philosophical understanding of economics, and that their omission from the *Treatise* came to represent for him a mistaken path in his early philosophical development. In particular, Keynes was to conclude that he had misunderstood the social dimension of intuition in his early thinking, and that the sorting out of this matter (which he had admitted on a number of occasions had troubled him for many years as much as anything else), enabled him to see both how Ramsey had been correct in his critique of Keynes's *Treatise* view of intuition, and how a proper understanding of the social dimension of intuition needed to underlie his new views in *The General Theory* regarding judgment and convention.

The early papers, then, enable us to explain Keynes's philosophical development, because they reveal Keynes's original philosophical ideas and concerns, and yet are also the subject of Keynes's own commentary on his most fundamental philosophical views after the completion of *The General Theory*. Indeed Keynes's early papers and his "My Early Beliefs" commentary upon them permit us to draw inferences regarding Keynes's later view of his arguments in the *Treatise*, which Keynes in his response to Ramsey had suggested were in important respects in need of adjustment. The *Treatise*, of course, was largely written before Keynes turned seriously to the study of economics. Thus it would not be unreasonable to suppose, lacking evidence to the contrary, that when Keynes wrote the *Treatise* he had not yet become sensitive to the complexities inherent in the ordinary exercise of intuition or judgment on the part of economic agents in concrete social historical contexts. Keynes's early professional path from philosophy to economics, it is thus assumed here, should itself be seen to have influenced the development of his philosophical thinking, and his "My Early Beliefs" statements regarding his early views should accordingly be taken as important evidence concerning Keynes's own opinion of his philosophical development. Indeed, precisely because Keynes left professional philosophy for economics after his first years at Cambridge, his rare, later philosophical comment such as appears in the memoir all the more deserves special attention.[2]

This all implies that Keynes ultimately came to distance himself from much of what was involved in the early Cambridge philosophy of Moore, Russell, and Wittgenstein, and from relatively early on was searching for additional philosophical resources for his developing analysis of economic life. The argument here is that, contrary to his early emphasis upon intuition and individual judgment, Keynes concluded in the 1930s when he working on *The General Theory* that it was necessary to invest greater significance in the operation of rules and conventions in economic life. This change in conviction takes on special importance for the analysis of Keynes's later philosophical thinking when one takes note of the fact that a similar conception of the importance of rules and conventions and the inadequacy of individual intuition was developed in connection with the understanding of language and meaning by the later Wittgenstein, Keynes's Cambridge colleague and friend. Keynes, it is now clear (Monk, 1990; Skidelsky, 1992), had many meetings with Wittgenstein in the period 1929 to 1935, indeed afterwards often complaining of exhaustion from long hours of discussion that were more monologue by Wittgenstein.

Wittgenstein's first statement of his later philosophy, *The Blue and Brown Books* (1958), circulated in typescript at Cambridge in 1933 through 1935, and though there is no clear evidence that Keynes read this material, it seems almost certain that its contents were related to Keynes by Wittgenstein in some fashion. Thus it is likely that Wittgenstein's focus on the problematical aspects of early Cambridge philosophy that both he and Keynes had previously shared influenced Keynes's own views of those early commitments. Recent research appears to support this (Coates, 1990). Precisely how the two thinkers influenced one another, however, can be reconstructed only through an examination of the positions they each adopted. This chapter accordingly extends the analysis of the last chapter regarding "language-games" to a further discussion of rules and conventions, in order to demonstrate that Keynes's attachment to rules and conventions in his later reflections upon his early reasoning bears important similarities to Wittgenstein's later views on the same subject.

The discussion focuses first upon an examination of four of Keynes's most important early papers, "Ethics in Relation to Conduct" of 1904, the related "Miscellanea Ethica" and "A Theory of Beauty" of 1905, and "Egoism" of 1906, and their relation to Keynes's *Treatise on Probability*. It then turns to an analysis of Keynes's "My Early Beliefs" both to demonstrate Keynes's renewed attachment to those ideas about the social dimension of intuition that he had put aside in the *Treatise*, and to emphasize the ways in which he came to believe he had been mistaken in his early thoughts on the subject. The discussion closes with a philosophical analysis of Keynes's thinking about rules and conventions, preparatory to a full statement of Keynes's later philosophy in the following chapter.

Keynes's early Apostles papers

Not all of Keynes's unpublished Apostles papers directly concern Moore's *Principia* (see Moggridge, 1992). Moore's ideas were nonetheless clearly the great intellectual influence in Keynes's first years at Cambridge, a fact which Keynes took pains to record and discuss in his "Early Beliefs" memoir after the completion of *The General Theory* (Keynes, X, p. 435). Those papers which did concern the *Principia*, moreover, are especially interesting in that each is largely devoted to (sympathetic) critique of a particular aspect of Moore's overall view. Though Keynes accepted the great bulk of the ideas which Moore believed had revolutionized moral thinking, he sought to make his own contribution to this new understanding by setting out where it stood in need of emendation. This, as it turned out, laid a foundation for his more substantive differences with early Cambridge philosophy in later years, differences which became more significant in light of the emotivists' response to Moore and the influence of this thinking on the ordinalists' natural science view of economics.

The four papers discussed here have been given special attention, because they reveal a crucial episode in the development of Keynes's early thinking about the nature of intuition, which left Keynes with problems he was both unable to resolve prior to beginning his work on probability theory for his fellowship dissertation of 1907, and which were to plague him for a number of years after the completion of the *Treatise*. Starting in 1904 in "Ethics in Relation to Conduct" Keynes identifies his philosophical starting point as the act of judgment or exercise of intuition presupposed in the making of probability statements. In the succeeding year in "Miscellanea Ethica" and "A Theory of Beauty," Keynes raises questions regarding the concept of intuition introduced in his 1904 paper that involved recognizing what might be termed the two-fold nature of intuition. In brief, Keynes saw intuition as possessing two dimensions, one individual and one social, with the latter guaranteeing the objectivity that is required in speaking about the rationality of moral judgments and probability statements. In his provocative 1906 "Egoism" paper, however, Keynes finds himself unable to resolve the conflicting ethical claims that arise in a two-fold view of intuition such as the one he had contemplated in the previous year. The 1906 paper forms an end-point of sorts to the set of questions Keynes began to investigate in 1904, because when he began work on his first fellowship dissertation, Keynes ignored his previous concerns about the nature of intuition, and took intuition *per se* to be rational and objective in the manner later given full statement in the *Treatise*. Keynes's two-fold view of intuition, however, re-emerged in considerably more sophisticated form in his later thinking, and this, it will be argued, reflected the development in Keynes's philosophical thinking brought on by his contact with economic reasoning.

"Ethics in Relation to Conduct"

In "Ethics in Relations to Conduct" (Keynes, 1904, UA/19) Keynes criticized Moore's understanding of probability relationships in ethical theory, and then advanced his first arguments about intuition and the meaning of probability.[3] Keynes objected that Moore's definition of right conduct as action producing good consequences, which Moore had combined with a recommendation to follow common sense rules of conduct when estimating the remote future effects of one's actions (Moore, 1903a, pp. 162–3), presupposed the cogency of the frequency theory of probability, since ordinary rules of conduct predict the likely effects of one's actions in future circumstances on the basis of the record of past experience. However, Keynes observed, past experience is hardly of much assistance to us in explaining the future likelihoods of events for which there is little historical record, and thus one cannot expect common sense rules of conduct to be of much value in determining moral duty in a good part of ordinary life. Indeed, he went on to argue, a proper account of right conduct ultimately depends upon developing a new view of the meaning of probability. Even when we look to past experience to predict the likely future effects of our actions, we necessarily exercise judgment in interpreting the record of the past. Probabilities, then, result from probability judgments, and by a probability statement, Keynes asserted,

I mean something of the nature 'I have more evidence in favour of A than in favour of B'; I am making some statement concerning the bearing of the evidence at my disposal; I am not stating that in the long-run A will happen more often than B for certain. (Keynes, 1904, UA/19)

An individual's probability statement, therefore, reflects that individual's judgment or intuition regarding the "bearing" of the available evidence upon some possible conclusion. Moreover, that individuals can and do intuit such judgments without a comprehensive knowledge of the relative frequencies with which events have occurred in the past demonstrates that probability statements do not possess certainty as their standard. Probability statements, rather, capture what Keynes believed to be the "rational ground for asserting [that] one of two alternatives was more likely than the other," and it was this foundation in rational belief that he believed needed to be better understood properly to explain our capacity to make probability judgments.

These ideas were reinforced for Keynes by his conviction that, despite the widely held belief that degrees of probability were by nature numerically measurable, it seemed "only a very limited class of questions are capable of numerical treatment."[4] Indeed, even in those cases in which a numerical treatment of probability relationships was appropriate, as in the case of the repeated flipping of a coin, the conclusion that the coin will turn up heads half of the time and tails half of the time does not depend simply upon the record of past trials. Rather it depends upon a reasoned judgment that a fair coin, flipped randomly so many times, with "precautions . . . taken to counteract any cause tending to produce predominance of either" heads or tails, makes a heads or a tails equiprobable on a subsequent flip of the coin. This is not to assert, Keynes insisted, that the evidence of repeated trials is unimportant in the determination of heads–tails probabilities. It is only to emphasize that such evidence takes on whatever significance it possesses in a particular act of judgment assessing the bearing of this evidence upon the conclusion at hand.

Thus "on the interpretation of probability which I have supported in this paper," Keynes asserted that, on any given occasion demanding right conduct, one is entitled to pursue just what one judges right to do, given one's rational beliefs regarding the likely future effects of one's actions. Indeed, supposing

we have evidence to show that an action will produce more good than not in the next year and have no reason for supposing either that it will produce more good than evil or the reverse after the end of that period, if, in fact, we are in complete ignorance as to all events subsequent to the end of the year, – in that case we have, in my opinion, more evidence to support the view that x is right than to support the contrary and hence we are justified in saying 'x is probably right'. (*Ibid.*)

Thus, while Keynes allowed that he had not yet fully analyzed the meaning of the concept of probability ("I do not claim to have put forward any precise definition of probability . . ."), he was nonetheless convinced that "in any particular case, we have far more evidence by which to form our judgment than in the general case . . ." Probability statements, that is, always presuppose an individual act of judgment concerning the "bearing of the evidence at [one's] disposal," and could not consequently be explained in terms of general rules formally derived from propositions expressing relationships between proportionate likelihoods. Probability judgements, accordingly, were not to be thought objective in virtue of their reflecting frequency relationships inherent in the very nature of the world, but rather understood to acquire their objectivity through the rationality of human judgment.

However, that Keynes's new treatment of probability combined the view that probability relationships were not simple reflections of past experience with the view that probabilities were apprehended in particular acts of judgment or intuition raised an interesting and difficult question for Keynes's subsequent thinking. Were probabilities not simply embedded in the observed frequency of events in the world, and were probabilities the product of an individual's act of judgment or intuition concerning the "bearing" of evidence at hand on a given conclusion, how precisely was it that a given probability statement did indeed reflect the "rational ground for asserting that one of two alternatives" was more likely, rather than an individual's mere subjective appraisal of that being the case? When, that is, were we entitled to claim that judgment was objective and rational, when it was apparent to all that judgment was often neither? Indeed, could one ever be confident in saying that our judgment attained the standard Keynes had claimed for it?

To understand the importance of these questions – perhaps the most fundamental of all philosophical questions for the early Keynes – and to understand them in relation to the development of Keynes's later thinking, it is important to take note of the fact that among philosophers at Cambridge in the first decade of the century the theory of judgment was in a state of upheaval. Idealists such as J. M. E. McTaggart had for many years made heavy use of the concept of judgment to characterize reality as mind-dependent. In 1903, however, Moore's influential "Refutation of Idealism" paper (Moore, 1903b) inaugurated a new tradition in realism at Cambridge by distinguishing the objective content of perception from the act of perceiving itself. The idea behind Moore's argument was soon extended to the theory of judgment in Moore and Russell's view that the objects of judgement, namely, propositions, were themselves really existing objects, distinct and separate from the acts of judgment in which they appeared, and analogous to the really existing objects of perception. Keynes, of course, acknowledged in the Preface to his *Treatise on Probability* (Keynes, VIII, p. 20) that he had been much influenced by both Moore and Russell, and was no doubt thinking of judgment in his own work along the lines that they had originally laid out. He thus found himself in his "Ethics in Relation to Conduct" paper criticizing a master who had lost sight of his initial insights concerning the nature of intuition and judgment developed in connection with his treatment of good, when later in the *Principia* relying on rules and the frequency theory of probability for the analysis of right conduct. On intuition, then, Keynes followed the realists Russell and Moore (where consistent) in adopting a position intermediate between the idealists' view of reality as mind-dependent and the sort of view commonly held by frequency theorists and many scientists that judgment was a comparatively passive element in the empirical identification of probability relationships. Judgment, that is, was both objective and rational for Keynes in that it was neither merely a matter of the mind's opinion nor the unexplained product of brute facts. That this view emerged with the development of a new philosophical movement at Cambridge intent upon countering the subjectivist implications of idealism and naive science arguably explains the fact that it was some time before Keynes (and Russell and Moore) was able to focus clearly on the questions concerning the objectivity and rationality of judgment.

The question of the objectivity and rationality of judgment nonetheless soon did become an important one in the new realist tradition at Cambridge, as Moore and Russell, having satisfied themselves vis-à-vis the idealists, further probed the implications of their new theory of judgment and intuition. Indeed by mid-decade Moore and Russell had not only come to deny that the objects of judgment, namely, propositions, were really existing entities like the things we perceive, but had also abandoned the associated (dyadic) theory of judgment (see, e.g., Hylton, 1992).[5] Keynes too, we will see, began to have doubts about this shared theory of judgment shortly after writing "Ethics in Relation to Conduct," and though he did not pursue the troublesome issues surrounding the idea that propositions were really existing entities as did Moore and Russell, he did come to believe that a proper account of moral duty required further emendation of Moore's treatment of the objects of intuition.

"Miscellanea Ethica" and "A Theory of Beauty"

Keynes advanced his second main critique of Moore's *Principia* in his "Miscellanea Ethica" and "A Theory of Beauty" papers, in this instance principally in regard to what Keynes characterized as speculative as opposed to practical ethics, or the investigation of what can be said to be good in and of itself. In this critique, Keynes began by suggesting that there were further reasons for thinking that Moore's account of moral intuition was unacceptable, and then went on to explore his own understanding of the act of judgment and how one intuits that which may be said intrinsically good. In particular, Keynes argued that Moore's understanding of the principle of organic unities (an idea of organic connection) was inimical to the successful determination of what may be said good in itself, and that a distinction Keynes himself subsequently developed between what he termed the "fitness" and the "goodness" of the objects of moral intuition overcame the chief difficulties in Moore's account.

In Moore's view, unless we understand the role which the principle of organic unities plays in our thinking, we are apt to be confused by the fact that many of the things we regard as intrinsically valuable are often accompanied by things we regard as intrinsically bad (and in other instances by things about which we are at best indifferent). The issue that naturally confronts us in such situations is whether the things we believe intrinsically good somehow lose or have their value negated in their being accompanied by intrinsically bad things. How could it be, one had to wonder, that something intrinsically good ceased to be altogether good, simply because of its (often incidental) accompaniment by something bad? For Moore, the answer depended upon grasping the paradoxical nature of organic unities.

There is . . . a vast number of different things, each of which has intrinsic value; there are also very many which are positively bad; and there is a still larger class of things, which appear to be indifferent. But a thing belonging to any of these three classes may occur as part of a whole . . . and these wholes, as such, may also have intrinsic value. The paradox, to which it is necessary to draw attention, is that *the value of such a whole bears no regular proportion to the sum of the values of its parts*. (Moore, 1903a, p. 27)

That the intrinsic value of a whole should be thought independent of the value of its parts suggested to Moore that one ought to direct one's efforts towards recognizing which wholes were of the greatest intrinisic value. Indeed, Moore believed, it seemed clear that we possessed the intuitive capacity to do this, and in his own estimation the whole of the greatest intrinsic value appeared to be that of the universe itself. Thus on his view of the operation of the principle of organic unities one aimed at things intrinsically good, and that involved aiming at the organic whole of the greatest intrinsic value, namely, the universe itself.

Not surprisingly Keynes found this view of duty altogether impractical. In "Miscellanea Ethica" (Keynes, 1905b, UA/21), he argued that since in the case of the universe as a whole "we never have the opportunity of direct inspection, it is impossible to tell what kinds of action increase the goodness of the Universe as a whole." On Moore's view of the principle of organic unities, it seemed impossible to determine what one ought to do, and "[w]e appear to be reduced to moral impotence from which nothing can save us short of a Revelation . . ." Moore also apparently thought it reasonable to suppose that an action producing "an improvement of a part gives a rational probability of an improvement of the whole." Keynes thought this would entail a full investigation of "the precise meaning of probability," which he suspected required extensive discussion, and accordingly elected to pursue "another way out of the difficulty" of speaking about duty where an organic connection existed. Keynes's way out of Moore's difficulty made use of the key distinction introduced in "Miscellanea Ethica" and "A Theory of Beauty," namely, that between the "fitness" and "goodness" of objects of moral intuition. Thus early in the first of these two linked papers Keynes states that the predicate "good" is employed

to express two notions which appear to me distinct. An object, towards which a valuable mental relation is possible, is liable to receive the same epithet as the mental relation it inspires. If the mental state which is "appropriate" to it is an unmixed good, then the object also is said to be good. Anything which is fit to inspire a good feeling is itself regarded as good . . . (Keynes, 1905b, UA/21)

Here Keynes made it clear that objects in the world really deserve the predicate "good" only on the condition that the mental states they inspire can themselves be said to be truly good. This made the business of identifying intrinsic goodness a matter of identifying good states of mind. Later Keynes goes on to further distinguish the object and the feeling it inspires by calling "the object of the feeling 'fit' and the feeling itself simply 'good.'" He concludes that the difficulties in Moore's account of duty stem from Moore's failure to appreciate that "the predicate of good is solely applicable to the mental states of conscious beings." Moore, in Keynes's view, had failed to appreciate that the object of a feeling should be thought to "fit" the feeling, not that the feeling should "fit" the object.

With this in mind, Keynes then argued, the confusion in Moore's account of duty is easily avoided. Since it cannot be said that the universe itself possesses mental states, restricting the predicate "good" to mental states implies that it no longer makes sense to speak of the good of the universe as an organic whole.

Now the Universe regarded as a whole is not a conscious being, nor is it capable of mental states. As an organic unity, therefore, it cannot be good, and regarded as an aggregate of conscious beings its goodness must be precisely equal to the sum of the goodness of the persons composing it. (*Ibid.*)

The greatest good at which it is our duty to aim, it follows, is not the good of the universe as a whole, but rather the greatest sum of good states of mind across individuals. Thus, Keynes emphasizes, in one of his most important philosophical doctrines,

In ethical calculation each individual's momentary state of mind is our sole unit. In so far as a state of mind has parts, to this extent I admit the principle of organic unities: it is the excellence of the state as a whole with which we are concerned. But beyond each individual the organic principle cannot reach. (*Ibid.*)

Quite simply then, should we confuse fitness and goodness "in the smallest degree," we find ourselves misapplying the principle of organic unities to the universe, and falling into Moore's error of believing that "dead inanimate nature" can have ethical value. In contrast, by restricting the scope of the principle of organic unities to the individual mind, our duty in promoting the greatest good becomes clear, since promoting the well-being of the greatest number of individuals is tantamount to promoting the greatest number of good states of mind. Indeed, Keynes speculates, it might be altogether simpler to "banish organic unities from the theory of ethics proper," since, though not incorrectly applied to individual minds taken one by one, the principle often seems to cause confusion concerning the nature of duty.[6]

Moore, it should be noted, was quite unwilling to follow Keynes's lead on this, though, as evidenced by his later abandonment of the frequency theory of probability in his *Ethics* (1912), he was not unwilling to accept criticism he thought justified. Thus, recalling his position in "Refutation of Idealism," Moore devoted the entire third chapter of his *Ethics* to arguing (against the emotivist philosopher C.L. Stevenson) that the predicate "good" applied only derivatively to individuals' mental states on the grounds that goodness is a quality existing objectively in the world whether or not perceived in acts of moral intuition. A view of this sort – generally labeled ethical objectivism – requires that the truth of an assertion about what might be thought good or bad holds independently of the experience or thinking of the individual making that assertion. In contrast, the view Keynes espouses in "Miscellanea Ethica," namely, that the predicate "good" is "solely applicable to the mental states of conscious beings," is generally characterized as ethical subjectivism in that it explains the truth of an assertion about what is thought good or bad precisely in terms of the experience or thinking of the individual making that assertion. On this view, what makes a particular thing good is not – as Moore would have it – that that thing possesses a simple quality of goodness that exists in and of itself, but rather that our awareness of that thing itself inspires genuinely good feelings in us.

That Keynes's thinking on this topic earns such a characterization may be surprising. In "Ethics in Relation to Conduct," Keynes argued that probability judgments were objective on the grounds that probability statements were not justified *a posteriori* in terms of the record of past events, but rather involved a rational grounding in logical relationships obtaining between evidence and conclusions. In "Miscellanea Ethica," goodness possesses a subjective dimension in that it does not exist apart from individuals' experience, but rather depends upon that experience. Yet Keynes had not really reversed his former position. Rather his attention to Moore's difficulties in connection with organic unities had driven him to emphasize the nature of judgment as humanly subjective. Logical relationships, though they were equally the product of human judgment, were more readily thought objective on account of their designation as rational. Judgments of what was objectively or intrinsically good, however, necessarily reflected a dependence upon human sensibility. In Keynes's own mind, this did not imply that such judgments were subjective in the sense of being relative to the individual. This emerges in an important passage at the end of his discussion of the principle of organic unities in "Miscellanea Ethica" where Keynes explained how he understood the relationship between individual judgment and rationality.

If the foregoing analysis is correct, it is plain that the idea and the emotion appropriate to any given sensation are partly dependent on the nature and past history of the individual who feels. This is obvious enough; we ought not all to have precisely similar states in similar physical circumstances; common sense and the commandments are agreed on that. But we can in many cases abstract that element which ought to vary from man to man. Assuming the approximate uniformity of human organs, we can often – if not near enough – say what, apart from peculiar circumstances, a man *ought* to think and feel: – not indeed what he *can* think and feel – that will *always* depend upon his nature and his part. In accordance, therefore, with what has gone before – those objects, which normally produce sensations in correspondence to which, in normal cases, a good state of mind potentially exists, are *fit*. It will be seen that such a scheme altogether lacks the precision which a metaphysician would desire. Subjective and relative elements are introduced. But I trust it will not conflict with its sole basis – the testimony of actual intuition and experience. (*Ibid.*)

Thus, though what an individual thinks and feels necessarily depends upon that individual's particular nature and past experience, because of an "approximate uniformity of human organs" across individuals Keynes still believed it was possible to say what an individual ought to think and feel in a given situation when thinking "normally," that is, rationally. From this perspective, it was also possible to say that though the objects of judgment themselves lacked the character that we attributed to them in judgment, those objects were nonetheless "fit" to be so characterized, and therefore could objectively be said to be as we asserted.

Keynes consequently combined rejection of a thoroughly relativist subjectivism with a signficant departure from the sort of realist view that Moore held. On Moore's view, since the good is a simple quality existing absolutely in and of itself, the good must be recognized in essentially the same way by every individual, and it made no sense to speak of an individual's own good or of good from that individual's perspective (Moore, 1903a, e.g. pp. 98–9).[7] For Keynes, however, the apprehension or intuition of good was essentially linked to experience, and experience is intrinsically individual whether one speaks of the good as it in fact appears to the individual or as it should normally appear to the individual. Thus, elsewhere in "Miscellanea Ethica" in his discussion of the fitness and goodness of objects of moral intuition Keynes emphasized the problem of getting beyond sense data to whatever might be thought to be said to exist objectively apart from experience for every individual.

I have spoken so far as if the quality of fitness was entirely objective and inherent in objects independently of the relations of the objects to us. But I am not clear that this is an assumption which will bear investigation. It turns, no doubt, on the question as to whether the sensations set up in us by external objects can, in any sense, be said to be *like* these objects. Our aesthetic feelings are evoked by the content of our perceptions; we must assume, therefore, *either* that similar objects always and in all persons evoke similar sensations, *or* that out of the various sensations evoked one can be said to be like the object in a sense in which the others are not. Neither of these assumptions, however, seems jusifiable . . . (*Ibid.*)

Keynes went on to cite David Hume's view that the eye is but a particular sort of lens which must give but one representation of the world of "external objects." Indeed, later in the paper, Keynes repeated these conclusions, and insisted that "we cannot usefully go behind the sense data." In regard to "external objects," ultimately appearance is in fact relative to him who looks: there is no such thing – or if there is, it has no relevance for ethics – as objective appearance (*Ibid.*).

This was not to say, it should be emphasized, that Keynes was claiming in classical idealist fashion that nothing actually exists apart from experience. Rather, his argument is that our characterization of what exists is inescapably dependent upon experience, and that it is a mistake to ignore this in one's account of intuition, as indeed Moore (and Russell) had originally done. In a more modern frame of reference, Keynes was only recognizing that the exercise of judgment presupposes some subjective capacity on the part of the individual, whereby we say that an individual possesses concepts appropriate to the judgments he or she makes (cf. e.g. Geach, 1957, pp. 7–13). Moore and Russell, in an effort to distance themselves from neo-Hegelian idealism, had regarded propositions and concepts as objectively existing entities. In so doing they invited the sort of response that Keynes found himself impelled to make in re-asserting the subjective aspects of judgment.

In "Miscellanea Ethica" and "A Theory of Beauty," then, Keynes expanded upon his "Ethics in Relation to Conduct" understanding of probability statements as objective products of acts of judgment by arguing that in judgment we distinguish between what a given individual actually thinks and feels and what an individual "*ought* to think and feel." While from time to time, he allowed, an individual may well misapprehend what is good or probable when misled by his or her own particular "nature and past history," we can still "abstract that element which ought to vary from man to man" – in virtue of the "approximate uniformity of human organs" – to speak of what would normally or rationally be thought good or probable. On the one hand, then, Keynes improved on Moore's understanding of intuition by sharpening Moore's theory of judgment and, it should be noted, by introducing a potential means of explaining error in judgment where none had existed in the *Principia*. For Keynes, a particular individual's feelings and experience need not accord with what might be normally anticipated in a given situation. For Moore, an individual's failure to intuit what is good or probable is virtually unexplainable. On the other hand, however, Keynes did not fully escape the dilemmas inherent in his "Ethics in Relation to Conduct" combination of particular judgment and the rational grounding of probabilities, since he did not explain in "Miscellanea Ethica" or "A Theory of Beauty" how what one ought normally to think and feel is related to what individuals actually do think and feel. In particular, in this new two-fold view of intuition, Keynes did not explain whether what an individual actually thinks and feels somehow ultimately emerges from what one ought to think and feel, or whether what one ought to think and feel somehow ultimately emerges from what individuals actually think and feel. Presumably Keynes wanted to claim that what an individual actually thinks and feels ultimately emerges from what one ought to think and feel, were judgment generally thought rational and there to exist an "approximate uniformity of human organs." However, his subsequent "Egoism" paper actually lent support to the opposite notion that what individuals "normally" thought and felt emerged from what they actually thought and felt. This placed far more weight on the "subjective and relative elements" of his analysis than he had wished to emphasize. It also began to suggest to Keynes the essentially ambiguous character of individual judgment as regards to its rationality and objectivity.

"Egoism"

In "Egoism" (Keynes, 1906, UA/26) Keynes argued against Moore (and on the side of Moore's teacher, Henry Sigwick) that ethical egoism is a defensible position. As noted above, Moore had claimed that the very notion of an individual private good was incoherent. Arguing a *reductio ad absurdum* against the egoist, Moore stipulated first that "when I talk of a thing as 'my own good' all that I can mean is that something which will be exclusively mine," and second that the "only reason I can have for aiming at 'my own good' is that it is *good absolutely* that what I so call should belong to me" (Moore, 1903a, p. 99). He then concluded:

If, therefore, it is true of *any* single man's 'interest' or 'happiness' that it ought to be his sole ultimate end, this can only mean that *that* man's 'interest' or 'happiness' is the *sole good*, the Universal Good, and the only thing that anybody ought to aim at. What Egoism holds, therefore, is that *each* man's happiness is the sole good – that a number of different things are *each* of them the only thing there is – an absolute contradiction!

That is, because each of us must aim at what is good absolutely, each of us must aim at the same, single good. To argue there are many private goods, then, is to deny that the good is good absolutely – a notion Moore thought incomprehensible in light of his understanding of definition and thus the very meaning of the term "good."

Keynes, however, was unimpressed with Moore's logic, and insisted that the "ordinary egoist of real unphilosophical life would scarcely feel his position properly undermined by the Mooristic attack . . ." Indeed, once one rejected Moore's premise that the individual private good could not be distinguished from the universal good (as Keynes had done in advancing his new two-fold view of intuition), it was difficult to see just why the universal good held a claim on the individual. Keynes thus noted that the representative egoist does *not* say that his own good is the sole good; he alleges that his own good is the only reasonable thing for *him* to aim at; he does not deny that other people are part of the good, or claim that everybody should aim at his good. He does not, in fact, admit the invariable and necessary connexion between universal good and ought; Moore in his refutation assumes this necessary connexion, whereas this is precisely what he has got to prove. (Keynes, 1906, UA/26)

Accordingly, that an individual's intuition of what was good might diverge from what might "normally" be thought good created a problem for Moore that he had never recognized, namely, how a particular individual's intuition of what he or she thought good was to be related to what was thought universally good (and thus a matter of right conduct), especially when the former had a clear basis in intuition while the latter, according to the argument of the *Principia*, was a matter of inference or argument. Since Moore had implicitly assumed the "necessary connexion between universal good and ought" in failing to distinguish individual and universal good, Keynes in turn charged him with a *petitio principii*, adding that Moore's "omission . . . runs through his whole system" since he everywhere thought this connection "self-evident" (*Ibid.*).

Keynes likely felt that his thinking of the previous year offered the promise of a solution of sorts to Moore's new problem. On his two-fold view of intuition, an individual's particular judgment could be thought potentially rational and objective in virtue of its possible correspondence to what one would normally be expected to think in the appropriate circumstances. This of course assumed that the "approximate uniformity of human organs" permitted one to speak about what one generally ought to think and feel by abstraction from what individuals actually think and feel. On this view, an individual could aim at what he or she thought and felt good (what the traditional view of egoism termed one's own good), and not need to have as one's object some abstract object on the order of Moore's absolute good. Certainly if the predicate "good" properly applied only to individual states of mind, as Keynes had previously concluded it must, then this seemed the only view possible. What was good was always a matter of individual judgment. Thus the logic – if not the spirit – of the egoist's thinking deserved attention.

This is the problem then. Is it intuitively rational, is it immediately obvious to the intelligence, that the pursuit of general good justifies itself as paramount simply because general good is general good? The egoist denies it; *he* admits the rationality of private good; it appears to him to be immediately obvious that he would be a fool if he did not make the goodness of his own states of mind as great as possible; he also allows, no doubt, that apparent sacrifice, sacrifice of his own happiness for instance, may increase his own goodness, and that he ought even at such a cost to make himself as good as possible. But at this point comes the crux;

he denies that he ought, on occasion, to make himself *bad* in order that others may be good. (*Ibid.*)

The tension, then, was between what Keynes termed "the obligation to *do* good" and the inherent rationality one detected in pursuing what seemed for the individual "to be good" (*Ibid.*). This, of course, recalled Keynes's previous arguments against Moore in "Ethics in Relation to Conduct" concerning the remote probable effects of action, since there too Keynes had thought that the immediate results of intuition were alone persuasive to the individual mind, and thus that Moore's inferential view of right conduct needed to be reconceived. Now in "Egoism" with the results of his more complex view of intuition from the previous year, Keynes apparently felt that he had both extended his earlier reasoning regarding right conduct and had also taken the sting out of the traditional message of egoism as narrowly self-interested.

Yet at the same time Keynes was not entirely satisfied with this result of his latest thinking, since, he candidly allowed, he still could not convincingly distinguish the selfish egoist from the philosophical egoist of his own argument. That would require some evidence that there was generally a coincidence and harmony between what one actually thought and felt – what he termed the matter of "being good" – and what one ought normally to think and feel – what he termed the matter of "doing good" – and he was painfully aware that his analysis still lacked sufficient resources for making such a claim.

Very often, of course, they will coincide; it is usually true that the best way to be good *is* to do good; but I confess I see no necessary connexion. Suppose they conflict: which is to be paramount? As they used to say in the eighteenth century, is authority to be given to rational self-love or to benevolence? (*Ibid.*)

Keynes's dilemma was that it made no sense on his view of intuition and judgment to say that the individual made some absolute or universal good his or her object, while at the same time he could not deny that the good possessed an objectivity that seemed to transcend what we actually think and feel. In effect, the flexibility his two-fold view of intuition brought him in dealing with Moore's organic unities problem also brought him two relatively independent standards for determining what was objectively good. "For my own goodness and the goodness of the Universe both seem to have a claim upon me and claims which I cannot easily reduce to common terms and weigh against one another upon a common balance." He consequently left himself with a dilemma between being good and doing good that would go unresolved in his thinking for many years: "I am a good friend of the Universe and I will do my best for it: but am I willing to go to the devil for it?" (*Ibid.*)

"Egoism," then, in important respects represented an unsatisfactory resolution of the development in thinking about judgment and intuition that Keynes began with his first serious reflections on philosophy. In the following year he began work on his first fellowship dissertation, and put aside these issues to return to his original idea that probability relationships are known intuitively. We might imagine Keynes thought that, though there were still important issues to be worked out in the theory of judgment, his initial insight regarding the essential meaning of probability was sound, and moreover placed him in the unique position of making an original contribution to the New Realist philosophy emerging at Cambridge by producing a "principia" of inductive logic to stand alongside the *Principia Mathematica* and the *Principia Ethica*. Indeed Russell and Moore themselves had yet to express doubts about the theory of judgment the three shared, and certainly the confidence and enthusiasm all felt in and for this new philosophy expected to displace the excesses of recent idealism were still strong. Perhaps not surprisingly, then, when Keynes did ultimately come in his *Treatise on Probability* to treat the philosophical issues surrounding intuition and judgment, he ignored possible complications in the notion and, with some arguably defensive adjustments, relied on his original view of the matter.

A Treatise on Probability

In the *Treatise*, Keynes carefully narrowed the acknowledged subjective dimensions of probability theory to "the relativity of knowledge to the individual" and the uneven powers of logical intuition across individuals (Keynes, VIII, p. 18), and proceeded as if intuition were unproblematic in nature. He accomplished this in large part by shifting the focus of his treatment of intuition from his two-fold view of intuition concerns to an adapted version of Russell's (1903, 1910–11) two-tier epistemology of acquaintance and description.[8] This change made possible two distinctions lacking in the earlier framework which had prevented Keynes from treating the good and probable in systematically objective terms, but which now enabled him to treat probability relationships in precisely those terms. On the one hand, Keynes distinguished between direct acquaintance with the materials of knowledge – sensations, meanings, and perceptions – and knowledge itself, identifying the objects of knowledge as propositions. On the other hand, he also distinguished between direct and indirect knowledge, or "between that part of our rational belief which we know directly and that part which we know by argument" (Keynes, VIII, p. 12).

Knowledge of probability relationships, Keynes then argued, was built up in the following manner. As a result of our contemplating the objects of acquaintance, we come to have a direct knowledge of propositions concerning those objects. Then,

> by the contemplation of propositions of which we have direct knowledge, we are able to pass indirectly to knowledge of or about other propositions. The mental process by which we pass from direct knowledge to indirect knowledge is in some cases and in some degree capable of analysis. We pass from a knowledge of the proposition *a* to a knowledge about the proposition by perceiving a logical relation between them. With this logical relation we have direct acquaintance. The logic of knowledge is mainly occupied with a study of the logical relations, direct acquaintance with which permits direct knowledge of the secondary proposition asserting the probability-relation, and so to indirect knowledge about, and in some cases of, the primary proposition. (p. 13)

A knowledge of probability relationships, accordingly, was to be understood as a (direct) knowledge of (secondary) propositions about previously known (primary) propositions, made possible by our "perceiving a logical relation" between these propositions. In this manner, Keynes made the perception of logical relations – a form of acquaintance not itself knowledge – the very basis of a knowledge of logical relations that itself took propositions rather than the content of intuition as its object.

The implications of this analysis for Keynes's previous view of probability relations are important to understand. In his earlier thinking Keynes had not quite known how to grant intuition the quality of legitimate insight, yet at the same time distinguish what one actually thinks and feels from what one ought normally to think and feel. By distinguishing acquaintance and knowledge, however, he was able to re-characterize intuition as an acquaintance whose object was not knowledge proper, but rather simply one's mental contents, and then go on to treat knowledge as a separate intellectual result, the objects of which were distinguished as truly existing propositions about what was rationally believed probable. In effect, Keynes took acquaintance to be a matter of what one actually thinks and feels in the individually subjective sense, and then re-characterized what had previously been a matter of what one ought normally to think and feel as knowledge about objectively existing propositions independent of particular individuals' subjective awareness.

At the same time, however, because Keynes did not – indeed could not in principle – explain the intuitive "mental process" by which one passed from direct to indirect knowledge in perceiving logical relations between propositions, it was not clear how effective his designating propositions the objects of knowledge could really be thought to be in resolving his basic problem of explaining the objectivity of probability relationships. Were it indeed the case that propositions about the world truly existed, then it might be said that logical relations between propositions were objective. On the other hand, were it not true that propositions truly existed, and were, say, our assertions meant to express such propositions only widely accepted linguistic expressions, then one would have to wonder whether what people widely claimed one ought to think and feel on any given occasion was really anchored in anything truly objective. The special difficulty for Keynes in this was that without such a grounding for rational belief, all that would remain of his adaptation of the Russellian two-tier epistemology was the "mental process" by which one intuited logical relations, and this, Keynes had clearly allowed on his view of experience, understanding, and perception as the forms of direct acquaintaince, was an indisputably subjective affair. Ironically, then, by the time Keynes was to publish the *Treatise*, Russell and Moore had abandoned the view that propositions actually existed, and had gone on to argue that their accompanying (dyadic) theory of judgment (as linking an act of judgment and the proposition judged) was fundamentally misconceived. This certainly was of no small consequence for Keynes's arguments, since the idea of an objectively existing proposition had enjoyed a very brief tenure in twentieth-century philosophical circles, and its philosophical standing was hardly so well established that it could easily survive abandonment by its chief proponents.

Not unrelated to these difficulties was the debate among moral philosophers over the sense and coherence of Moore's concept of intuition in ethics discussed in the previous chapter. Moore's view that intuition was a form of cognitive insight, we saw, was contested by the emotivists who regarded normative judgment as affective response to our emotional states. Keynes's own view of judgment and organic unities, it turned out, was not so far removed from the emotivists' view, since he emphasized that the predicates we apply to the world derive from our mental states, namely, from what we think and feel to be the case. Keynes, it is fair to say, was not himself in any way predisposed to emotivist arguments, since he clearly believed one could say what individuals should normally or rationally think and feel in various circumstances. Yet, at the same time, on his two-fold view of intuition he had never explained how rational and actual judgment were related, and thus he remained vulnerable, as was Moore, to the emotivist critique. Indeed, it might be said that Keynes's re-interpretation of Moore's theory of intuition in terms of fitness and mental states provided just the reading of Moore that the emotivists had argued Moore's view ultimately collapsed upon. Thus, though Keynes was not sympathetic to the emotivists' subjectivism and relativism, his receptivity to the idea that human sensibility played a necessary role in judgment would have made it difficult for him to persuasively distinguish his position from theirs. His own hesitancy on this score is best manifested in his "Egoism" paper.

Yet that Keynes did not, and could not in principle, explain the intuitive "mental process" by which one passed from direct to indirect knowledge also signaled his difficulties in connection with the issues discussed at the end of the first chapter above. The realist turn in Cambridge philosophy in the first decade of the twentieth century, we saw, depended upon the view that facts existed atomistically or were externally related, and were thus known to us by self-evident intuition. In the history of philosophy, however, principles of self-evidence have generally suffered a dilemma of explanation. Should something be thought self-evident or known by intuition, then there is precious little to be said to justify that insight as knowledge, since self-evidence must by nature be taken at face value. Alternatively, should one attempt some analysis of one's intuitions in order to legitimate their claims as insight, then one undermines the principle of self-evidence, and at the same time brings into question the epistemic standing of intuition as a form of cognitive insight. Keynes, of course, made the principle of self-evidence central to his original critique of Moore's probability thinking in his reliance on an immediate and incorrigible intuition as a foundation for probability judgments. But his later two-fold view of intuition injected a dimension of social evaluation into his understanding of individual judgment, and raised questions about what intuition amounted to. We will see shortly that expanding this latter theme became the principal means by which he registered his revised view of intuition and individual judgment in "My Early Beliefs."

By the time that the much delayed *Treatise* was to appear, however, Keynes had already overstayed his immediate interest in philosophical questions, and economics (and politics) had become his primary concern. Accordingly, the philosophical thinking that emerges from Keynes's early years has a mixed character. While Keynes wished to treat probability relationships as objective, his basis for doing so is not solid. This does not imply, it should be emphasized, either that Keynes was entirely unjustified in believing probability relationships objective, or that Keynes himself ceased to believe them to be so. It does imply that Keynes was not as successful in this regard as he intended to be, and this, it is fair to suggest, must have made him somewhat circumspect about claims concerning the objectivity of probabilities and about what could be said to be good. In what follows, we will look at how Keynes's philosophical thinking was to develop in succeeding years through the lens of his own opinions of his early efforts.

"My Early Beliefs"

Keynes's earlier frustration over the difficulty he had detected in linking the matter of "doing good" with the matter of "being good" re-surfaced after the *Treatise* had been published, and he had turned to questions of politics and economics. In a letter of April 1928 to F.L. Lucas regarding the often tragic nature of everyday life, he asserted that "All this is connected with my favourite dilemma – the difficulty or impossibility of both being good and doing good" (Keynes, 1928, pp/45). Similarly, in 1930 in the *Nation* he went on at more length.

Moreover, is it not the highest virtue to 'do evil that good may come'? For is this not what we mean by 'doing good' as distinct from 'being good'? 'Doing good', as I understand the phrase, means to forgo the best in oneself in order that others may have an opportunity to be good, which is the completest form of self-sacrifice. That is the choice which has to be made. For it is given to very few in this awkward world both to do good and to be good. Or is it true that to do good is the only way to be good? I ask questions, both *num and nonne*. (Keynes, XX, pp. 467–8)

Whether it might be the case that "to do good is the only way to be good," however, represented a speculation somewhat removed from the tone of Keynes's remarks in 1906 in "Egoism." There the emphasis had been firmly upon the intuitive plausibility of always "being good" and doubts regarding whether this might link up with the possibility of "doing good." Keynes's shift in emphasis is perhaps explainable in terms of his transition from undergraduate life to the world of international economic policy and diplomacy. Right conduct, naturally enough, would have bulked larger in his thinking after such a change, while his concern with what was involved in the individual's "being good" would no doubt have occupied him less strongly. But this change in emphasis might also have signaled a change in Keynes's views regarding the pre-eminent role he had earlier assigned to individual judgment and intuition, especially since eight years later in his "My Early Beliefs" he indeed did conclude that he had placed too much importance on individual judgment and intuition and too little on the explanation of right conduct.

"My Early Beliefs" represented an effort on Keynes's part to summarize and explain the nature of the influence Moore's *Principia Ethica* had had upon Keynes and his friends in their first years at Cambridge. Above all, Keynes wanted to emphasize the tremendous impact of Moore and the *Principia*: "The influence was not only overwhelming . . . it was exciting, exhilarating, the beginning of a renaissance, the opening of a new heaven on a new earth . . ." (Keynes, X, p. 435). Yet at the same time it was an uneven influence, and in Keynes's view this was the key to understanding the path that his thinking (and that of a number of the others) was to take in succeeding years.

Now what we got from Moore was by no means entirely what he offered us. He had one foot on the threshold of the new heaven, but the other foot in Sidgwick and the Benthamite calculus and the general rules of correct behaviour. There was one chapter in the *Principia* of which we took not the slightest notice. We accepted Moore's religion, so to speak, and discarded his morals. Indeed, in our opinion, one of the greatest advantages of his religion, was that it made morals unnecessary – meaning by 'religion' one's attitude towards oneself and the ultimate and by 'morals' one's attitude towards the outside world and the intermediate. To the consequences of having a religion and no morals I return later. (p. 436)

The chapter in the *Principia* they overlooked was the fifth, "Ethics in Relation to Conduct," in which Moore analyzed right conduct in utilitarian and frequency theory terms, and which Keynes had made the subject of his first Apostles paper critique of the *Principia*. In contrast, Moore's "religion" concerned the intuition of things intrinsically good, for Keynes, that is, individuals' good states of mind regarding "love, the creation and enjoyment of aesthetic experience and the pursuit of knowledge" (pp. 436–7). By 1938, Keynes had come to believe this selective appreciation of Moore's thinking sufficiently unfortunate that he thought it necessary to make some statement about where he and his friends had gone wrong.

In the first place, Keynes began, in this "religion" of intrinsic values "[t]here was not a very intimate connection between 'being good' and 'doing good'; and we had a feeling that there was some risk that in practice the latter might interfere with the former" (p. 437). This was indeed Keynes's original concern in 1904 when in his "Ethics in Relation to Conduct" critique of Moore's theory of "morals" he disputed Moore's claim that common sense rules of conduct ought to supplant intuition when one was concerned to estimate the future effects of one's actions. It had become even more a matter of concern for Keynes by the time of his "Egoism" paper two years later when he argued that Moore had failed to demonstrate the "necessary connexion between universal good and ought." For Keynes and his friends, it was almost as if the business of knowing what was good had come to represent the exclusive subject matter of ethics, subsuming the theory of right conduct as but an added dimension of how we intuited the good. Though this clearly placed a considerable burden on individuals' intuitive capacities, at the time Keynes and his friends did not hesitate to believe they possessed unfailing intuitive insight: "How did we know what states of mind were good? This was a matter of direct inspection, of direct unanalysable intuition about which it was useless and impossible to argue" (p. 437). Indeed Keynes again likened the intuition of what was good to the simple perception of color: "[o]ur apprehension of good was exactly the same as our apprehension of green, and we purported to handle it with the same logical and analytical technique which was appropriate to the latter" (p. 438).

Thus, Keynes admitted, though he and his friends would once have "been very angry" at the idea, it would really have been more appropriate to call "this faith a religion," since it had amounted to little more than an uncritical "neo-platonism" that "combined a dogmatic treatment as to the nature of experience with a method of handling it which was extravagantly scholastic" (p. 438). And, despite their early confidence in their intuitive powers, an intuition that was incontestable and incontrovertible could hardly offer an objective and rational foundation for ethics, when differences in judgment between individuals in the final analysis seemed always to mean that "victory was with those who could speak with the greatest appearance of clear, undoubting conviction and could best use the accents of infallibility" (*Ibid.*). This, Keynes confessed, "was hardly a state of mind which a grown-up person in his senses could sustain literally" (p. 442), and thus though he and his friends had been convinced in their first years at Cambridge that their view of the *Principia* had been solidly worked out, it was now clear, he thought, that their early views were really in need of significant revision, especially in regard to their understanding of the nature of intuition. Just how, then, did Keynes understand this needed revision?

Moore's "religion," especially as captured in the final chapter of the *Principia* entitled "The Ideal," Keynes still asserted to be his own. That is, Keynes still adhered to Moore's view of the content of the good, and believed it truly the basis for the good life. Good states of mind relating to the experience of love and friendship, the appreciation of art, and the enjoyment of knowledge and learning comprised a full life for Keynes, as well attested to by his biographers. At the same time, he added, "one cannot live today secure in the undisturbed individualism which was the extraordinary achievement of the early Edwardian days," and unfortunately these values "furnish a justification of experience wholly independent of outside events" (p. 444). More was needed, accordingly, were these values to continue to have meaning, and clearly this would somehow involve a changed view of the place of right conduct in one's overall conception of ethics. Moore of course had gone to some trouble to "distinguish between goodness as an attribute of states of mind and rightness as an attribute of actions," but his characterization of right conduct had made use of a consequentialist (ideal) utilitarian reasoning and had employed general rules of common sense, both of which Keynes and his friends had thought fundamentally misguided. Thus

we set on one side, not only that part of Moore's fifth chapter on 'Ethics in Relation to Conduct' which dealt with the obligation so to act as to produce by causal connection the most probable maximum of eventual good through the whole procession of future ages (a discussion which was indeed riddled with fallacies), but also the part which discussed the duty of the individual to obey general rules. We entirely repudiated a personal liability on us to obey general rules. We claimed the right to judge every individual case on its merits, and the wisdom, experience and self-control to do so successfully. (p. 446)

This approach to right conduct, Keynes had come to realize, was not only naive, but more importantly would never serve to reconcile "being good" and "doing good." It was not surprising that this was also the verdict of most of those who knew Keynes and his friends in their early years, and that their espousing such views

resulted in a general, widespread, though partly covert, suspicion affecting ourselves, our motives and our behaviour. This suspicion still persists to a certain extent, and it always will. It has deeply coloured the course of our lives in relation to the outside world. It is, I now think, a justifiable suspicion. (pp. 446–7)

The only possible response, then, was to produce a new account of the principles governing right conduct, and this, it turned out, demanded re-thinking of a number of deeply held commitments.

Here Keynes was quite specific about the source of his difficulties. Most importantly, his misunderstanding of right conduct, he had come to believe, "was flimsily based . . . on an *a priori* view of what human nature is like, both other people's and our own, which was disastrously mistaken." He and his friends, who were in his estimation "among the last of the Utopians, or meliorists as they are sometimes called," had mistakenly concluded that history was making possible

a continuing moral progress by virtue of which the human race already consists of reliable, rational, decent people, influenced by truth and objective standards, who can be safely released from the outward restraints of convention and traditional standards and inflexible rules of conduct, and left, from now onwards, to their own sensible devices, pure motives and reliable intuitions of the good. The view that human nature is reasonable had in 1903 quite a long history behind it. It underlay the ethics of self-interest – rational self-interest as it was called . . . and it was because self-interest was *rational* that the egoistic and altruistic systems were supposed to work out in practice to the same conclusions. (p. 447)

However, that history had not achieved this result, and that individuals were not always decent and rational, meant that the "egoistic and altruistic systems," that is, the business of "being good" and "doing good," could not be counted upon to "work out in practice to the same conclusions." In effect, that "approximate uniformity of human organs" across individuals, that Keynes had thought explained the tendency for what an individual actually thought and felt to coincide with what one ought normally to think and feel, had yet to emerge in history, if it ever was to. Individuals, Keynes had come to appreciate, exhibited such a wide variety of motives, feelings, and beliefs about what they ought to do, that there was very little the philosopher could say *a priori* about human nature and individual judgment. Accordingly, his earlier "pseudo-rational view of human nature led to a thinness, a superficiality, not only of judgment, but also of feeling," so that his "attribution of rationality to human nature, instead of enriching it . . . seem[ed] . . . to have impoverished it" (p. 448).

Intuition, obviously then, could be thought to be but part of that which explained what individuals did and thought they ought to do. But what was there beyond individual judgment that might additionally explain the relationship between what individuals actually thought and did and what they ought to think and do? Here, Keynes insisted, we must rely upon "convention and traditional standards and inflexible rules of conduct." Indeed it was best, he emphasized, to proceed on the assumption that "civilisation was a thin precarious crust erected by the personality and the will of a very few, and only maintained by rules and conventions skilfully put across and guilefully preserved" (p. 447), if we are to fully appreciate the fundamental significance of a society's rules and conventions. Then we will understand that when individuals exercise good judgment, it is in good part because they are able to rely upon the guidance provided by a society's rules and conventions. It is true that a society's rules and conventions have themselves emerged from the individual efforts of those skilled in foresight and judgment. Yet even these efforts, one should not forget, were themselves made possible by earlier, pre-existing rules and conventions. For Keynes, then, the principal discovery he felt impelled to register in his late-career, post-*General Theory* memoir, was that individual judgment combined with rules and conventions in explaining what people did and thought they ought to do. It is this combination of judgment and rules, and specifically the way that they interact with one another, then, that we need to better understand if we are to explain Keynes's later philosophical thinking.

Judgment and rules

Preparatory to turning to the analysis of Keynes's later philosophical thinking, however, it will be helpful to link the discussion of the last two chapters to Keynes's changed view of rules and conventions in "My Early

Beliefs." An issue that immediately arises in this connection is whether Keynes's new position amounted to a complete reversal of his earlier critique of Moore on rules. In fact, Keynes's new view remained consistent with his argument regarding rules advanced originally in "Ethics in Relation to Conduct." Moore, recall, had thought it virtually impossible to ascertain the full range of future consequences of one's actions in determining right conduct, and had consequently recommended recourse to general, common sense rules of conduct on the grounds that the probable effects of one's actions were reasonably predicted from the frequency of past effects of similar actions. Keynes, however, still had little use for the frequency theory of probability, and was thus still prepared to argue that rules, as mere descriptive summaries of past behavior, were an inadequate foundation for explaining right conduct. Indeed, the rules and conventions emphasized in "My Early Beliefs" are clearly something more than simple compilations of past information in that they possess an important element of obligatoriness. Better put, the rules and conventions of "My Early Beliefs" are prescriptive rather than descriptive in nature, and are therefore not just rules of thumb which one might choose to consult when concerned about the likely effects of one's actions. Rules and conventions in Keynes's sense, rather, genuinely affect the scope and nature of individual judgment, and are altogether different from the sorts of rules Moore had imagined.

This difference, it should be emphasized, goes a considerable distance towards freeing Keynes from the subjectivist and relativist views that the emotivists had read into Moore's understanding of intuition. Recall that Robbins's view of taste and preference, which shared this emotivist emphasis, could not explain rule-governed language use, because its view of taste and preference as intrinsically private made it impossible to account for the successful following of rules in language. On Wittgenstein's later thinking, however, successfully following a rule involves a commitment to participate in a "language-game", and this implies that rule-following is understood not in descriptive, inductive terms, but prescriptively. Keynes's own later understanding of rules and conventions, it can be seen, closely resembles Wittgenstein's view, because Keynes also credited rules with a command which individuals embrace should they be able to exercise individual judgment.

Following a rule or observing a convention, it is fair to say, involves an individual in a two-sided endeavor (Winch, 1958, pp. 29–33). On the one hand, that individual's behavior itself must be considered from the vantage point of the rule or convention at issue. On the other hand, in addition to the actions of this individual, the reactions of other people to this individual's behavior are central to determining whether a rule or convention has been observed. In effect, an individual relies upon the judgment of others to interpret rules and conventions (as others of course do as well), so that rule-following is necessarily a social activity. The important implication of this for Keynes is that his "My Early Beliefs" reconceptualization of rules and conventions as prescriptive and implicitly social transformed his early view of intuition by making it possible to speak about errors in individual judgment. In contrast to his early conception of intuition as immediate, incontrovertible insight, Keynes's later view of judgment as bearing a social dimension allowed for the revision of individual intuition in virtue of the role rule-following played in the making of judgment. Quite simply, when one takes into account others' reactions to one's behavior in determining whether one is correctly following a rule, one necessarily adopts the notion of being able to be in error. Indeed, the very question of whether one can successfully follow a rule demands evaluation of what is being done, so that the prescriptive character of rules entails some theory of error and its correction.

We can, it should be emphasized, still comfortably speak about intuition, insight, and self-evidence in this new context. Individual judgment, even when reliant upon rules and conventions, we know, still possesses an immediacy that is not wrongly characterized as intuitive. Yet what theory of intuition one adopts is highly significant, since to understand intuition as presupposing rules and conventions is to explain its basis in a manner that is justifiable and appropriate to our experience in observing social practice. Keynes signaled in his "My Early Beliefs" that his old view of intuition was inadequate, and that he felt it necessary to understand individual judgment in conjunction with rules and conventions. In this he rendered a verdict on his early Apostle papers and philosophy in the *Treatise on Probability* that also declared *The General Theory* the location of his new philosophical thinking. The following chapter is devoted to explaining just how Keynes's new view of judgment and intuition tranformed his early philosophical commitments. The chapter following that pursues these new commitments in *The General Theory*.

4   Keynes's later philosophy

Since the revival of interest in J.M. Keynes's philosophical thinking with Skidelsky's (1983) introduction to Keynes's early unpublished papers, two studies of Keynes's philosophical thought in particular, one by Anna Carabelli (1988) and one by Rod O'Donnell (1989), have attracted attention from scholars.[1] The Carabelli and O'Donnell books, however, are difficult to compare, since each locates Keynes's philosophy in a different Cambridge paradigm, O'Donnell in the early Cambridge paradigm of Moore, Russell, and the early Wittgenstein, and Carabelli in the later Cambridge paradigm of the later Wittgenstein. Readers of both books expecting to gain greater insight into Keynes's economics from his philosophical thinking may find this distressing should they wonder how to connect these arguments, since their interpretations of Keynes's philosophy are in so many respects opposed to one another (see Bateman, 1991a; Davis, 1995b).

One solution to this dilemma could be thought to rest in investigating how Keynes's philosophical thinking might have changed and developed over Keynes's lifetime. This is the argument adopted in the present work. Both Carabelli and O'Donnell recognize the existence of change in Keynes's philosophical thinking, but each regard it as minor and emphasize the continuity in Keynes's philosophy. Were one consequently to argue that there were significant areas of development in Keynes's philosophical thinking, then the Carabelli and O'Donnell books might well be seen to have focused on different stages of this thinking according to the emphasis they respectively place on Keynes's later and earlier periods of thinking. This chapter, then, sets out to explain how Keynes's philosophical thinking might have evolved over his intellectual career, where the principal change in Keynes's philosophical thinking involved the adoption of a social theory of judgment and belief and the abandonment of Moore's beginning-of-the century epistemology of rational intuition. The discussion is primarily devoted to explaining what Keynes's later philosophical views actually amounted to and how they emerged from his earlier views. It first re-examines the tensions in Keynes's early thinking regarding the concept of intuition as brought out in the exchange with Ramsey, uses this to briefly review Keynes's changed view of intuition as it emerged in his post-*General Theory* "My Early Beliefs," then moves on to Keynes's view of economics as a moral science expressed in correspondence with Harrod in 1938, and finally traces the outlines of Keynes's later philosophical thinking as it developed out of Keynes's early Apostles papers' concerns and ideas.

Keynes's early epistemological dilemma

Though Keynes turned his attention almost entirely to economics and politics after completing the *Treatise on Probability*, so that very few of his later writings are specifically devoted to philosophical issues, nonetheless in his 1930 response to Ramsey's critique of the *Treatise* and in his 1938 "My Early Beliefs" memoir, Keynes quite clearly indicated that he thought his early philosophical views were mistaken in important respects. In response to Ramsey's charge that there was no evidence that probability relations were perceived in acts of intuition, Keynes agreed that Ramsey was correct – "I think he is right" (Keynes, X, pp. 338–9; c.f. also Bateman, 1987, and Cottrell, 1993) – while in his "My Early Beliefs" he insisted that he had given too much emphasis to intuition in his early thinking, and that he had come to think that conventions merited greater consideration. How, then, did Ramsey's critique impact on Keynes's early philosophical views as basically inherited from Moore, Russell, and the early Wittgenstein? To see this, it will be helpful to review the tone and character of Keynes's early philosophical allegiances.

The point of departure for Moore, Russell, and the early Wittgenstein, we saw, was their critique of British neo-Hegelian idealism as developed by Bradley, Bosanquet, Green, and McTaggart. For these philosophers, the ideal or mind-dependent character of the world implied that all things and objects were internally related, and that the truth of any given proposition ultimately depended upon the truth of all other propositions. On this view knowledge always constituted an interconnected or organic whole, and since the whole of knowledge could clearly never be comprehended at once, the pursuit of individual items of knowledge in the ordinary, traditional sense – facts and truths – amounted to an endeavor less rational than contemplation of the whole of thought and being. For Moore, Russell, and Wittgenstein, this conception of the tasks of philosophy appeared hopelessly mistaken and all but irresponsible. They were convinced that particular facts and truths could be established individually irrespective of the limited character of knowledge in general, and took as one of their first fundamental philosophical tasks the setting out of a new theory of judgment alternative to that embraced by the idealists. Moore's 1903 "Refutation of Idealism," which distinguished the act of judgment from the object of judgment, laid the basis for this new view of judgment, and in the process contributed to the initiation of a metaphysics of individual or atomic facts about the world, for which it appeared reasonable to suppose one should set forth a parallel epistemology of individual or atomic truths captured by individual propositions.

This new tradition in philosophy at Cambridge, however, was soon exposed to a number of powerful critiques, both on the part of its own representatives and by philosophers of competing traditions. As seen above, in ethics Moore's *Principia Ethica* underwent a subjectivist critique by the emotivists in the 1920s and thirties that brought Keynes's early ethical attachments into question in ways related to his own hesitations over the nature of intuition. Ramsey's critique of Keynes on probability, coming originally in 1922, was also subjectivist, or – more accurately – was part of the development of a general trend in philosophical thinking at the time that involved a reaction to the objectivist New Realism at Cambridge just as that philosophy had involved a reaction against the idealism of the last decades of the previous century.[2] Together with Bruno De Finetti (1937), Ramsey was responsible for developing the early foundations of the subjective theory of probability. Relatedly, in mathematics, L.E.J. Brouwer contested Russell and Whitehead's attempt to reduce mathematics to logic with an extreme subjectivism of his own.

Thus, while it is quite reasonable to say that Moore, Russell, and Wittgenstein were right to think that the idealists had mistakenly carried their view of the internally related character of reality beyond the point at which their conclusions made a contribution to philosophical understanding, the particular doctrines they themselves adopted concerning the nature of what was considered real and objective is by most accounts highly problematic. This became perhaps most evident in connection with Moore's theory of definition discussed at length above. Here Moore employed the referential theory of meaning in arguing that simple terms pick out simple qualities and relations actually in the world. At the same time, because for Moore simple qualities and relations were necessarily indefinable in terms of other properties or characteristics of the world, it followed that they needed to be regarded as non-natural constituents of the world's ontology. As such, they could be apprehended only in acts of simple insight, the possibility of which implied that individuals universally possessed a faculty of intuition they each exercised autonomously on account of the character of intuition as a pure unmediated vision.

Keynes adopted Moore's indefinability argument concerning the meaning of probability and thus also its associated doctrine of what was real and objective. Taking the world, like Moore, to possess an underlying structure of simple, non-natural qualities and relations, Keynes concluded that the probability of a particular proposition derived from there existing a corresponding probability relation in the world that was knowable *a priori* through the unassisted exercise of one's intuitive powers. Probability was thus a degree of rational belief that all beings with the same body of knowledge would equally entertain. Like Moore, Keynes was especially interested in the metaphysical doctrine at issue, or in his case the view that probability relations underlay determinate and objective probability judgments, and thus much less interested in – especially as he moved on after 1907 to concentrate on study of the probability calculus itself – the associated epistemological theory of intuition and judgment. Perhaps not surprisingly, then, it was Keynes's objectivist view of the meaning of probability statements that was the subject of the critical remarks Ramsey made about the *Treatise*, when, commenting on the business of intuiting logical relations, he went straight to the heart of the matter in saying, "I do not perceive them, and . . . I . . . suspect that others do not perceive them either . . ." (Ramsey, 1978, p. 63).[3] On Ramsey's subjectivist view, then, probability was still a degree of belief, but different individuals could have the same knowledge and still entertain different views regarding likelihoods.

That Keynes was indeed primarily interested in the first component of the New Cambridge Realism, or the view that it was possible to set out what was real and objective in a series of individual judgments, emerges perhaps most clearly in his own, later response to Ramsey. Acknowledging that Ramsey had in fact demonstrated that "the calculus of probabilities simply amounts to a set of rules for ensuring that the system of degrees of belief which we hold shall be a *consistent* system" (what came to be the central claim of the subjectivist view of probability), Keynes still questioned whether Ramsey had adequately distinguished mere belief from rational belief, concluding that he did not think Ramsey had been "quite successful" (Keynes, X, pp. 338–9). That is, for Keynes, it continued to make sense to say that rational belief based on what was objective or really the case could or should somehow be differentiated from mere opinion. Moore's original arguments against the idealists had been premised upon the possibility of there being a way to set out what was determinate and objective, and Keynes still found this persuasive. However, since in writing the *Treatise* Keynes had largely taken over a modified version of the terminology and reasoning of Russell's account of knowledge by acquaintance and description, when he finally came to answer Ramsey he had essentially no idea about how he might go about justifying his objectivist view of probability judgments. In effect, like Moore and Russell, Keynes had been so convinced that his starting point was correct that he gave little thought to the possible difficulties in the Moore–Russell–Wittgenstein epistemic linkage between intuition and its associated atomic view of the nature of the real.

These particular difficulties, moreover, impinged directly on Keynes's attempt to set out a new view of probability statements in the *Treatise*. In his earlier "Ethics in Relation to Conduct" paper, Keynes had concluded that the frequency theory of probability was mistaken, because it defined probabilities in terms of relative frequencies. Definition of probability as a relative frequency committed what Moore in his *Principia Ethica* (in connection with various proposed definitions of the good) had termed the naturalistic (or simply definist) fallacy. For Moore, simple qualities and relations could not be defined, but only recognized through intuition. Keynes had embraced this argument by insisting on the indefinability of the probability relation. Probability relations were real, unchanging features of the world to be grasped only through intuition. Moreover, were probabilities defined in terms of the relative frequencies of events, then they might continually be revised as more information concerning those events became available. This suggested that there was nothing substantial and permanent behind the play of phenomena, since what was probable at one point could cease to be so at a later date when experience had changed.

A key issue for Keynes in the *Treatise* regarding the interpretation of probability statements, consequently, was whether the accession of new information concerning subjects about which probability judgments had been made in the past led to altogether new probability judgements, rather than to the revision of those past probability judgments. His response was to distinguish probability judgments and judgments concerning the weight of evidence at hand, so that upon acquiring more evidence on a given subject an individual might re-assess his or her view of the relevant likelihood (VIII, pp. 77, 84; and see Runde, 1990). But judgments of weight were, like probability judgments, intuitions for Keynes, so that though one might change one's view of the likelihood of some event, this need not imply a revision of a probability judgment, rather only the having of additional intuitions regarding the evidence relevant to the case at hand. This preserved Keynes's attachment to Moore's indefinability view, and distinguished Keynes's understanding from the frequency theory approach which allowed for the continual revision of past probability judgments upon the accession of new information. Unfortunately for Keynes, however, his position still depended upon the same infallibilist view of intuition he had inherited from Moore, and as Ramsey had demonstrated, there seemed to be nothing behind this view in the way of underlying relations and qualities to anchor an individual's claims. Thus Keynes not only failed to provide an alternative to the frequency theory, but his efforts at doing so seemed to point toward Ramsey's subjectivist theory of probability.

To distinguish his objectivist approach to probabilities from the frequency theory view, Keynes had made use of an epistemology of intuition that lacked a theory of error. Though the frequency theory might be said to possess an implicit theory of error and its potential correction in the method of continual revision of probabilities with the accession of new information, on Keynes's view this conception was unable to demonstrate that individual probability judgments were rational and objective. And it was this requirement that the New Realist movement in philosophy had insisted upon, since it seemed that to fail to do so left one open to the idealists' argument that individual judgments were always conditional upon further judgments. However, whether or not individual judgments could or should be thought rational and objective, an epistemology that lacks a theory of error is questionable in the extreme, since the minimum requirement of any epistemology must certainly be that it enables one to say how one rules out being in error. This is not possible in a theory of intuition as direct insight, because error on this view is simply the unexplained absence of intuition. Such was the essential implication of Ramsey's criticism, since Ramsey had been prepared from the outset to regard intuition as fully subjective, thus abandoning the issue of the rationality and objectivity of intuition altogether. Indeed, because he had addressed his criticism directly to Keynes, who had emphasized in the *Treatise* that intuition was "some mental process of which it is difficult to give an account" (Keynes, VIII, p. 13), Ramsey made it particularly clear that the early Cambridge theory of intuition was obscure as well as implausible as an epistemology.

Keynes's particular dilemma, then, was that Ramsey's disarming critique of the concept of intuition left the objectivist interpretation of probability judgments unstably positioned between the frequency theory and the new subjectivist approach. He could, it thus seemed, either retreat to what he believed to be an inadequate foundation for the explanation of probability relations in the previously forsworn frequency approach (inadequate not only for philosophical reasons, but also because many probability judgments were non-numerical in his view), or he could retain intuition, though now as subjective, and follow Ramsey in the elaboration of mere belief. Keynes never believed that the frequency approach applied in but the most exceptional circumstances. He also continued to have doubts about Ramsey's not distinguishing mere belief from something more substantial. The latter might not possess the strong objectivist characteristics Keynes had originally attributed to it, but it still struck him as fundamental, even if it became necessary to conclude, he responded to Ramsey, that "the *a priori* probabilities, as they used to be called [are rather] part of our human outfit, perhaps given to us by natural selection, analogous to our perceptions and our memories rather than formal logic" (Keynes, X, pp. 338–9). Indeed, Ramsey had not actually demonstrated that probability judgments had to be subjective, or that they were solely a function of individual opinion. He had only shown that Keynes had failed to discover just how they might be thought objective. What, then, was Keynes's response to the dilemma in which he found himself? The key to answering this question lies in understanding Keynes's revised view of intuition and emphasis upon convention signaled most prominently in his "My Early Beliefs."

Intuition from Keynes's perspective in "My Early Beliefs"

As we saw above, while noting the tremendous impact of Moore and the *Principia* – "overwhelming . . . exciting, exhilarating" (X, p. 435) – Keynes also emphasized that the particular understanding of intuition Moore had offered as a means for knowing what things might be thought good in themselves was unequal to its assigned task. For Moore, the answer to "How did we know what states of mind were good?" was that "This was a matter of direct inspection, of direct unanalysable intuition about which it was useless and impossible to argue" (X, p. 437). However, it soon became apparent, Keynes recalled, that what was truly good was more a function of "who could speak with the greatest appearance of clear, undoubting conviction and could best use the accents of infallibility" (p. 438), and this, Keynes added, "was hardly a state of mind which a grown-up person in his senses could sustain literally" (p. 442). Thus, since good judgment clearly had to involve more than simple acts of pure, unmediated insight, what more did Keynes require to explain intuition and the grounding of individual judgment?

"My Early Beliefs" has generally attracted the most attention from recent scholars (Bateman, 1991b; Shionoya, 1991) for Keynes's reversal of his early view that it was not necessary to think that "the individual ought to obey general rules" (p. 446). For Keynes, this admitted error was traceable to a view of human nature he had earlier held that he had come to believe "disastrously mistaken" (447). It was mistaken in the sense that it presupposed the idea that "the human race already consists of reliable, decent people, influenced by truth and objective standards, who can be safely released from the outward restraints of convention and traditional standards and inflexible rules of conduct, and left, from now onwards, to their own sensible devices, pure motives and reliable intuitions of the good" (p. 447). In fact, Keynes concluded, individual judgment required an anchoring in "convention and traditional standards and inflexible rules of conduct." Human nature was not such that individuals might be expected to exercise a "direct unanalysable intuition" without fear of error, and the only available resource upon which they apparently might draw to correct individual errors in judgment rested in a society's accumulated conventions, standards, and rules.

In this conclusion, Keynes demonstrated the outlines of a resolution to the dilemma to which he had been exposed following Ramsey's critique of the *Treatise*. A society's conventions, standards, and rules went beyond the simple summaries of past experience that the frequency approach made central to probability, because they possessed a normative character over and above their quality as statistical description. At the same time, a society's conventions, standards, and rules possess an objectivity of sorts overlooked in Ramsey's subjectivist view of judgment as mere belief, in that individuals' recognition of conventions, standards, and rules typically acted as both a guide and express point of departure for individual judgment. This social objectivity, as it might be termed, was of course an imperfect standard for objective judgment compared to the rather imposing metaphysical one that underlying logical relations and simple qualities had possessed for Moore and the early Keynes. But as philosophical argument had suggested that that earlier Platonist standard was possibly incoherent, Keynes was not unwise to seek as an alternative conception the idea that a society's conventions, standards, and rules functioned as a center of gravity for individual judgment and intuition. How they might function in this capacity, and precisely what it was that would justify characterizing them as objective, were questions that admittedly went unanswered in "My Early Beliefs." But, given the central role the question of error implicitly possessed in Ramsey's critique of the *Treatise*, the beginnings of an answer to just how conventions, standards, and rules might be objective rested on an account of how individuals revised their judgments when coming into contact with the judgments of others.

Thus, it is worth noting that when an individual abides by a society's conventions, standards, and rules, this involves both attention to the apparent requirements of the principle in question and also attention to other individuals' opinions regarding whether such action fulfills the requirements of the principle in question. A single individual, consequently, depends upon others for assistance in determining when his or her actions measure up to what is required. But of course all other individuals are in the identical situation, so that a society's conventions, standards, and rules have less the character of well-defined, monolithic institutions, and more the character of on-going systems of understanding that depend upon an interpersonal exchange of thinking about proper action. Behind Keynes's greater attachment to rules and conventions, accordingly, emerges the idea of an interpersonal exchange and comparison of ideas that constitutes something of a foundation of individual judgment. Individuals are able to revise their judgments and correct errors in their thinking if able to compare their ideas with those of others, and this capacity to correct errors in judgment signals a potential objectivity in judgment distinct in nature from what Keynes had earlier sought. Since Keynes defended interpersonal comparisons (though not of utility) against Robbins in his remarks to Harrod about economics being a moral science, further understanding of how Keynes's thinking developed in this regard can be found by turning to this exchange.

Keynes's view of economics as a moral science

Keynes's remarks on the nature of economics as a moral science are especially valuable for the present discussion in that Keynes made them with the clear intent of distinguishing his view of economics from what he termed the natural science view advanced by Lionel Robbins, which had itself equated the conventional and the subjective (Keynes, XIV, p. 297).[4] Robbins had developed his methodological individualist view of economics in *An Essay on the Nature and Significance of Economic Science* (1935), arguing in his last chapter that interpersonal comparisons of utility were based on value judgments which were subjective because conventional. This occasioned a response from Harrod in his Presidential Address to Section F of the British Association, "Scope and Method of Economics," which was published in the September 1938 *Economic Journal*. Keynes had corresponded with Harrod about the nature of economics prior to the latter's August 1938 presentation of the Address. Robbins later responded to Harrod in a comment in the December *Economic Journal*.

In his letters to Harrod, Keynes insisted that judgments of value and introspection were legitimate in economics, and then attributed this to the special character of its subject matter.

I also want to emphasise strongly the point about economics being a moral science. I mentioned before that it deals with introspection and with values. I might have added that it deals with motives, expectations, psychological uncertainties. One has to be constantly on guard against treating the material as constant and homogeneous. (Keynes, XIV, p. 300)

Keynes thus emphasized that economists employ introspection and judgments of value, because economics deals with "motives, expectations, [and] psychological uncertainties." Taking Keynes to mean by this that individuals' "motives, expectations, [and] psychological uncertainties" reflect their inner intentions, whose manifestation in observable movements, apparent actions, and visible economic behavior is neither "constant" nor "homogeneous" (presumably both because of the variety of motives that inspire action and because of the generally complex relation between intention and action), for Keynes a reliance on introspection and judgments of value as reliable methods of investigation in economics enables the economist to explain individuals' observed behavior in terms of its foundation in their inner intentions by way of comparison with the economist's own inner motives and intentions imagined in similar circumstances. On Keynes's view of the subject matter of economics, that is, introspection and judgments of value are simply the methods one naturally employs when reasoning about individuals whose motives and intentions are generally obscure and inaccessible. Interpersonal comparisons are presupposed in the use of introspection and judgments of value, where introspection involves consulting one's own case to establish a relationship between behavior and intention as a possible model for another's behavior, and judgments of value pertain to the determination of the strength of a commitment that might be thought to obtain between individuals' behavior and intention.[5]

Robbins, of course, also allowed a place for introspection in economics, since he believed it involved assuming individuals could always say what their preferences were. However, for Keynes Robbins's natural science view of economics implied that the subject matter of economics is always "constant and homogeneous," such that for Robbins there was in effect no real difficulty in relating individuals' observed behavior and their inner motives and intentions. More specifically, since for Robbins an individual's inner preference rankings are perfectly reflected in the scarcity prices that that individual would pay, individuals' observed behavior is effectively transparent. In contrast, for Keynes, with his early study of Moore's ethics of good states of mind and right conduct, human motivation was far too complex to be thought so straightforwardly correlated with individual behavior and action, and economics accordingly needed to make use of additional means of analysis to be able to explain economic behavior properly.

It should be noted at once, however, that the method Keynes thinks appropriate for economists' analysis of economic agents' beliefs and reasons for acting as they do is a method available to those agents themselves as well. Thus, just as the economist looks to his or her own case to explain the behavior of individuals in economic life, so also individuals can equally be expected to consult their own motives and actions in their evaluations of others' motives and actions, particularly when considering the advisability of a given course of action. On the assumption that Keynes was alive to this, this implies that a key object of economics as a moral science for Keynes is to set out that structure of interdependent economic beliefs that reflects individuals' mutual evaluations of one another's behavior and courses of action. Such a structure of interdependent beliefs postulates numerous individuals, who, finding themselves in similar circumstances, each pair their own recognized, linked motives and actions with what they conjecture to be similar pairings of motive and action in others. Indeed, because the analogical methods involved in doing this are necessarily conjectural, in that a given individual can never be entirely certain how well his or her own motives correspond to those attributed to others, individuals can at best be thought to form sets of mutual expectations regarding one another's beliefs about future courses of action. For Keynes, therefore, economics as a moral science would naturally have this system (or systems) of interdependent belief expectations among individuals (or groups of individuals) as a primary object of investigation.

This, clearly, has important implications for understanding the nature of individual judgment in Keynes's later thinking, as perhaps can best be seen by means of a simple account of how individual judgment might be thought to emerge within a structure of interdependent beliefs. When an individual initially thinks something to be the case, say some proposition concerning something believed or that something might be desirable to do, this amounts to an individual judgment or intuition regarding the contents of this particular proposition. Suppose the individual then looks to the actions and apparent motives of others who hold like beliefs. On Keynes's moral science view that beliefs are constituted within a structure of interdependent beliefs, this individual would hypothesize about these latter individuals' reasons for holding a similar belief, and compare his or her own reasons and motivations with theirs to add plausible reasons for believing the proposition in question. Of course most cases of belief evaluation would be much more complex than this, since individuals often abandon and change their initial beliefs on exposure to the beliefs of others, while at the same time other individuals are simultaneously evaluating and adjusting their beliefs as well. The simple case nonetheless demonstrates that Keynes's moral science view of interdependent belief expectations involves a fundamentally different view of intuition and individual judgment from that which existed in his early philosophy: first, because in contrast to his early view, intuition and belief in this latter conception can now fairly be termed social in that they are arrived at through an intersubjective epistemic process, and secondly, because to suppose that individuals generally form their beliefs through introspection and judgments of value in this analogical fashion is to implicitly incorporate a theory of error in one's account of intuition and individual judgment, something that was missing from Keynes's early thinking.

In *The General Theory*, completed several years before Keynes's moral science remarks, this view of interdependent individual judgment is of course most explicitly embedded in Keynes's twelfth chapter treatment of the conventions governing long-term expectations, where speculators "devote [their] intelligences to anticipating what average opinion expects average opinion to be" (Keynes, VII, p. 156). It is also central, as will be seen in the following chapter, to Keynes's analysis of liquidity and short-term producer expectations, where conventions also operate for Keynes, if less prominently than in his account of investment. This suggests that the theme of interdependent expectations occupies an important place in the overall analysis of *The General Theory*, and that Keynes's new theory of individual judgment and expected belief is a central underlying philosophical theme of that work. It should be noted, however, that the particular interpretation given expectations here differs from the more traditional view of expectations in *The General Theory* which concentrates upon the typical individual's expectations of genuinely uncertain events, since the emphasis here is rather upon agents' expectations of each other's expectations regarding genuinely uncertain events. In effect, on the view of individual judgment and belief that arises out of Keynes's moral science philosophy, uncertainty is in the final analysis less a metaphysical absolute bound up with the unknowability of the future, and more a matter of a particular kind of structure of interdependent belief expectations. This in fact is what distinguishes Keynes's view of uncertainty in his *Treatise on Probability* from his view of uncertainty in *The General Theory*.[6] In the latter book, then, and in Keynes's later philosophy generally, uncertainty is ultimately a social relation. Individuals are uncertain about each other as much as about future events, and thus understanding uncertainty ultimately requires understanding the stability and instability of different structures of interdependent belief expectations and the systems of social relations involved.

Can it truly be said, however, that individuals do indeed reason successfully in analogical fashion about one another's beliefs in the manner suggested? Does the error correction process that belief adjustment implicitly presupposes offer us good reason to think individual judgment is still somehow objective, if not as in the *Treatise*, then in some other manner? Certainly there is something paradoxical about supposing that individuals may place themselves in the places of others, since should individuals be sufficiently distinct so that putting oneself in another's place is truly informative, then one has to wonder whether individuals can indeed put themselves in others' places at all. In effect, to say that analogical reasoning is a coherent epistemic endeavor, it must be possible, paradoxically, to say at the same time that one is both essentially similar to and different from the individual whose case is being consulted. Did Keynes have reason to think that this was a coherent enterprise? To answer this question, it is necessary to uncover and investigate the broader philosophical framework underlying his account of judgment and belief, since from the time of his early "Ethics in Relation to Conduct" paper to the Apostles to the time when he was to write to Townshend in 1938 that "the economic problem is . . . only a particular department of the general principles of conduct" (Keynes, XXIX, p. 289), Keynes sustained an abiding interest in a general theory of human conduct that subsumed specific views on individuality and the most basic relationships between individuals.

Keynes's dual conception of individuality and sociality

Keynes's deeper philosophical views concerning individuals and their relationships to one another, we saw above, first began to emerge in his critical analysis of Moore's treatment of right conduct in the latter's *Principia Ethica*. The principal argument Keynes advanced in his early "Ethics in Relation to Conduct" paper was that Moore's intuitionist view of good needed to be extended to include an intuitionist analysis of right conduct. As argued above, however, it was also apparent to Keynes that Moore's view of the nature of good (to which in its essentials Keynes himself subscribed) created additional difficulties for Keynes's proposed analysis of right conduct that were associated with Moore's interpretation of the principle of organic unities. On Moore's view of organic unities, because the good and bad effects of one's actions were generally inseparable, it followed that it was one's duty to aim in action at organic wholes of the greatest intrinsic value. Yet in Moore's view the organic whole of the greatest intrinsic value was evidently the entire universe itself, and this consequently implied that right conduct could take only the good of the universe as its object. Keynes found this conclusion absurd, and he thus argued in his 1905 "Miscellanea Ethica" that Moore had been mistaken in extending the principle of organic unities beyond the scope of the individual mind.

In ethical calculation each individual's momentary state of mind is our sole unit. In so far as a state of mind has parts, to this extent I admit the principle of organic unities: it is the excellence of the state as a whole with which we are concerned. But beyond each individual the organic principle cannot reach. (Keynes, 1905b, UA/21)

Given that organic connection obtained only within the confines of the individual mind, right conduct would involve nothing more than an obligation to bring about the greatest sum of individual good states of mind possible. This made the analysis of moral obligation a far more intelligible affair, since, in contrast to the hopelessly confusing task of taking the good of the universe as one's object, it was a reasonably practical matter to concern oneself with the greatest number of good states of mind summed across all individuals.

At the same time, however, Keynes's critique of Moore also held important implications for a wider set of philosophical issues that concerned the nature of individual identity and the most basic relationships between individuals. Philosophers have long sought to determine what explains individuals' distinct identities as agents, in order to then go on to explain belief and the capacity for action on the part of individuals (see, e.g., Parfit, 1984). Moreover, since delimiting the sphere of individual life *pari passu* goes some distance towards explaining the avenues remaining for relationships between individuals, the adoption of a particular theory of individual identity also typically implies specific views regarding the nature of social relationships. More generally, just as a theory of individual identity implies some theory of social relationships, conversely a theory of social relationships typically presupposes some theory of individual identity. Combined, a view of the nature of individual identity and the corresponding relationships between individuals constitutes what might be termed a dual conception of individuality and sociality.

Keynes's view of the proper scope of the organic principle raised just these sorts of issues since it implied a particular understanding of the boundaries delimiting individuality. Thus, to produce the greatest sum of good states of mind across individuals, one had to be able to say at the very least what distinguished one individual from another. Yet this at the same time then entailed some analysis of what did not distinguish individuals, or alternatively of what they possessed in common or was tallied across individuals. Keynes's early view of right conduct can thus be seen to reflect precisely the sort of dual conception of individuality and sociality that has long preoccupied philosophers. Both of the dimensions it involves deserve further attention, to better understand the later development in his philosophical thinking.

First, then, if in Keynes's view organic unity obtains only within the confines of the individual mind, such that each individual's thoughts and feelings are organically connected, and such that no two individuals' thoughts and feelings are organically related, then it follows that the organic connection of each individual's thoughts and feelings must also distinguish each individual as a distinct, separate being. For Keynes, that is, an individual's distinct individual identity is essentially determined by the mutual dependence of all that individual's thoughts and feelings upon one another. Each individual's own thoughts and feelings, it might be said, are so much connected to one another in the mind of the individual to whom they belong that the organization they thus assume effectively distinguishes that individual from all other individuals, who at the same time are similarly distinguished as individual identities.

Hints of this thinking first appeared in Keynes's early insistence in "Ethics in Relation to Conduct" that individuals not be bound by general rules of conduct, but rather rely on individual intuitive insight regarding right and wrong. Essentially, general rules do not connect up well with those situations demanding right conduct, whereas, within the ambit of the single individual's mind, an understanding of the context of duty and the judgment of a desired action cohere because organically related. That intuition was a preferable approach to determining right conduct, then, depended ultimately upon the individual mind possessing a cohesiveness and integrity that Keynes understood as an organic unity. It can be argued that Keynes retained the view that organic connection pertained to the mind alone throughout his intellectual career (Davis, 1989), and that it is a mistake to attribute to Keynes the view that organic connection pertained rather to the economy as a whole (Davis, 1989–90).[7] Perhaps more importantly, however, it can be seen that the view that the mind is an organic unity is also central to Keynes's later moral science thinking. When Keynes urges the economist to draw upon his or her own unique experience to make sense of the behavior of others, he ascribes an integrity to the investigator's mind that parallels a like integrity in the mind of the individual studied. The world of action on the face of things lacks evident coherence. Thus, one employs a method of analogical reasoning, with its underlying assumption that individual minds constitute distinct identities, because the world of action becomes meaningful only when the organic connection between intention and action is made manifest.

Secondly, however, if for Keynes the particular organic connection of each individual's ideas alone establishes that individual's own distinct identity, then it follows that ideas in the abstract, or taken a priori and apart from the sense and meaning ideas assume within each individual's own experience and distinct intellectual organization, do not distinguish individuals from one another, but rather constitute the common ground for the relationships between individuals. Indeed, should individuals be distinguished from one another by the ways in which they each incorporate abstract ideas within their own modes of intellectual organization, then shared abstract ideas by nature transcend individual understanding. For Keynes, then, there exists a body of thoughts and ideas about the world which is independent of particular individuals' experience, and which constitutes an essential binding element in the relationships between individuals. Shared abstract ideas, it might thus be said, are the substance of social relationships.

This doctrine was implicit in Keynes's thinking from the time of his first reading of Moore's *Principia*, when he accepted Moore's view that good states of mind were things good in themselves. On this view, one experiences a truly good state of mind (as when one enjoys another's friendship) only when one's object is something intrinsically good or good for its own sake (that is, friendship *per se*). Accordingly, while individuals' thoughts and ideas continue to possess particular significance for the individuals to whom they belong, to the extent that they take aim at intrinsically valuable objects, they possess an objective standing over and above their significance for particular individuals. Importantly, this view also underlay Keynes's *Treatise* view of probability relations and the objectivity of probability judgments. For Keynes, probability relations were knowable *a priori*, and this knowledge constituted a knowledge of abstract ideas. Individual probability judgments and the intuition of probability relations were thus objective to the extent that they were based upon the individual's accurate perception of real probability relations, that is, upon a grasp of abstract ideas reflecting real probability relations.

But if Keynes's early view of individuals as distinct identities, the first component of his early dual conception of individualty and sociality, can be seen to reappear in his later moral science thinking, is it also the case that the second component of this conception, namely, shared abstract ideas as the substance of social relationships, reappears there as well? This is especially important for any interpretation of Keynes's later moral science view, since a dual conception of individuality and sociality, by emphasizing the linkages between these two aspects of being, might well begin to resolve the paradoxes that naturally arise when one attempts to understand how individuals imagine themselves in the places of others while yet remaining distinct and separate beings. Specifically, then, is it the case for Keynes's later moral science thinking that individuals engaging in an analogical reasoning process about the motives and thinking of others somehow presuppose some body of shared conceptual materials on the order of the abstract ideas of Keynes's early ethics and the *Treatise*?

Keynes's later moral science view, it is fair to say, makes one very obvious departure from Keynes's earlier thinking. Whereas Keynes's early view presents an essentially static conception of individuals and their relationships to one another, his later moral science view in comparison is clearly dynamical in its emphasis on a process of interdependent belief adjustment. On Keynes's later understanding, individuals revise and change their beliefs when in contact with one another, and this interaction contributes to the determination of their respective beliefs (as, for example, when individual speculators "devote [their] intelligences to anticipating what average opinion expects average opinion to be" [Keynes, VII, p. 156]). In his early thinking, in contrast, since intuition and individual judgment do not depend upon the interaction of individuals, that individuals share certain abstract ideas is strictly a function of the existence of those underlying objective relations in the world which these ideas concern. In effect, that individuals share such ideas derives not from their possessing some distinctive social nature, but rather from their simply co-occupying the same world.

Put in this way, it may not be surprising that Keynes early on felt there were difficulties with his initial views. As I have argued previously, an important manifestation of Keynes's early pre-*Treatise* difficulties with the concept of intuition stemmed from his inability to explain the presumed objective basis of individual judgment or intuition. Indeed, in the conclusion of his "Miscellanea Ethica" paper, Keynes himself allowed that while "we can often say what . . . a man *ought* to think and feel" (that is, what intuition or individual judgment objectively required), on the grounds that there seemed to exist an "approximate uniformity of human organs" across individuals, he nonetheless felt himself unable to explain just how a sameness in human nature had anything to do with individuals sharing abstract ideas about such things as intrinsic value and *a priori* logical relations. Thus, he was never able to say on his early view whether what individuals actually thought and felt from their own particular points of view somehow depended upon what they ought to think and feel, or alternatively whether what they ought to think and feel somehow depended upon what they actually did think and feel. That is, Keynes was unable to explain the relationship between abstract ideas and their understanding by particular individuals, and was thus ultimately unable to explain individuals' shared social substance as a body of abstract ideas.

Ramsey, of course, drew attention to these problems in Keynes's early thought by insisting that individuals did not perceive probability relations, and thus likely did not intuit abstract ideas in the manner that Keynes had imagined. Keynes later echoed Ramsey's critique of intuition in his "My

Early Beliefs" memoir, and added that his errors in this regard were associated with the fact that his early view of human nature had been "disastrously mistaken" (X, p. 447). Indeed, he went on, because human nature was so much more complex and variable than he and his friends had originally believed, he now recommended respect – indeed even "reverence" – for society's "rules and conventions," "traditional wisdom," and "the restraints of custom." Clearly, then, the sameness of human nature contemplated in "Miscellanea Ethica," that had there justified the notion that one could often say what an individual ought to think and feel, now dwindled in significance in comparison with the role society's rules and conventions played in assisting individual judgment. Indeed, Keynes was now doubtful that one could speak comfortably at all about what constituted human nature. And, where before Keynes had characterized individuals' common social substance in terms of a shared body of abstract ideas, by the time of *The General Theory* individuals' shared social substance had clearly come to be constituted out of a collection of inherited rules, practices, conventions, and institutions, which each individual might grasp and apply in the context of their respective circumstances.

Put in terms of the dynamical moral science conception of Keynes's later thinking, Keynes modified his early dual conception of individuality and sociality by re-interpreting the latter dimension as the relatively settled product of accumulated historical judgment and experience bound up in rules and conventions. Rules and conventions emerge from a history of past judgments, which are themselves rooted in past systems of interdependent belief. Moreover, since individuals always share an understanding of and act on existing rules and conventions, rules and conventions themselves are continually undergoing change, if slowly, within existing systems of interdependent belief. Just as, then, Keynes's moral science view required that individual judgment be understood in terms of a process of interdependent belief adjustment, so also individuals' shared social substance on this later view, their rules, practices, and conventions, similarly needed to be understood to be the product of an historical, social process. More simply, a society's rules and conventions were in effect the semi-permanent structures of systems of interdependent belief expectations.

Given this, the analogical reasoning process Keynes's moral science thinking attributes to individuals seems perhaps somewhat less paradoxical. Individuals can imagine themselves in each other's places, because they share common sets of assumptions about the connections between action and motivation that derive from their shared social substance, the rules and conventions that operate in their time and society. Indeed, that a society's rules and conventions themselves derive from a history of past interdependent judgment suggests that these common assumptions are not remote from the concerns of on-going judgment, and thus that individuals' conjectures about one another's thinking and behavior are often reasonable. Particularly relevant here is the emphasis Keynes places in "My Early Beliefs" on the normative character of rules and conventions as standards of conduct. In contrast to Moore's view of rules as statistical summaries earlier critiqued by Keynes, rules on Keynes's later view, had a compellingness or obligatoriness to them, especially in light of the fact that they had been "skilfully put across and guilefully preserved" to create a "thin and precarious crust" of "civilisation" (X, p. 447). Individual judgment, consequently, received considerable direction from a society's rules and conventions, and this had to be particularly valuable when it came to individuals' assessments of each other's rationales for action.

Keynes's later moral science thinking, then, represented a methodology for economics and view of the economy that had deep roots in his early ideas about the nature of individuality and sociality. His early dual conception of individuality and sociality, however, was flawed by a view of judgment as rational intuition that made the idea of a shared social substance (as a collection of abstract ideas) questionable in the extreme. Ramsey drew attention to this, and Keynes himself ultimately came to regard his early view of intuition as misconceived. Upon reconsidering what was truly involved in individual judgment – especially in his efforts to explain real economic behavior – he grasped the mutual dependence of individual belief expectations, and thus came to appreciate the place and role of conventions and rules in the economy. This permitted him to give his early dual conception of individuality and sociality a reasonable reformulation, thus giving credence to his moral science methodological recommendations and view of the economy as being based on sets of interdependent belief expectations.

Keynes's later philosophy

Keynes's philosophical thinking across his career thus reflects a pattern of development and change which has important implications for its understanding. That Keynes was introduced to philosophy when Moore, Russell, and the early Wittgenstein were transforming the reigning philosophical theory of judgment meant that his own initial philosophical thinking reflected the characteristics and dilemmas of their thought. Yet that Keynes's primary interests soon shifted away from traditional philosophy meant that his own response to the questions raised about early Cambridge philosophy was to assume a relatively unique path. In particular, Keynes's study of economics made the structure of judgment in an economy a preferred vehicle for the investigation of the nature of judgment, so that Keynes was ultimately to seek an explanation of what grounded judgment not in the abstract philosophical discourse of early Cambridge, but in the practical operation of different individuals' judgments in an interactive context.

This meant that, in contrast to the view of intuition in early Cambridge as a necessarily individual form of pre-epistemic insight unmediated or conditioned in any sense by the thinking of others, intuition or individual judgment in Keynes's later thinking bears an inescapable social component in its functioning within a system of interdependent individual expectations. In the *Treatise* Keynes had developed a general theory of rational belief premised on the idea that intuition permits direct insight into the underlying nature of the world. This implied that

When once the facts are given which determine our knowledge, what is probable or improbable in these circumstances has been fixed objectively and is independent of our opinion. The theory of probability is logical, therefore, because it is concerned with the degree of belief which it is *rational* to entertain in given conditions, and not merely with the actual beliefs of particular individuals, which may or may not be rational. (VIII, p. 4).

But on his later understanding, individual judgment as individual expectation takes the judgments of others at the very least as a point of departure, and "opinion" and the "actual beliefs of particular individuals" then very much factor into the formation of individual beliefs. Consequently, it is difficult to see how on Keynes's later thinking judgment has as its object the underlying nature of the world, or, in the case of an uncertain future, sets of logical probability relations making up the essential structure of the world. It is also difficult to say that the beliefs individuals ultimately arrive at should still be considered "rational" on Keynes's later view. Indeed, one searches in vain in his later writings for expressions of concern regarding either an underlying logical reality or the promise of rational belief. The tone of Keynes's later views, quite simply, is no longer reminiscent of his early writings.

However, whether individual judgment might yet be thought objective raises different questions, since though there is little reason to suppose that the later Keynes still thought judgment objective in the manner of rational intuition, this would not preclude one's arguing it to be objective in some other fashion. Keynes, unfortunately, was never again to address the traditional philosophical topic of the objectivity of judgment in the manner of his early thinking. But it is fair to suggest that he was able to establish a reasonable, alternative case for explaining when and how interdependent judgment might be objective in historical economies. In the first place, this was a matter of addressing the fundamental weakness of Moore's theory of intuition, namely, that in its fundamentally abstract character it lacked a theory of error. For Keynes, that individuals possessed a means of evaluating their respective judgments – through an analogical reasoning process – meant that it was possible, at least in principle, to distinguish good and bad judgments. Secondly, because Keynes was able to draw upon and develop his early views of the nature of individuality and sociality, he was able to place this revised view of intuition in a framework that explained the general limits surrounding judgment. Specifically, that individuals possessed a tangible sociality in their shared rules and conventions meant that what they ought to think and do always constituted a consideration relevant to their determination of what they in fact thought and did. This permitted an objectivity of sorts to judgment, though clearly not of the order provided by a transcendent world of logical forms.

Perhaps this case is clearest if contrasted to the distinctively non-objectivist views of some of Keynes's contemporaries. First of all, Keynes's later view remained consistent with his insistence against Ramsey that one must still find something more substantial than mere belief to explain the nature of judgment. Ramsey's subjectivism, where only consistency of bets need obtain, falls short of what Keynes later believed assisted individual judgment in the form of a society's conventions and rules.[8] For Ramsey, individuals were free from occasion to occasion to form whatever beliefs and convictions struck them as appropriate, so that a society's rules and conventions were at best rules of thumb they might consult, but which otherwise lacked any compelling quality. Secondly, Keynes's later thinking needs also to be distinguished from the emotivist psychology which we saw above introduced a comprehensive subjectivism into ethics and economics in the 1930s. While it is true that a society's rules and conventions are not infrequently irrational and arbitrary in their rootedness in past practice and custom, nonetheless recourse to rules and conventions is quite contrary to the subjectivist theme of a free-floating individual opinion. Keynes, it seems fair to add, apparently did not believe that a society's rules and conventions were on balance irrational or arbitrary. Thus, as a counterweight to emotivist and subjectivist judgment, they provided objective standards of sorts for individual judgment.

Keynes thus changed his understanding of the very concept of what made judgment objective, rather than abandon the notion of objectivity altogether. As already noted, philosophy in Cambridge was to pursue a path in this regard not unlike Keynes's. Wittgenstein, who came to dominate Cambridge philosophy by the 1930s as did Keynes its economics, produced arguments in his *Philosophical Investigations* (1953), especially regarding convention and the notion of intention, that bear considerable resemblance to those Keynes developed.[9] This convergence in views may have been the product of a shared critique of early Cambridge thinking. Thus, in discussing his own early views in his 1935 Lent Term lectures (taken down by Alice Ambrose), Wittgenstein expanded his self-critique to include Keynes's previous positions:

One calls a lot of things propositions. If one sees this, then one can discard the idea that Russell and Frege had that logic is a science of certain objects – and that logic is like a natural science such as zoology and talks about these objects as zoology talks of animals. Like a natural science, it could supposedly discover certain relations. For example, Keynes claimed to discover a probability relation which was like implication, yet not quite like implication. But logic is a calculus, not a natural science, and in it one can make inventions but not discoveries. (Ambrose, 1979, pp. 138–9)

Wittgenstein's words, "logic is a calculus" in which "one can make inventions," echo Keynes's own admission to Ramsey five years earlier that "the calculus of probabilities simply amount to a set of rules for ensuring that the system of degrees of belief which we hold shall be a *consistent* system" (Keynes, X, pp. 338–9). Both thinkers, moreover, were close friends of the Italian economist Piero Sraffa, who was instrumental in influencing Wittgenstein to abandon his original philosophical views in favor of his forms of life views.[10] Sraffa himself had adopted Antonio Gramsci's Marxist ideas regarding society and state, and these presumably were not of negligible interest to Wittgenstein, who had made a mild commitment to socialism. Thus while it would certainly be wrong to say that Keynes, Wittgenstein, and Sraffa were in close agreement on the specific issues that occupied their different works, it is clearly arguable that they all agreed that the objectivity of individual judgment depended in good part upon society's historical systems of organization such as were involved in a society's conventions, rules, and practices. Their work, it might be said, represented a reaction to the subjectivist currents in philosophy and social science that arose in the 1920s and early thirties, which were also beginning to face resistance in the later Vienna Circle writings of Neurath and Rudolph Carnap, as well in the rise of conventionalist mathematics in the work of the formalist David Hilbert.

With this in view, it remains to look to *The General Theory* to see how Keynes's later philosophy became embedded in his later economics. A brief review of the stages through which the argument has moved in previous chapters will assist this transition. In the first chapter, it was argued that Keynes's early theory of judgment, inherited from Moore and others at Cambridge, was central to his early philosophical thinking, though that early theory was flawed in important respects. In the second chapter, it was argued that emotivist and subjectivist views that emerged in critique of the theory of judgment employed by Moore and Keynes were themselves flawed. Wittgenstein was responsible for bringing out these subsequent difficulties, and his own arguments demonstrated that the requirements of communication and language were incompatible with the thinking of Ayer and Robbins. In the third chapter, Keynes's own doubts about his early ideas were shown to premise rules and conventions. Like Wittgenstein with his notions of forms of life and language games, then, Keynes came to appreciate the idea that social historical practices provided frameworks in which individuals formed judgments and communicated with one another. Indeed, this latter orientation was argued in the present chapter to provide philosophical grounds for a reformulated view of judgment and intuition that made belief adjustment and error correction intrinsic features of a system of interdependent belief expectations. Conventions and rules, then, operate upon individual belief expectations. How this is so in *The General Theory* will make the later philosophical conception of Keynes yet more understandable, and in addition permit insights into such topics as the role of habit, animal spirits, and the place of the concept of the rational agent in Keynes's later economics.

5   The philosophical thinking of *The General Theory*

The criticisms addressed to Keynes's earlier philosophical thinking as initiated by Ramsey together with Keynes's own sense of the limitations of his earlier philosophy led Keynes to reformulate the central concept of his early philosophy, the concept of intuition. Yet clearly what dominated Keynes's intellectual development in the years subsequent to his initial concern with philosophy was his struggle with the problems of economic theory and policy (Clarke, 1989; Moggridge, 1992; Skidelsky, 1992). This conceptual terrain was almost entirely removed from the language and interests of Keynes's early philosophy, and indeed philosophy in general, so that it cannot be said that Keynes's intellectual development was directly focused upon matters of philosophical significance, as might have been the case had his career taken the path upon which it had originally embarked. Keynes's philosophical development, it could indeed be said, proceeded at two removes from the usual objects and preoccupations of philosophy. It did not make the traditional problems of philosophy its primary vehicle, and it also required translation behind the scenes, as it were, from one set of issues and way of thinking about economics to another. Despite this, Keynes's attachment to philosophical thinking as established in his first years at Cambridge, together with his natural talent for abstract thought, rendered the philosophical dimensions of his later work always immediate to his overall reasoning process. Accordingly, though his philosophical conclusions became increasingly implicit in his later writing, they were no less serious commitments on his part, only more difficult to discern.

This implies that though one can trace the outlines of Keynes's later philosophical development by marking its occasional signposts in Keynes's infrequent philosophical comments, to fully understand this development it is necessary to read off its expression in theoretical matters of a quite different nature, namely, Keynes's economics. It would be a mistake to say that Keynes was not alive to the philosophical implications of his economic reasoning. Yet at the same time this philosophical thinking was informed by the issues and different logic of economics. The task of those who seek to explain Keynes's philosophical thinking, therefore, is to demonstrate how Keynes resolved problems specifically in economics as a philosophically self-conscious thinker. This is to explain the philosophical commitments of Keynes's later economics in a manner consistent with Keynes's apparent later philosophical interests and history of philosophical thinking.

To proceed on this score is to turn attention to *The General Theory*. Keynes's conception of the workings of the economy in *The General Theory* will be set forth here with special attention to his emphasis upon convention. The concept of convention is both central to the argument of *The General Theory* regarding equilibrium unemployment, and was also, we saw above, singled out by Keynes in "My Early Beliefs" as one of his chief later philosophical concerns. Further, its treatment in the locations in *The General Theory* in which it appears recalls Keynes's comments to Harrod about economic method. This coincidence of philosophical and economic concerns arguably holds significant potential for explaining Keynes's later economics itself. In essence, if Keynes's argument regarding equilibrium unemployment ultimately turns on his concept of convention, and if this concept bears specific philosophical import for Keynes, then in the final analysis Keynes's fundamental conclusions in *The General Theory* themselves turn upon deep-rooted philosophical convictions he developed in his later years.

The argument of *The General Theory*

In recent years there have been renewed efforts to explain Keynes's thinking in *The General Theory*.[1] Keynes himself summarized his argument in his eighteenth chapter, "The General Theory of Employment Re-stated." He starts out by identifying the factors that are given, the independent variables, and the dependent variables. The "ultimate independent variables" are

(1) the three fundamental psychological factors, namely, the psychological propensity to consume, the psychological attitude to liquidity and the psychological expectation of future yield from capital assets, (2) the wage-unit as determined by the bargains reached between employers and employed, and (3) the quantity of money as determined by the action of the central bank. (VII, pp. 246–7)

These variables determine at any one time an economy's national income and its quantity of employment, the dependent variables whose explanation is the primary object of *The General Theory*. They are also variables that Keynes says are susceptible to influence and in some instances subject to deliberate control or management by central authorities to promote full employment levels of national income and output. Keynes then summarized his argument as follows (pp. 247–9).

Focusing upon new investment as the crucial form of aggregate expenditure, Keynes notes that new investment proceeds to the point at which the supply price of each type of capital asset, taken together with its expected yield in the future earnings it is likely to generate, makes the marginal efficiency of capital equal to the rate of interest. This immediately presupposes states of activity for three of the independent variables noted above, the "psychological expectation of future yield from capital assets," or as Keynes also describes it, the "state of confidence" (p. 248) concerning prospective yields, the psychological attitude to liquidity, and the quantity of money as determined by the actions of the central bank, which together thus determine the rate of new investment. New investment then brings forth new consumption, yet, according to the marginal propensity to consume, another of Keynes's independent variables, in an increment smaller than the increment to income stemming from the new investment. The ratio of new investment to additional income is termed the investment multiplier. Using it to proxy an associated employment multiplier, the increment to employment attendant upon the new investment can be established. Higher income then raises the schedule of liquidity preference by increasing the demand for money, which, given the quantity of money as determined by actions of the central bank, raises the rate of interest until new investment is halted.

The position of equilibrium, with values for national income and employment, need not of course be a full employment equilibrium. Indeed, in Keynes's view, the capitalist economic system is "capable of remaining in a chronic condition of sub-normal activity for a considerable period without any marked tendency either towards recovery or towards complete collapse" (p. 249). This state of affairs, importantly, derives from the levels achieved by the independent variables Keynes isolates, or more specifically, from the states of activity exhibited by the psychological propensities or attitudes he believes of central importance. But what does it mean to say that a particular psychological propensity or attitude, for example, the psychological attitude toward liquidity, exhibits a certain state of activity? In determining equilibrium income and employment this question does not arise, since the levels of the independent variables, and the state of activity of each psychological propensity, are taken as given for that purpose. Yet *The General Theory* does more than demonstrate that unemployment may exist in equilibrium. It also considers how this state of affairs is tied to the development of a monetary economy which has made the psychological propensities Keynes isolates the chief determinants of income and employment. From this perspective, the question of how the psychological propensities isolated achieve their respective states of activity becomes important, and more thus needs to be said about the philosophical thinking underlying Keynes's understanding of an economy's chief psychological propensities and attitudes and their states of activity.

To begin, it helps to recognize that Keynes's summary view of his argument, with its focus upon new investment expenditure, gives primary attention to two of the three "fundamental" psychological factors he identifies, the psychological attitude toward liquidity and psychological attitude toward or state of confidence concerning the future yields from capital assets. These attitudes, moreover, are also the subject of Keynes's most emphatic assertions about economic behavior being essentially conventional in character. In his discussion of the incentives to liquidity Keynes asserts, "[i]t might be more accurate, perhaps, to say that the rate of interest is a highly conventional, rather than a highly psychological, phenomenon. For its actual value is largely governed by the prevailing view as to what its value is expected to be" (p. 203). In discussing long-term investment expectations, Keynes states that the valuation of investments cannot be accomplished solely through mathematical calculation, but depends upon a convention in organized investment markets that "the existing state of affairs will continue indefinitely, except in so far as we have specific reasons to expect a change" (p. 152). The chief psychological propensities at issue in Keynes's view of the economy, then, are thought to require explanation in terms of the notion of a convention. Keynes's Chapter 18 summary view of the operation of the capitalist market economy, accordingly, itself needs to be understood in this way. How is this to be done?

In *Macroeconomics after Keynes*, Vicky Chick asserts that at an important point in the transition from his thinking in the *Treatise on Money* to that in *The General Theory* Keynes came "to the astonishing conclusion that the chief cause of unemployment is not so much that the real wage is too high, but that the rate of interest is too high" (1983, p. 10).[2] That the rate of interest could be too high meant for Keynes that the array of empirical, psychological, and institutional factors (such as bank policy, lenders' and borrowers' attitudes toward risk and liquidity, etc.) which determined the rate of interest possessed a configuration relative to the configuration of those empirical, psychological, and institutional factors which determined the wage-unit (such as employers' and employees' bargaining strengths, relative wages, etc.) that left income and output below full employment levels. Put differently, that there existed unemployment was ultimately to be explained by the inertial evolution of conventional attitudes and predispositions regarding finance and the labor market that locked the interest rate and the real wage in non-market clearing relations to one another. As emphasized by Colin Rogers (1989), for Keynes the Wicksellian notion that there exists a real or natural long-term rate of interest that constitutes a center of gravity to which all other variables ultimately freely adjust was without foundation. It is market forces, rather, which the historical evidence demonstrates are constrained to adjust to conventional non-market, historically-and socially-determined institutional arrangements, and it is these, accordingly, that constitute the center of gravity for the economic system as a whole. Should, then, the demand for liquidity as determined by such forces be especially high, it is because of institutional and psychological developments in the historical evolution of financial markets that, given long-standing, conventionally established levels for real and relative wages, leave the interest rate too high to justify the new investment needed for full employment.

Income and employment are then determined by the level of effective demand this state of affairs permits. Here Keynes's argument and view of market forces in the labor market is familiar.

The propensity to consume and the rate of new investment determine between them the volume of employment, and the volume of employment is uniquely related to a given level of real wages – not the other way round. If the propensity to consume and the rate of new investment result in a deficient effective demand, the actual level of employment will fall short of the supply of labor potentially available at the existing real wage, and the equilibrium real wage will be *greater* than the marginal disutility of the equilibrium level of employment. (VII, p. 30)

The principle of effective demand, by way of the dependence of investment upon conventional attitudes toward liquidity and prospective yield, is thus in significant degree detached from the logic of market forces. Indeed, when entrepreneurs determine their offers of employment in light of their (short-term) expectations of sales and earnings, they put aside concern with the effects of possible wage changes on desired output, and focus their primary concern simply upon the level of expected sales. Relatedly, from the perspective of the economy as a whole, Keynes often emphasized that any economy-wide wage deflation might well negatively affect effective demand. In combination, then, the attitude toward liquidity, with its effect on the interest rate, and the attitude toward prospective yields, with its impact on long-term expectations, jointly serve to determine income and employment, and both behaviors, clearly, are for Keynes preeminently conventional in nature.

That Keynes's argument in *The General Theory* takes this form is not always well appreciated. No doubt this is partly due to the fact that the short-period equilibrium focus of the book makes investigation of the further determinants of the argument's independent variables, or what might explain the states of activity the different psychological propensities and attitudes exhibit, a less immediate objective. But surely also important is the fact that this latter investigation is largely an historical–social one that lacks the well-defined, formal character of the income determination argument.[3] As Keynes emphasized to Harrod, economics is an art or way of thinking that makes unusual demands upon the economist, and "Good economists are scarce, because the gift for using 'vigilant observation' to choose good models, although it does not require a highly specialised intellectual technique, appears to be a very rare one" (XIV, p. 297). Here, the successful exercise of this "art or way of thinking" is taken to require a deeper understanding of the psychological attitudes and propensities Keynes believed central to the determination of income and employment, and "vigilant observation" in choosing such models to depend upon grasping the precise role that conventions play in establishing the state of activity of these attitudes and propensities. More can be understood about Keynes's own thinking in this regard by turning to his analysis of average expectation and its role in determining the structure of a convention.

Average expectation and the structure of a convention

For Keynes, an economy's conventions are responsible for determining the levels or states of activity displayed by the psychological propensities and attitudes at work in the economy. Yet certainly these psychological propensities and attitudes manifest themselves in varying degrees in different individuals, and thus it is more useful and more informative to say that Keynes's interest in conventions was ultimately directed toward explaining how conventions act to structure different individuals' psychological propensities and attitudes in relation to one another, or alternatively how conventions relate the degrees to which psychological propensities and attitudes operate across different individuals. This is borne out most clearly in Keynes's often-cited Chapter 12 explanation of the role convention assumes in determining long-term investment expectations. It can readily be seen, however, that Keynes's analysis there is quite general, and as such, might well be applied in similar fashion to his treatments of the differences between individuals regarding the attitude toward liquidity, the propensity to consume, relative wages, and entrepreneurial behavior in the short period.[4] Just how, then, does Keynes understand convention in his account of long-term expectations?

This question is best approached by first asking why it should be the case that the convention governing investment valuation – "that the existing state of affairs will continue indefinitely, except in so far as we have specific reasons to expect a change" (p. 152) – assumes the form that Keynes says it does. Why is it the case, that is, that organized investment markets tend to preserve the status quo – "the existing state of affairs" – rather than, say, constantly challenge it? Keynes's characterization of the convention that operates in investment markets has as background a number of important statements he makes regarding the origins of speculative activity in equity markets and stock exchanges.[5] Chief among these is his statement that at the end of the nineteenth century capital markets were not nearly so highly developed as they came to be in the first decades of the twentieth century when there emerged a significant separation between ownership and management in the typical business firm. Prior to that separation – when "enterprises were mainly owned by those who undertook them or by their friends and associates" (p. 150) – close involvement with the affairs of a business, and with the fundamentals of its operations, typically meant a steady commitment to that firm's growth. "Decisions to invest in private business of the old-fashioned type were . . . decisions largely irrevocable, not only for the community as a whole, but also for the individual" (*Ibid.*). This decentralized, atomistic world of business, in which individuals had little interaction with one another in regard to decisions to invest and grow, was largely displaced by the emergence of a more mobile and versatile form of capital ownership, which permitted the daily transfer of wealth from one investment to another, and which threw investors together on centralized stock exchanges in their common pursuit of speculative gains and losses. In this change in the site and character of investment activity, investors lost both their former isolation from one another, and their former hands-on knowledge of the operations of business. They gained the opportunity to compare daily their judgments with those of others, so that the modern investment process made investors far more interdependent, though at the same time less well acquainted by past standards with those considerations specific to particular firms' investment strategies.

In these circumstances, Keynes tells us, what constituted a good or bad investment came to be "governed by the average expectation of those who deal on the Stock Exchange as revealed by the price of shares, rather than by the genuine expectations of the professional entrepreneur" (p. 151). While one might be tempted to think that the reference to good or bad investment implies that the "energies and skill of the professional investor and speculator" are to be largely devoted to acquiring a better knowledge than widely available, so as to permit "superior long-term forecasts of the probable yield of an investment over its whole life," in Keynes's view the investor's "energies and skill" are rather almost entirely devoted to "foreseeing changes in the conventional basis of valuation a short time ahead of the general public" (p. 154). Thus, while "the social object of skilled investment should be to defeat the dark forces of time and ignorance which envelop our future . . . the actual, private object of the most skilled investment to-day is 'to beat the gun,' as the Americans so well express it, to outwit the crowd, and to pass the bad, or depreciating, half-crown to the other fellow" (p. 155). Average expectation regarding the worth of various investments is thus not only removed from an informed acquaintance with the underlying facts relevant to those investments, but really represents no more than an average opinion of their worth – or, to put it more accurately, Keynes asserts, an opinion of "what average opinion expects average opinion to be" (p. 156).

Nonetheless, in such circumstances, or "under the influence of a mass psychology" as not surprisingly develops when average opinion seeks to determine average opinion, the professional investor's "behaviour is not the outcome of a wrong-headed propensity," but rather the inevitable "result of an investment market organised along the lines described" (p. 155). This average expectation of an investment's prospective yield, of course, subsumes different individual expectations of prospective yields both above and below that average. Different individuals accordingly have different views of the value of any given investment, and their taking action in regard to any particular investment opportunity depends upon their recognizing how their particular expectations differ from the average. Different individuals might thus be said to position themselves in investment markets relative to average opinion in those markets, though, despite the importance of this distribution for the daily play of trade between different investors, in the final analysis it is average expectation – the end-of-the-day mean result of any given distribution of individual investors acting upon their different, particular expectations – that is always visible to investors *en masse* in the form of the final price that clears the market.[6]

The historical background to Keynes's treatment of the convention operating around investment, then, emphasizes the role of average expectation as a force in determining long-term expectations. How are the "daily, even hourly, revaluations of existing investments carried out in practice? In practice, we have tacitly agreed, as a rule, to fall back on what is, in truth, a *convention*. The essence of this convention . . . lies in assuming that the existing state of affairs will continue indefinitely, except in so far as we have specific reasons to expect a change" (pp. 151–2). More accurately, the convention in place regarding investment behavior is that average expectation is fairly taken to be correct, except insofar as particular individuals find that their own special circumstances give them reason to think otherwise. Alternatively, any standing or broadly accepted interpretation of the existing state of affairs is correct as representing the best, general knowledge or understanding available, and incorrect to the extent that particular individuals have special knowledge associated with their own individual circumstances which justifies their thinking otherwise. Put in these terms, a convention might be said to combine two different sorts of knowledge – a general form and an individual form – both of which individuals utilize to plan their different courses of action.

These two sorts of knowledge which conventions involve, it is fair to say, each have their respective advantages and disadvantages. The general knowledge that average expectation provides has the advantage that, because investors are less able to interpret the fundamentals of firms' operations than formerly, a knowledge of these firms' average performance gains in relative importance. The disadvantage of this form of knowledge is that, as but a summary form of thinking, average expectation naturally subsumes a variety of individual views, some of which, no doubt, represent a more accurate estimation of the value of various investments. In contrast, the special knowledge particular individuals possess has as its advantage the greater possibility of being better founded on the true determinants of an investment's value. The disadvantage of this sort of knowledge derives from the fact that, with the separation of ownership and management, this individual knowledge is still deficient by comparison with the standard of close, in-house acquaintance with firm operations that explained individual knowledge before the modern separation of ownership and management.

In light of these comparative advantages and disadvantages, two sets of counterbalancing considerations dictate the way in which the conventional valuation of investments is established. Thus, on the one hand, we recognize that average expectation is ever-changing, and accordingly do not "really believe that the existing state of affairs will continue indefinitely. We know from extensive experience that this is most unlikely" (p. 152), and this reminds us that average expectation at best approximates a good knowledge of an investment's worth. Nonetheless, at the same time, "we are assuming, in effect, that the existing market valuation, however arrived at, is uniquely *correct* in relation to our existing knowledge of the facts which will influence the yield of investment, and that it will only change in proportion to changes in this knowledge; though, philosophically speaking, it cannot be uniquely correct, since our existing knowledge does not provide a sufficient basis for a calculated mathematical expectation" (*Ibid.*). That is, average expectation is still fairly taken to be "correct," despite its evident deficiency, on account of the fact that that standard by which it might be discounted, namely, "calculated mathematical expectation," is not typically available to us on "our existing knowledge."

Indeed, a "calculated mathematical expectation," were it to be possible or appropriate, would at the very least reflect an individual knowledge of the specific facts surrounding a particular investment. Yet since the separation of ownership and management, the in-house acquaintance with firm operations necessary for this knowledge and such a calculation rarely exists for most investors. Ironically, with this separation, the method of mathematical expectation gains in reputation with investors who, now distant from particular facts in their firm-specific contexts, seek a technique of judging the significance of collections of the various facts available to them that will improve on average expectation. As a result of this overall state of affairs, investment valuation becomes the product of an unstable balance between an average expectation that is invariably wrong yet accepted and each individual's specific judgments which lack firm foundation yet offer at least the promise of doing better than average thinking. It is this combination that makes it necessary to regard a convention as a structure of expectations – a structure, it should still be emphasized, that is always rooted in a specific historical setting.

A conventional valuation of investments – indeed convention generally in *The General Theory*, it can be argued – thus emerges from a structure of diverse opinion that bears a complex relationship to average opinion as its central reference. In this structure, it is the significance of average expectation as a central reference that explains why conventions favor the status quo. More will be said below about the relative autonomy of individual expectation and opinion in such a structure of expectations. Here it is necessary to emphasize only that a convention is a form of practical interaction between individuals, where average opinion exercises regulative effects on individual opinion while still accommodating judgment and action that departs from this central reference. It can be seen that such a structure is normative in the most general sense in that it imposes an orientation upon individual behavior without at the same time making that orientation binding. This is also reflected in the fact that the content of ruling conventions typically changes over time. What a particular investment is worth may generally be agreed upon to be one thing on one occasion, and yet generally agreed upon on another occasion to be something quite different. Convention seen from this perspective is a dynamical structure. In essence, the competing rationales which average and individual expectation offer guarantee regular change in the content of any convention, and this places a considerable premium upon "vigilant observation" as central to the economist's craft.

Keynes addressed the important topic of the dynamics which conventions exhibit in connection with the issue of their stability and precariousness. Fundamental in this is his emphasis on the role played by the state of confidence, which, with the decline in "the element of real knowledge in the valuation of investments" attendant upon the separation of ownership and management (p. 153), emerges as a factor "to which practical men always pay the closest and most anxious attention" (p. 148). In these circumstances, ephemeral and insignificant matters often disturb an investment community's attachment to the notion that average opinion genuinely represents a reasonable valuation of a particular investment. Confidence thus emerges as significant with the very emergence of average expectation as a central reference in investment valuation. Accordingly, as it is increasingly average opinion seeking average opinion that characterizes such markets, a "conventional valuation . . . established as the outcome of the mass psychology of a large number of ignorant individuals is liable to change violently as the result of a sudden fluctuation of opinion due to factors which do not really make much difference to the prospective yield" (p. 154). In this ever more insubstantial world, even the more skilled individual, "who, unperturbed by the prevailing pastime, continues to purchase investments on the best genuine long-term expectations he can frame" (p. 156), is likely to be a casualty of the general change in character of the modern investment process, which more and more makes for the outsider "Investment based on genuine long-term expectation . . . so difficult to-day as to be scarcely practicable" (p. 157).

The state of confidence regarding any given investment option in an age of speculation, then, could not be said impressive by comparison with the full play and expression of animal spirits that Keynes believed characterized a former era of enterprise. Though entrepreneurs in the past undoubtedly also acted on the assumption that what obtained in the past was an important guide for their decisions about the future, this was "business as a way of life" (p. 150), where life in business was embedded in lifelong commitments to particular firms. Average expectation lacked meaning in this historical context, so that the state of confidence also lacked significance. In short, investment markets assume a different complexion as speculation and the pursuit of short-term gain come to dominate enterprise and the long-term project of forecasting the prospective yields of assets. Perhaps this is nowhere more sharply expressed by Keynes than in his comparison of the investment process and a newspaper beauty contest.

Professional investment may be likened to those newspaper competitions in which the competitors have to pick out the six prettiest faces from a hundred photographs, the prize being awarded to the competitor whose choice most nearly corresponds to the average preferences of the competitors as a whole; so that each competitor has to pick, not those faces which he himself finds prettiest, but those which he himself thinks likeliest to catch the fancy of the other competitors, all of whom are looking at the problem from the same point of view. It is not a case of choosing those which, to the best of one's judgment, are really the prettiest, nor even those which average opinion genuinely thinks the prettiest. We have reached the third degree where we devote our intelligences to anticipating what average opinion expects average opinion to be. And there are some, I believe, who practise the fourth, fifth and higher degrees. (p. 156)

The professional investor neither asks what might be intrinsically the "prettiest" or best investment, nor even what average opinion will take to be the "prettiest" or best investment, but rather what other investors believe other investors believe to be the "prettiest" or best investment. In these circumstances, investors' expectations display a flimsy attachment to their central reference in average expectation – the necessary, though hardly all-dominating moment in a structure of interdependent beliefs regarding good investments. In such circumstances, the state of confidence is inevitably a shifting phenomenon, and long-term investment commitments are often and easily abandoned. The result is that the level of investment is generally lower than would likely be the case were the spirit of enterprise more dominant.

Given, then, that "[t]hese tendencies are a scarcely avoidable outcome of our having successfully organised 'liquid' investment markets" (p. 159), Keynes concludes that the modern world faces a dilemma. While

The spectacle of modern investment markets has sometimes moved me towards the conclusion that to make the purchase of an investment permanent and indissoluble, like marriage, except by reason of death or other grave cause, might be a useful remedy for our contemporary evils . . . But a little consideration of this expedient brings us up against a dilemma, and shows us how the liquidity of investment markets often facilitates, though it sometimes impedes, the course of new investment. For the fact that each individual investor flatters himself that his commitment is 'liquid' . . . calms his nerves and makes him much more willing to run a risk. If individual purchases of investments were rendered illiquid, this might seriously impede new investment, so long as *alternative ways* in which to hold his savings are available. This is the dilemma. So long as it is open to the individual to employ his wealth in hoarding or lending *money*, the alternative of purchasing actual capital assets cannot be rendered sufficiently attractive . . . (p. 160)

The liquid character of investment markets enhances investment activity, while the availability of money investments that are comparatively attractive hampers it. It is true, as Richard Kahn has noted (1984), that Keynes's account here does not distinguish clearly between decisions regarding real capital formation and decisions taken on stock exchanges, so that there is some ambiguity in his thinking concerning just how decisions made in the latter case come to affect decisions made in the former. Keynes's general view, nonetheless, is clear. The increasing importance of speculative activity pursuant upon the historic separation of ownership and management had, and was likely to continue to have, decidedly negative effects on the level of investment expenditure.

Historically speaking, this could all well be seen to flow from the diminished role remaining in economic life for the full play and exercise of animal spirits, that "spontaneous urge to action rather than inaction" (p. 161) that was more fully in evidence in that earlier period when business enterprise was more dominant.[7] Speculation, in contrast, with its greater emphasis upon the immediate, foreseeable return, places heavy weight upon the estimation of probable gain. Yet because the consequences of so many of the long-term projects business contemplates are fundamentally uncertain – as Keynes puts it, really no clearer at the outset in their ultimate upshot than "an expedition to the South Pole" (p. 162)[8] – the occasions available for "calculated mathematical expectation" are rare, so that the increasing role for speculation changes the character of the investment process for the worse. Long-term investment, where uncertainty about the future is inescapable, makes it clear that "individual initiative will only be adequate when reasonable calculation is supplemented and supported by animal spirits" (*Ibid.*) and the "spontaneous optimism" (p. 161) they manifest.

From this perspective, then, chronic unemployment results from the interest rate being too high, because the short-term gains available to those whose wealth is ready and liquid sustain a demand for money that keeps interest rates high relative to the marginal efficiency of capital and investor animal spirits. Two sets of interdependent expectations operate here, one around long-term investment and one around the long rate of interest. Investors' attitudes toward prospective yields are structured around average expectation so as to tend to sustain the past valuation of investments, albeit given the forces for change embodied in individual expectations. The level and volume of this investment, however, is influenced by the level of the rate of interest, which is also conventionally determined for Keynes. Attitudes toward liquidity are also structured around an average expectation of the interest rate, much as attitudes toward prospective yields on investments are structured around their average expectation. In the case of the interest rate, "its actual value is largely governed by the prevailing view as to what its value is expected to be. *Any* level of interest which is accepted with sufficient conviction as *likely* to be durable *will* be durable; subject, of course, in a changing society to fluctuations for all kinds of reasons round the expected normal" (p. 203). Any particular interest rate, that is, reveals a balance of expectations across individuals with different views of the value of money, a balance which manifests itself in an average, central reference value in terms of which individuals form their respective expectations regarding the value of money. The reigning interest rate, accordingly, is conventional in that it is expected to obtain unless there are reasons to expect otherwise. And like investment expectations, the average expectation of the interest rate "is not rooted in secure knowledge," is not rooted in any objective understanding of the true value of money, and thus "may fluctuate for decades about a level which is chronically too high for full employment" (p. 204).

Keynes's general conception of the economy, thus, is one in which these two fundamental sets of psychological attitudes, the attitude toward prospective yields and the attitude toward liquidity, are structured as dynamic, interactive systems of interdependent belief. In each case, an average expectation, though changeable in content, reigns as a conventional, central reference for the range of particular expectations different individuals form regarding prospective yields or future interest rates. The state of average expectation in the money market relative to the state of average expectation regarding future yields determines the interest rate relative to the determination of firms' investment demand schedules, and jointly they determine the level of effective demand, income, and employment. Should the actual contents of these two conventions change relative to one another, then demand, income, and employment will change. A condition of chronic unemployment is thus the result of a particular balance between these two, key sets of psychological attitudes in particular circumstances at a particular point in history, where the desire for liquidity is strong relative to the confidence in prospective yields. A full explanation of the existence of chronic unemployment, consequently, incorporates an historical–institutional analysis of the structuring of these two, key sets of psychological attitudes to account for the particular balance these conventional systems of interdependent beliefs have attained at any given time.

Confidence and individual expectation

To link these conclusions to Keynes's later philosophical thinking regarding intuition and judgment, more now needs to be said about how different individuals come to form their respective expectations in a system of interdependent expectations taking average expectation as a central reference. We saw that when writing to Harrod about the nature of economics as a moral science, Keynes had emphasized that the subject matter of economics is neither "constant" nor "homogeneous," because it deals with individuals' "motives, expectations, [and] psychological uncertainties" (XIV, p. 300). He might well have added that individuals' "motives, expectations, [and] psychological uncertainties" are variegated and diverse, because individuals find themselves in different circumstances when it comes to such things as their respective views regarding the prospective yields on various investments and perceptions of the relative desirability of holding money. This point in fact received special attention in *The General Theory* discussion of "bulls" and "bears" in the money market.

> Just as we found that the marginal efficiency of capital is fixed, not by the 'best' opinion, but by the market valuation as determined by mass psychology, so also expectations as to the future of the rate of interest as fixed by mass psychology have their reactions on liquidity-preference; – but with this addition that the individual, who believes that future rates of interest will be above the rates assumed by the market, has a reason for keeping actual liquid cash . . . whilst the individual who differs from the market in the other direction will have a motive for borrowing money for short periods in order to purchase debts of longer term. The market price will be fixed at the point at which the sales of the 'bears' and the purchases of the 'bulls' are balanced. (p. 170)

A structure of individual expectations, then, not only has average expectation as its central reference, but also, as this passage emphasizes, somehow emerges from and is dependent upon a pattern of divergent individual expectations. Such an emphasis clearly places less weight on the gravitational aspects of average expectation as a central reference. Indeed it invites us to investigate those principles that produce various distributions of individual expectations about a mean. Given the greater attention Keynes devotes to investment, it will be easiest to do this in regard to investors' different attitudes toward prospective yields.

   In equity markets, the average expectation of a particular stock's value emerges through a brokered trading process between buyers and sellers of that stock, whereby offers to buy and sell a stock reflect individual expectations regarding the direction of movement of a stock's value, or expectations regarding the direction of movement of the average expectation of its value. The quoted price or reigning value of a stock, from this perspective, is less a central reference and more a point of departure for subsequent offers to buy and sell the stock. The convention that "the existing state of affairs will continue indefinitely, except in so far as we have specific reasons to expect a change" thus means different things to different individuals according to their different perspectives on how they believe average expectation is likely to change. When individuals have "specific reasons to expect a change" in average expectation based on their own particular circumstances, views, and information, they act upon those "reasons" making offers to buy and sell stocks, in the process helping to determine a new average expectation of these stocks' values.

Indeed, individuals hope that it will not be the case that "the existing state of affairs will continue indefinitely," since they optimistically believe that their particular, special perspective on the market will put them in a position "to outwit the crowd, and to pass the bad, or depreciating, half-crown to the other fellow" (p. 155).

Yet how is it that individual traders feel justified in expecting some particular direction of change in average expection? They cannot rely on the collective wisdom that average expectation embodies, since average expectation continually changes. And, that an individual hopes "to outwit the crowd" hardly implies he or she can do so. Of course entertaining the expectation of a certain direction of movement in a stock's value generally depends upon being in the possession of some special information or view not widely distributed among those participating in the market. The distribution of individual expectations about an average is thus in the first instance a function of a differential possession of information or knowledge about the market on the part of different individuals. But being in such possession, while important, cannot by itself explain how individuals are able to judge a market likely to move in one direction or another, since, in a world where ownership and management are separated, individual knowledge possesses limitations associated with the individual investor's detachment from firm operations.

Keynes, however, provides an additional explanation for the distribution of individual expectations around average expectation. In his account of the development of speculation and the decline of enterprise, he argues that the professional investor comes to be less and less concerned with the underlying fundamentals of an investment, and more and more with anticipating the mood or psychology of the market surrounding that investment. Indeed in his metaphor of the newspaper beauty contest, the goal of the professional investor is not merely to estimate average opinion, but rather to estimate "what average opinion expects the average opinion to be" (p. 156). Investors, then, judge the desirability of offers to buy and sell according to their views of the psychology of the market in regard to average opinion. In the context of the discussion here, transactions between particular traders turn upon these individuals' mutual opinions of each other's individual expectations (in effect, their opinions of each other's psychology), since it is these individual expectations that embody views of what average opinion is likely to be. This implies that when individual traders actually enter the market in anticipation of a certain change in price, they have come to share – as Keynes also puts it – a confidence of sorts with other traders regarding the desirability of entering the market. Their individual reasons for entering the market, accordingly, are supplemented by this shared confidence, and it is thus confidence – specifically a confidence distributed and shared differentially according to the different intentions of different groups of traders – that constitutes the sufficient condition for there being a distribution of expectations among traders in a market.[9]

The notion of a shared confidence, clearly, has affinities to Keynes's thinking about introspection and value judgments as methods employed in economics understood as a moral science. In the previous chapter, it was argued that these methods of investigation important for economic science are equally at the disposal of individuals in the economy, and that Keynes's moral science thinking involves the idea that individuals form interdependent belief expectations when consulting their own cases to judge the likely motives of others. In *The General Theory*, Keynes's reference to "what average opinion expects the average opinion to be" displays a preoccupation with essentially just this same sort of interdependence. Professional investors consider offers to buy and sell stocks, and in important degree determine the desirability of acting upon certain courses of action according to the perceived interest and willingness of those with like goals to do so as well. Indeed, on account of the decline in "the element of real knowledge in the valuation of investments" resulting from the separation of ownership and management (p. 153), for Keynes the state of confidence was central to any explanation of the movement in the market, since that movement depended upon (dominant) groups of individuals sharing a confidence regarding the hoped-for direction of the market. More generally, the movement and direction of the market resulted from a distribution of confidence across different individuals, and this determined how "the sales of the 'bears' and the purchases of the 'bulls' are balanced" (p. 170).

To better understand how this reciprocal interaction of judgments actually occurs, it might be helpful to expand briefly on Keynes's account from the perspective of a more recent literature. We have seen that in an analogical reasoning process governing potential traders, each individual attempts to understand the thinking of other traders by reference to what he or she imagines would be his or her own thinking put in their places. Yet each trader is also aware that just as he or she is attempting to replicate the reasoning of others, so other traders are simultaneously attempting to do the same. This means that to properly understand other traders' thinking each trader must also attempt to replicate other traders' attempts at replication, so that, in addition to estimating their reasoning, each must also estimate how his or her own reasoning appears to others. Higher-order replications may be imagined, but they do not add materially to the basic conception of interdependence at hand. On this conception, interdependent decision-making contexts might be likened to what recent game-theoretic literature treats as coordination problems (e.g., Lewis, 1969).[10] Individuals making independent yet interdependent decisions are said to be capable of coordinating their separate and sometimes conflicting objectives (here, for example, bulls' different goals in buying a given stock) by arriving at a system of concordant mutual expectations of first and higher orders regarding each other's aims and thinking. However, that individual circumstances and strategies continue to differentiate different traders (as they differentiate a market's bulls) means that coordination failures are a still regular occurrence. In Keynes's terms, a state of shared confidence among a set of traders is as often disrupted as it is established. For both Keynes and this more modern literature, then, a principal issue concerns specification of those conditions that make such coordination possible.

In the game-theoretic literature, this has sometimes been characterized in terms of the idea of salient solutions (Schelling, 1960). If, say, difficulties in communication constitute an obstacle forestalling coordination of independent plans, individuals may reach coordination equilibria that stand out from other courses of action in virtue of their conspicuousness. The salient or conspicuous solution need not be uniquely good or have any other particularly remarkable characteristics. It need only be something that permits interacting individuals to expect each other to expect each other to pursue some particular solution to their mutual coordination problem. Precedent, in particular, counts as an important source of salience and means of achieving coordination. Individuals sharing similar experiences tend to succeed more often in coordinating their respective plans than do individuals without shared experience. A precedent, from this perspective, is only some commonly recognized pattern that offers a guide to individual expectations.

In this light, one of Keynes's central concerns in the twelfth chapter of *The General Theory* was whether there were notable sources of salience for the coordination problems implicitly facing groups of investors in equity markets. Because interdependent belief expectations governing investment are sensitive to shared states of confidence, for Keynes it was well possible that investors in an age of speculation would often hesitate before committing themselves to long-term investments. Difficulties in establishing shared confidence, that is, tended to reduce levels of investment, and such difficulties were presumably not rare in times of change and turmoil with their disruptive effects on precedent and other commonly recognized sources of salience. Put in this light, the special attention Keynes devotes to conventions and the state of confidence in the twelfth chapter of *The General Theory* indicates less a concern that investors in an age of speculation no longer possessed the will or the needed quantity of animal spirits to commit themselves to long-term investments, and more a suspicion that the states of shared confidence associated with the convention determining investment tended not to support a high level of investor commitment to equity investment plans.[11] Generally speaking, then, investors in the age of speculation become more reluctant to gamble on possible movements in the equity market, and more inclined to maintain high levels of financial holdings in their wealth portfolios. Investment, on this view, is not high by the standards of the era of enterprise, and the associated level of income accordingly often insufficient for the full employment of labor, simply because, in the language of contemporary game theory, coordination equilibria are increasingly difficult to achieve.[12]

Keynes's later philosophy in the context of *The General Theory*

In the last chapter, the general path of Keynes's philosophical development was described. Now in the context of *The General Theory* it is possible to look again at Keynes's later philosophy as it emerged in Keynes's economics. Three themes are treated: Keynes's new view of judgment, the philosophical import of his characterization of economic behavior in terms of dispositions, tendencies, and propensities, and finally his view of induction.

Judgment

Individual expectation in *The General Theory* operates as a form of judgment exercised by individuals within systems of interdependent judgment. As such, it takes average expectation as a point of departure, and depends crucially on the state of confidence obtaining between individuals who face like decisions. When Keynes said of the convention appropriate to investment that "the existing state of affairs will continue indefinitely, except in so far as we have specific reasons to expect a change" (p. 152), he drew upon these different dimensions of this system of interdependent judgment to explain investor behavior. Similar accounts were appropriate to his treatment of the other independent variables of *The General Theory*, including the attitude toward liquidity, relative wages, and short-period producer expectations. Nowhere in this method of analysis, however, is there any reference to intuition as some form of pre-epistemic mental insight by which one might have "direct acquaintance" with one's "sensations, meanings, and perceptions" (VIII, p. 12). Indeed, the idea of intuition as a necessarily individual affair, direct, unmediated, and unconditioned in any sense by the ideas or thinking of others is far distant from Keynes's later thinking. Rather, in a system of interdependent individual expectations, each individual's judgment is influenced by the judgment of those individuals with whom he or she interacts since individuals evaluate their own thinking in the light of what others think, recognizing that others do the same.

Presumably Keynes's new understanding of intuition and judgment first began to develop as he acquired personal experience in financial markets where an interdependence of judgment between traders was readily apparent. Removed from the austere and artifical life of a Cambridge undergraduate, Moore's view of judgment (if not his values) would hardly have still seemed tenable. Keynes had nonetheless been aware in even his early Apostles papers that difficulties surrounded the concept of intuition, and he also could not have failed to be acquainted with the break-up in the twenties of the beginning-of-the-century consensus among Analytic Cambridge philosophers regarding the theory of judgment. When, then, did Keynes's thinking about interdependent judgment begin to mature? The idea that judgment was interdependent in important respects had been important to his treatment of relative wages in "The Economic Consequences of Mr. Churchill" which followed several years' argument about Britain's return to gold. And in the *Treatise on Money* Keynes advanced many of the propositions about bulls and bears that appear in *The General Theory*. Yet it is really only in the latter work that convention gains real prominence in Keynes's thinking. Thus, though undoubtedly his thinking about judgment underwent a fairly long evolution, its more systematic treatment within a system of interdependent judgment appears to have emerged only relatively late in Keynes's work.

In any event, the philosophy of *The General Theory* is hardly the theory of rational belief Keynes employed in the *Treatise on Probability*. Individuals may of course still seek a knowledge of probability relationships,[13] but this was no longer a matter of direct insight into an underlying structure of the world where objectively existing logical relations serve as the rational ground for our probability statements. Rather, since individual expectation takes average expectation as its ground and central reference, and then departs from this as individual knowledge and shared confidence permit, what is generally taken to be the case, as registered by average expectation, is in a continual state of change. Keynes gives no indication in his *General Theory* thinking that anything more substantial than average expectation grounds individual judgment. His discussion of convention in "My Early Beliefs" does suggest that social and cultural conventions possess a greater degree of solidity, but on his model of convention as a system of interdependent expectation in *The General Theory* even cultural traditions must constantly be changing (if more slowly than those surrounding investment valuation). Thus, though philosophers may think Keynes's view inadequate as an account of what grounds judgment, Keynes nonetheless clearly changed his model of the objective from the notion of an underlying external ground or anchor in a transcendent reality to the idea of an objectivity internal to a system of judgment. In this, his thinking was very much like Wittgenstein's later forms of life conception that tied "language game" meanings to the practices in which they functioned. Each, it might be said, came to doubt the meaningfulness of an external Platonic reality of timeless relations and qualities that earlier Cambridge philosophy had pursued, and accordingly each found it more worthwhile to turn their efforts to explaining individual judgment in terms of the systems of judgment in which it came to be embedded.[14]

Dispositions, tendencies, propensities

That judgment in *The General Theory* is no longer conceived on the model of rational intuition is perhaps most evident, however, in Keynes's characterization of behavior as dispositional or tendential. Indeed, his emphasis there is less on the episodic nature of successive, individual acts of judgment and more upon agents' decision-making as an on-going process reflected in terms of the states of activity achieved by *The General Theory*'s independent variables. That these independent variables are understood as having levels or states of activity implies that individual acts of judgment ultimately take on their meaning within patterns of judgment. This should be understood both in terms of single individuals continually revising their thinking and judgment, and in terms of collections of individuals revising their judgments upon coming into contact with one another. The notion of behavior as dispositional or tendential, it might thus be said, derives from the idea of there being an iterative process of individual belief adjustment when individuals' judgments mutually affect one another. Individuals continually approximate understanding of the subjects that concern them, and this means that their behavior is better characterized in terms of propensities, rather than in terms of rational belief.

That Keynes frames his treatment of his independent variables in terms of their characterization as dispositions and propensities has often been explained as an attempt to accommodate non-rational, animal spirits-type motives in his account of individual behavior (e.g., recently, Matthews, 1991). The argument here puts a different light on the idea of a disposition or propensity to behave in some particular way. On the view here, a disposition or tendency to act in some manner or another for Keynes reflects an element of flexibility in the process of individual belief formation captured by the idea that individuals in contact with one another continually revise their beliefs. If we emphasize this idea of individuals having a special capacity to do this, for Keynes an adequate treatment of behavior as tendential would need to reflect individuals' constant preparedness for multiple possible courses of action that they may reasonably expect to encounter. There are of course realms of behavior where our actions are relatively isolated and their effects are comparatively determinate and predictable. In such instances our actions might not need to be characterized in terms of tendencies. Yet after he came to invest greater significance in the fact of fundamental uncertainty, Keynes became particularly interested in those realms of behavior involving considerable agent interaction. In such circumstances, a behavior that was dispositional was a behavior that reflected a capacity for adapting to unforeseen eventualities.

In more modern terms, the decision logic of individuals whose behavior is to be explained in this manner is a counterfactual or other-possible-worlds logic. In traditional logic, conditional propositions are not contrary to fact. In many modern modal logics, however, conditional propositions are contrary to fact in that one considers what might be the case, were something true which is not the case (see, e.g., Stalnaker, 1968). Counterfactual reasoning, of course, is hardly a new form of human thought, but it has always been difficult to formalize, and has only recently gained the attention of philosophers and logicians attempting to give it systematic expression (cf. Passmore, 1985). Its chief value resides in the fact that human intention regularly comprehends counterfactual possibilities in a wide variety of contexts. Keynes's preoccupation with uncertainty indicates a concern with precisely this sort of reasoning, and thus it is fair to conclude that his emphasis upon behavior as dispositional or tendential reflects an effort to capture the important element of counterfactuality in individual decision-making. Individuals accordingly do not behave dispositionally so much because they are inconsistent or less than rational in their behavior (though Keynes also allows for such possibilities). They behave dispositionally because they always consider a variety of available alternative paths according to how events and their interactions with others may transpire.

A number of commentators on Keynes's economics have emphasized Keynes's awareness of an historical dimension to the economy. Asimakopulos, recently, has argued that Keynes blended equilibrium thinking and historical methodology in allowing for the possibility that changes in a system's independent variables might determine not only changes in its dependent variables but also changes in the system's parameter values as well (1991, pp. 122ff). Keynes reasoned in this way, Asimakopulos argues, so as to approximate the behavior of changing, real world economies with static equilibrium thinking. His occasion for his doing so, it is claimed here, was essentially to allow for the effects of interactions between individuals on the formation of individual plans, as in the important case of the formation of long-term expectations. From this perspective, Keynes's conception of equilibrium method required the notion of shifting equilibrium (Kregel, 1976; Amadeo, 1989), and his approach in *The General Theory* was thus, as he himself put it, a "study of the forces which determine changes in the scale of output and employment" rather than simply a study of the determination of their equilibrium values (VII, p. vii).

Induction

This naturally brings up a final issue appropriate to a consideration of Keynes's later philosophy. The existence of a fundamental uncertainty in the economy raises questions about the predictability of future events. Moreover, arguably the most important objective of the *Treatise on Probability* was to produce an account of the inductive practices of science that would both explain the nature of prediction, and "solve the induction problem which had been set by David Hume" (Klant, 1985, p. 83). Following a quotation from Hume's *Philosophical Essays Concerning Human Understanding*, Keynes had begun the third and perhaps most important part of the *Treatise* with the following statement:

I have described probability as comprising that part of logic which deals with arguments which are rational but not conclusive. By far the most important types of such arguments are those which are based on the methods of induction and analogy. Almost all empirical science rests on these. And the decisions dictated by experience in the ordinary conduct of life generally depend upon them. To the analysis and logical justification of these methods the following chapters are directed. (VIII, p. 241)

Keynes's analysis of induction, of course, depended upon his understanding of probability as the intuition of logical relations between propositions, a point he was at pains to emphasize.

The fundamental connection between inductive method and probability deserves all the emphasis that I can give it. Many writers, it is true, have recognised that the conclusions which we reach by inductive argument are probable and inconclusive . . . But it has been seldom apprehended clearly, either by these writers or by others, that the validity of every induction, strictly interpreted, depends, not on a matter of fact, but on the existence of a relation of probability. (VIII, p. 245)

Was it the case, then, that Keynes's abandonment of the early Cambridge view of intuition meant that he no longer adhered to his *Treatise* view of induction, or that perhaps he came to accept some alternative understanding of induction?

Here it seems necessary to give some attention to Keynes's remarks about statistical methods in his debate with Jan Tinbergen after the publication of *The General Theory*. Tinbergen had developed an early multivariate analysis of the trade cycle in his *A Method and its Application to Investment Activity* (1939), and Keynes had critically reviewed the book in the September 1939 *Economic Journal*. An exchange of comments later took place between the two, while at about the same time Keynes was advancing his views about the nature of economics as a moral science in an independent correspondence with Harrod. Keynes's concern with Tinbergen's work was chiefly focused upon the question of the scope for proper inductive methods: "There is first of all the central question of methodology, – the logic of applying the method of multiple correlation to unanalysed economic material, which we know to be nonhomogeneous through time" (XIV, pp. 285–6). And central to this was the issue of whether Tinbergen was really doing anything more than producing "a piece of historical curve-fitting and [statistical] description," and mistaking this for "inductive claims with reference to the future as well as the past" (p. 315). Keynes, it appears, did not fully dismiss inductive methods, despite his conviction that the "economic material" was "nonhomogeneous through time" (a claim that recurred in his remarks on economics as a moral science), since he still encouraged Tinbergen in his work (Bateman, 1990). But clearly he felt considerable skepticism about Tinbergen's efforts to explain the trade cycle in such a fashion as to account for future trends. Why he felt this way is perhaps clearest from his own discussion of the trade cycle in the twenty-second chapter of *The General Theory*.

Two questions Keynes raised in correspondence at this time regarding his review of Tinbergen signal the nature of his own view: "Is it assumed that the future is a determinate function of *past statistics*? What place is left for expectation and the state of confidence relating to the future?" (XIV, p. 287). Keynes, of course, did not follow Harrod in extending his short-period analysis to a long-period dynamic model of the economy, essentially because he did not believe that long-term expectations could be accurately modeled from past data. This emerged most explicitly in his 1937 correspondence with Hugh Townshend, when Keynes affirmed Townshend's assertion that for Keynes the "prospect of future returns . . . is not expressible as a *mathematical* expectation" (XXIX, pp. 257, 258). In *The General Theory* this was reflected in terms of the fundamental complexity of the trade cycle, especially as regarded fluctuations in the marginal efficiency of capital. Keynes was prepared to speculate about the nature of the trade cycle, but his own treatment made it clear that the role expectations played precluded an inductive analysis of the order sought by Tinbergen.

His account begins with the later stages of an expansion shortly before a downturn. Though productive capacity is increasing, the production costs for capital assets are rising, interest rates are higher, and optimistic long-term expectations, driven by speculation and the rising prices of equities, continue to feed the expansion for a time. Keynes comments:

It is of the nature of organised investment markets, under the influence of purchasers largely ignorant of what they are buying and of speculators who are more concerned with forecasting the next shift of market sentiment than with a reasonable estimate of the future yield of capital-assets, that, when disillusion falls upon an over-optimistic and over-bought market, it should fall with sudden and even catastrophic force. (VII, pp. 315–16)

The subsequent collapse of equity prices depresses the marginal efficiency of capital, and the downturn ensues. A turnaround occurs only when there is a recovery of the marginal efficiency of capital, and this, Keynes emphasizes, is typically brought about by the return of confidence and a restoration of optimistic long-term expectations. In short, the psychology of the market is crucial to the analysis of the trade cycle, but its essential unpredictability (or the inability to model long-term expectations) precludes anything more than the most general characterization of the economy's likely future.

That the future is not a function of "past statistics" and that one must always leave a place for "expectation and the state of confidence relating to the future" thus suggests that Keynes did not believe that there was much scope for inductive methods in economics. But the matter really goes much deeper than the question of the scope left for induction, since Keynes's complaint is not just that the trade cycle is highly complex, but rather that long-term expectations and the attendant state of confidence really defy any determinate analysis whatsoever. Essentially, individuals form their expectations in interaction with one another, and the resulting interdependence of expectations precludes any truly precise analysis of when (or even why) they will again become optimistic or regain confidence. This is because individual judgment, or more properly individual expectation, is an at best tendential affair in Keynes's later thinking, inasmuch as its objects are themselves ultimately contingent upon individuals' interaction with one another. In contrast, intuition in Keynes's earlier philosophy always possessed a determinate, indeed timeless object, namely, the underlying probability relation that justified rational belief in a given probability statement. After Ramsey's criticism Keynes gave up this conception. This naturally implied that his view of induction, or what was involved in saying how the future was based on the past, would change as well.

Interpreting the place of induction in Keynes's later thinking, then, turns ultimately upon recognizing the deep-seated implications of Keynes's abandonment of the ideal Platonic realm of timeless forms and relations. In effect, without an anchor in a transcendent objective reality, judgment or expectation must obtain what leverage it can in a changing world of individual interaction. Keynes had previously tried to explain induction on the assumption that his analysis of the meaning of probability, as a relation justifying rational belief in arguments that were non-demonstrative and inconclusive, was correct. But, without the intuition of probability relations, this understanding of probability meant to function as a foundation for inductive argument was no longer available. The leverage individual judgment or expectation did possess, Keynes came to see as he struggled with explaining finance and investment, rested in the logic of convention and average expectation in a changing historical world. Were one, thus, to say how the future depended upon the past in this historical world, one would need to explain how individual expectation operated upon this particular foundation, remembering at all times, of course, that individual expectations were generally structured in systems of interdependent expectations that took average expectation as a central reference.

This conception of convention and average expectation, it should now be emphasized, possesses an important attribute touched upon briefly in earlier chapters. A convention as a structure of expectations, it has been argued, exercises a regulatory or normative influence on individuals in their respective decisions and judgments in that it exhibits implicitly recommended courses of action, while yet clearly leaving space for individual discretion. This notion of a normative force possessed by conventions, we saw above, has also been argued to be central to Wittgenstein's characterization of language use (Kripke, 1982). The issue of language use itself arose above in connection with a discussion of emotivism and Robbins's implicit acceptance of the emotivist view of ethics in his famous critique of interpersonal utility comparisons. What is relevant here from that discussion is the idea that conventions play a role alternative to inductive methods in enabling us to account for how the future is based on the past.

The view of language that Wittgenstein himself criticized can be termed the induction model of language. On that view, an individual applies a given term or expression when the facts that obtain on that occasion are the same as existed when the term or expression was employed on a previous occasion. According to this interpretation, Wittgenstein believed that one can never find facts that will quite do this job. Accordingly, he reasoned, language use must possess an alternative non-descriptive, non-inductive basis in individuals' intentions to communicate with one another. More broadly, individuals communicate by adopting conventions concerning language use that signal widely held expectations concerning communication. By observing these conventions, they are able to make particular adjustments in meaning appropriate to the particular contexts in which they find themselves, because those with whom they communicate are able to understand and interpret departures from a generally expected meaning when those departures presuppose that general meaning. In this fashion, the future is linked to the past, but not in virtue of any statistical regularity that would be required on the traditional model of induction.

Keynes, in his emphasis upon convention in his later thinking, can be understood to be reasoning in similar terms when he spoke of inductive methods. That is, whether individuals feel able to make claims about the future based on the past depends crucially on conventional views of what is believed likely to transpire. This is not to say that individuals always agree in their inductive claims. Since individuals depart from average expectation when they feel individually justified in doing so, their predictions can vary considerably. Yet the idea of induction as a formal technique of prediction identically applied to any and all information contexts he essentially set aside. Induction, rather, had to be understood as being relative to the reasoning particular individuals exercised in particular historical contexts. In this respect, Keynes's strategy was closely connected to the strategy which he adopted regarding the concept of probability. Though he was aware that individuals spoke about what was probable, and though he himself continued to use such language from time to time, his thinking as it emerged in *The General Theory* required that what could be said more or less probable ultimately depended upon the way in which average expectation and individual expectation interacted in systems of interdependent judgment.

The change in Keynes's philosophy

In Keynes's later career, then, the effort to explain the operation of the economic world produced a change in philosophical thinking that forced abandonment, modification, and replacement of much that Keynes had previously believed. Intuition in the Moorean sense was replaced by individual expectation. The focus on probability became secondary to the focus on convention. Rational behavior as a principal concern in the analysis of individual judgment was supplanted by a preoccupation with the effects of interdependence and uncertainty. These paradigmatic changes and developments can be observed at work in *The General Theory*. Unfortunately, Keynes never clearly articulated his philosophical conversion, largely no doubt on account of the tremendous demands upon his time made by economics and policy. There simply was too much to do in the practical world, especially when attention to philosophical questions would inevitably require comment upon his past positions and subsequent developments in philosophy to which he had devoted little time.

None of this, however, should suggest that Keynes's later philosophical thinking was an incidental accompaniment to his economic thinking. Those economists Keynes termed Classical in their reasoning generally worked with the idea of a non-interdependent individual judgment, and so naturally adopted market-clearing concepts of equilibrium to argue that unemployment could not exist in the absence of wage and price rigidities. Keynes, in contrast, took individual judgment to be embedded in systems of interdependent judgment, and accordingly adopted a view of equilibrium as a relatively settled state of affairs in which unemployment might prevail. In effect, that actual markets did not adjust as Classical economists claimed was to be explained in terms of the way conventions locked individuals into states of activity where a trend in average expectation constrained individual judgment and behavior. This sort of thinking was not available to those whose implicit philosophical presuppositions made judgment a fully individual affair, and thus the fact that Keynes's philosophical presuppositions changed as he worked to explain the economy as a whole was central to the way in which he came to work out his argument in *The General Theory*.

Of course, in addition to being an economist Keynes was also engaged in the design and formulation of economic and social policy from the time of his involvement at the Versailles conference after the First World War. Thus it is appropriate to carry the discussion here of his later philosophical thinking one step further to treat its relation to his views on policy. The following chapter pursues this through an investigation of how Keynes's later philosophical thinking emerged in his later ethics and policy views.

6   Ethics and policy

The argument thus far has been principally about the development of Keynes's epistemological thinking and the implications of this for his later economics. However, Keynes's earliest philosophical thinking concerned the ethics of Moore's *Principia Ethica,* and his subsequent thinking about ethics clearly remained a fundamental dimension of his overall thought, as his recent biographers have shown (Skidelsky, 1983, 1992; Moggridge, 1992). An important matter that thus remains to be investigated in an examination of Keynes's philosophical development is how Keynes's ethics and policy thinking developed together with his changing epistemological commitments. Here it will be argued that just as the developments in Keynes's epistemological thinking had important implications for his later economics, so the developments in Keynes's ethical thinking had important implications for his later view of economic policy. More specifically, it will be argued that some of Keynes's most far-reaching long-term policy proposals, as they emerged at the end of *The General Theory* and in his later wartime statements, can be seen to have emerged only upon the resolution of a "favorite" dilemma Keynes early encountered in the view of ethics he advanced in critique of Moore, namely, the dilemma of how to reconcile being good and doing good.

In what follows, this early dilemma will first be briefly reviewed, setting it forth this time in relation to the critique of Moore's ethics advanced by the emotivist philosophers of the logical positivist movement in the 1930s. From this vantage point, Keynes's resolution of his "favorite" dilemma and reversal of his initial opinions about rules of conduct can then be understood in a manner that will allow us to go on to explain the philosophical thinking behind his long-term policy proposal for "a somewhat comprehensive socialisation of investment." The general development of Keynes's philosophical thinking, it will emerge, depended upon two reversals in his early thinking: the first, as already discussed at length, regarding the theory of judgment and intuition, and the second, a related yet independent change in thinking that concerned his understanding of conventions and the rules of conduct. It was this latter reversal that, predicated on a new understanding of being good and doing good, was the basis for Keynes's most far-reaching economic policy proposal and key to his later social philosophy of individuality and sociality.

The dilemma of being good and doing good

Recall that originally Keynes accepted Moore's argument regarding the indefinability of the good, and hence the need for its intuitive apprehension, but had rejected Moore's argument about duty and the nature of right conduct. Right conduct for Moore was not a simple quality, and could in fact be defined in terms of intrinsic good as that action producing the greatest possible balance of good over bad consequences. Unfortunately, Moore noted, it was practically impossible to account fully for all the future consequences of a given act, and thus one did best to follow general rules of conduct or rules of thumb people customarily adopted in determining what was right to do. Keynes, we have seen, rejected this argument on account of its foundation in the frequency theory of probability, claiming that one might intuit what was right to do though certainty regarding all the future effects of one's actions was unavailable. Moore, in Keynes's view, had been inconsistent when it came to the application of his understanding of intuition, since, in addition to an intuitive recognition of what was good in itself, individuals also had the capacity for intuitive recognition of right conduct.

The importance of this argument in the development of Keynes's early thought is now well appreciated, especially in light of its role, as Keynes himself was to note (X, p. 445), in stimulating his initial interest in the study of probability theory. Yet Keynes's early thinking about ethics departed from Moore's *Principia Ethica* in a further respect, one, however, which constituted more of an amplification and extension of Moore's views than a point of disagreement. In connection with the matter of being good, or the topic of what things individuals found good in themselves, Moore had written of aesthetic enjoyment and the pleasures of friendship as good states of affairs (1903a, pp. 183ff). Keynes put another interpretation upon these same goods, and treated them as valuable only in virtue of the states of mind to which they gave rise. As he argued in "Miscellanea Ethica," good could be properly spoken of only in terms of good states of mind, and those objects which gave rise to good states of mind were properly described as "fit." This modest change in Moore's view seemed only to add precision where Moore had been vague. As it turned out, however, Keynes's emendation inadvertently exposed a significant vulnerability in Moore's intuitionism that was later targeted in the emotivist critiques of Moore's ethics by Ayer and Stevenson. Keynes's own personal dilemma regarding being good and doing good needs to be understood in this larger context.[1]

The emotivists, as logical positivists, had been intent upon challenging what they saw as any attempt to ground ethics in metaphysics, and accordingly were quick to dispute Moore's view that a judgment concerning what was good picked out some transcendent, objective quality in the world whose existence justified that judgment. In their view, the Platonist metaphysics of transcendent qualities and relations that Moore thought intuition apprehended was specious and unscientific, and ethical statements rather amounted to no more than subjective expressions of feeling. Moore, we saw, was at a loss for an effective way to respond to these arguments, and allowed that he had not appreciated how his conception of intuitive judgment might be interpreted in such subjectivistic fashion. Keynes, moreover, had offered precisely the elucidation of Moore's ideals that verified the emotivists' worst suspicions of intuitionism. It thus seemed reasonable to conclude that if those ideals to which Moore referred were ultimately nothing but states of mind, then ethical statements regarding what was good or bad could only reflect individual states of mind. Ethical statements were nothing but expressions of feeling, expressions of approval or disapproval, and in this capacity they clearly lacked the sort of objective foundation that was attributable to empirical statements based in fact.

Keynes was evidently well aware of the general nature of the controversy over the *Principia* in which his former teacher had become embroiled. He later suggested that something very much like the emotivist view of ethical statements might sometimes well apply in his "My Early Beliefs" sarcastic reference to the airs and nuances he and his early friends employed when debating the nature of the good (X, p. 438), and was of course fully cognizant of the general attack on Platonism with its metaphysics of transcendent qualities and relations as a result of critiques like Ramsey's. Indeed, it would be remarkable to think Keynes was unaware of the decline in fortune Moore's ethics experienced in the twenties and thirties or of the general rise of subjectivism that accompanied the sudden enthusiasm for positivist thinking in the same period, especially when this general movement was influential from the outset at Cambridge through the instrumentality of such figures as Ayer and later Hutchison. An important issue in the development of Keynes's ethics, then, is how his reaction to the emotivist critiques of Moore affected his own concern over the seeming irreconcilability of being good and doing good.

We saw in Chapter 3 that the problem of reconciling being good and doing good arose for Keynes within the ambit of his own interpretation of

Moore's ethics. In "Miscellanea Ethica" he had differentiated between what an individual might actually think and feel and what an individual ought to think and feel without determining the relationship between these two conceptions. Being good, the intuition of what an individual actually apprehended as good in itself, seemed to require some relation to doing good, the intuition of what an individual ought to do and apprehend as right, but having abandoned Moore's linking of the two notions through the definition of right conduct in terms of (an indefinable) good, Keynes found himself with two separate, competing sources of intuitive insight, each by assumption necessarily irreducible to the other (or lacking any "intimate connection," as he later put it [X, p. 437]). Essentially, having permitted himself multiple, independent objects of intuition, Keynes had precluded any argument concerning their ultimate relation.[2] While initially this seemed a reasonable implication of his extension of intuition to right conduct, Keynes was soon to confess in his "Egoism" paper that this also led to seemingly intractable practical conflicts between being good and doing good. Keynes admitted he was unable to resolve these conflicts, and was for a time afterwards resigned to labeling conflicts of this sort his "favorite" dilemma. At best, he later related, he had had to believe in a general coincidence of being good and doing good in a society so happily constituted that "the egoistic and altruistic systems" worked out in practice to the same conclusions (X, p. 447).[3]

Keynes's early ethics, therefore, was beset by two important difficulties. Its two departures from Moore's *Principia* had made it arguably subjectivistic (in its emphasis upon intrinsic good as a state of mind) and seemingly arbitrary (in its inability to weigh and integrate his two fundamental ethical requirements of being good and doing good). Yet there is no evidence that Keynes thought that good was ultimately just a matter of taste or that ethics was as hopeless an affair as his favorite dilemma appeared to imply. How ultimately, then, did he address these twin difficulties? The answer to this question can best be approached through a consideration of how Keynes ultimately confronted his "favorite" dilemma, since it was to this matter that he explicitly returned in his "My Early Beliefs" review of his early ethical views when he commented upon where he thought he had been misguided in his early philosophy.

Social rules and conventions

As we have seen, Keynes's verdict in "My Early Beliefs" regarding his early views was that he had been overly optimistic about moral progress and human nature, and had as a result placed too little emphasis upon the restraining role played by society's rules and conventions. Thus Keynes thought that his critique of Moore on rules and right conduct had in important respects been mistaken, and believed that confronting his dilemma over being good and doing good depended upon re-evaluating the nature and significance of doing good and right conduct. Yet it would not be quite correct to say that Keynes simply abandoned his early critique of Moore to re-embrace the latter's *Principia* view that rules for right conduct were explainable as those means which promoted the greatest balance of good consequences over bad. Keynes never went on to assert, as Moore had, that general rules deserve our attention for the reason that they tend to promote the greatest good. He also never gave serious attention to the frequency view of probability upon which Moore had relied to elaborate his consequentialist defense of general rules, and which Keynes continued to believe reflected an unfortunate attachment to the "Benthamite calculus" (X, p. 436).

More importantly, the social rules and conventions Keynes recognized in "My Early Beliefs" possessed a status quite different from Moore's general rules or rules of thumb. On Moore's view, rules are empirical regularities, and as such possess the most limited authority over individuals, who may consult them should they find it pragmatic to do so, but who are under no obligation to pay them any heed. In contrast, for Keynes in "My Early Beliefs" a society's rules and conventions possess an authority over individuals in virtue of their standing as norms, standards, and moral principles. A society's rules and conventions, that is, are normative in and of themselves, and consequently possess a *prima facie* obligatoriness that contrasts sharply with Moore's view of rules as mere consultable means to a possible determination of the greatest good. In terms of Keynes's early language, a society's rules and conventions possess intrinsic value in the same respect that things truly good are said to possess intrinsic value. Thus, though right conduct often did require that one try to produce the maximum balance of good over bad consequences by one's actions, this was neither a necessary feature of a society's rules and conventions nor the source of their status as intrinsically valuable.

That a society's rules and conventions came to be intrinsically valuable for Keynes was closely linked to how Keynes's later understanding of intuition and judgment made rules and conventions a point of departure for individual judgment. We have seen that Keynes gave up his early view of intuition as pure, unmediated insight, and adopted an understanding of intuition as judgment functioning within a system of interdependent beliefs. That judgment and intuition function within a system of interdependent beliefs, however, lends an open-endedness to each individual's judgments that contrasts with their purported definiteness or determinacy under their Moorean characterization as pure, unmediated insight. Because an individual forms his or her judgment on a given subject with an eye to like thinking on the part of others, and because other individuals are also engaged in doing the same thing, judgment and intuition always possess a conjectural or expectational nature. In this framework, conventions and social rules function normatively in that, like average expectation in the equity market, they constitute broadly accepted points of reference that ground the system of interdependent judgment. Put differently, the command and authority that social rules and conventions possess derives from fact that they constitute the respected results of a multitude of past individual judgments. On Moore's view, in contrast, general rules and individual judgment lack any close relation to one another. General rules appear to reflect past judgments, but as mere empirical regularities or rules of thumb they are really only poor substitutes for a desired yet unachievable certain insight into the precise balance of good over bad consequences. As such they lack, as Keynes had grasped at the outset, any real normative command over individuals.

Given this, it is now possible to see both how the relationship between being good and doing good changed in Keynes's later ethical thinking, and how Keynes escaped his "favorite" dilemma. Whereas in his early view judgments of being good and doing good bore no real relation to one another and might well often contradict one another, in his later thinking being good and doing good are bound together within a single system of interdependent individual judgment in which individuals formulated their respective conceptions of being good with an eye to society's rules and conventions concerning doing good. Keynes speaks in "My Early Beliefs" of "the restraints of convention and traditional standards and inflexible rules of conduct" for individuals' "intuitions of the good" (X, p. 447). Right conduct, then, as society itself came to understand the requirements for doing good in its myriad social rules and conventions, counted for Keynes as that framework which created and defined the allowable domain of judgment regarding being good. While being good and doing good remained fundamentally distinct and irreducible normative concerns – since it was left to individuals to pursue the good, while society in the form of inherited rules and conventions provided the terms of right conduct for doing good – these two notions nonetheless acquired a clear relation to one another in Keynes's later thinking as coordinate elements in the system of interdependent individual judgment.

It should be emphasized, however, that Keynes's philosophical reconciliation of being good and doing good hardly implied that individual judgments of the good and society's standards for right conduct were never in conflict. On the contrary, since society's rules and conventions were but points of departure and a framework that individuals were obliged to consider, their judgments regarding right conduct, as derived from their respective judgments of what was good, were as likely as not to differ from what society appeared to prescribe. How much so, and in what respects this might be the case constituted the sorts of questions one would investigate in an ethics that took as its subject matter contemporary moral dilemmas. Keynes's reconciliation of being good and doing good, it might thus be said, had as an implicit agenda the investigation of how our fundamental normative concerns interacted in a system of interdependent judgment that continually settled, unsettled, and re-settled itself in its rules and conventions. He thus escaped his former "favorite" dilemma in the specific sense that what had previously appeared an intractable, metaphysical dilemma was now a matter of understanding the continually changing balance between a society's constraints on right conduct and individuals' judgments of good. This, importantly, created space for a politics of reform, where before there had only been an ethics of eternal paradoxes.

For Keynes, then, it is central that social rules and conventions were intrinsically valuable. From this it follows that Keynes's ethical view is not correctly characterized as a form of act-consequentialism (O'Donnell, 1989, p. 107), since such a characterization overlooks the intrinsic normative significance Keynes invested in social rules and conventions in his later thinking. It is true that Keynes originally thought right conduct a matter of good consequences (intuitively apprehended), and he was certainly concerned with the potential consequences of action throughout his life. But to say he was therefore an act-consequentialist is to suppose he remained wedded to his early rejection of general rules, did not re-embrace rules as intrinsically valuable, and never wrote "My Early Beliefs." At the same time, it would also be a mistake to assert that Keynes's ethical view was a form of rule-consequentialism (Braithwaite, 1975, pp. 242-5), or that he thought the normative significance of social rules and conventions was an instrumental means to good consequences. Rather, social rules and conventions deserve our attention, because they are intrinsically valuable in and of themselves. Again, they may well often produce good consequences, and are often thought by many to deserve credit and attention accordingly. But for Keynes their moral significance in the first instance rested on the fact that they represent principles and norms "skilfully put across and guilefully preserved" that were "the extraordinary accomplishment of our predecessors in the ordering of life" (X, pp. 447, 448).

To be sure, Keynes's view is not easily understood today in light of the assumption on the part of many that ethics must ultimately be understood in consequentialist terms, and that a society's rules are only instrumentally valuable in enabling us to obtain some presupposed good. Indeed, Keynes himself reasoned consequentially in his early years, and only later, after considerable thinking, came to regard social rules and conventions as intrinsically valuable in themselves. To understand better how he came to this conclusion, his process of reasoning can be reconstructed as follows. Being good and doing good are each normative concerns of the most fundamental moral importance. It is unacceptable, therefore, to suppose that their claims upon us are irreconcilable in principle. One strategy for addressing this problem would be to reduce what it meant to do good to intuitions about what was involved in being good. Keynes adopted this strategy in his initial critique of Moore, but was forced to conclude by the time of his early "Egoism" paper that this strategy really did not account for what doing good required. Barring this reduction, then, one could only hope to show that somehow being good and doing good were in principle compatible with one another. Moreover, it should be added, barring such a reduction, each notion also had to possess intrinsic moral significance in and of itself. Thus, upon conceiving being good and doing good to function in coordination in a system of interdependent judgment dominated by conventions, Keynes became committed to both the idea that being good and doing good were in principle compatible, and to the view that the social rules and conventions that this system produced were intrinsically valuable. Put differently, a society's rules and conventions were intrinsically valuable, because they were the vehicle by which being good and doing good were reconciled. Keynes commented, one must thus owe "reverence" to those who had "skilfully put across" society's rules and conventions which were responsible for this fundamental "ordering of life" (X, pp. 447, 448).

Keynes's later ethical view, then, was essentially a rule-intuitionist ethical philosophy. We will see below that this intuitionism extended beyond a society's rules and conventions in one significant respect. Here first it is worth noting as a comment on the history of ethics that the development of Keynes's ethical philosophy in some ways resembled another, better known intuitionist development of Moore's ethics, namely, that which occurred at Oxford in the 1930s. The philosophers H.A. Prichard (1929) and W.D. Ross (1930) argued, as had the early Keynes, that Moore had been wrong not to treat right conduct as the subject of intuition. Moreover, Prichard and Ross went on to explain duty and right conduct in terms of conformity to the conventional rules of ordinary morality, irrespective of whether such rules tended to produce a maximum balance of good over bad consequences. There is no evidence, however, that Keynes was aware of this parallel development and effort to revise Moore's intuitionism, and indeed Keynes's own view of social rules and conventions was arguably richer than that of his Oxford counterparts in being rooted in Keynes's special understanding of judgment as expectational. Moreover, Keynes's view, as we have just seen, was also tied to his conviction that we possessed two distinct, fundamental normative concerns in need of reconciliation, and that a society's rules and conventions were intrinsically valuable because they expressed this reconciliation.

The important and obvious change in Keynes's ethics, then, concerned the new significance attributed to rules and conventions. A less obvious, though not less important change in Keynes's later ethics concerned his conception of the very objects of intuition, the business of being good (cf. Lawson, 1993). Whereas in his early thinking the object of intuition had been a single metaphysical quality, namely, simple intrinsic goodness, which one might locate in such things as aesthetic enjoyment and the pleasures of friendship, in his later thinking Keynes abandoned the notion of a transcendent goodness, and expanded his conception of the good to include a variety of different sorts of good objects, whose intrinsic value was in each case to be explained more by "the qualities of the life of action and of the pattern of life as a whole" than by the "timeless ecstasy" and "emotions of the moment" of the philosopher in his study (X, p. 443). As Keynes commented, "I see no reason to shift from the fundamental intuitions of *Principia Ethica*; though they are much too few and too narrow to fit actual experience which provides a richer and more various content" (X, p. 444). The "fundamental intuitions of *Principia Ethica*" concerned the centrality of intrinsic value in ethics. On the other hand, the "richer and more various content" of "actual experience" is given to us by "the qualities of the life of action and the pattern of life as a whole," or, that heterogeneous set of values regarding things good in themselves that are thrown up by the play of interdependent judgment of individuals active in daily, worldly concerns. From this perspective, Moore's shortsightedness about intrinsic value came down to the simple fact that he reasoned as if isolated individuals could fully grasp the full complexity of goodness through the use of some special analytic method (as we saw in Chapter 1, his analytical method of definition). Keynes's public experience beyond Cambridge taught him that there were more good things under the sun (and bad things) than a single, isolated individual might theorize in his study, so that in the judgment of things of intrinsic value, individuals were necessarily dependent upon one another to extend and develop their intellectual horizons in ways that did not occur to them separately.

That for the later Keynes a single individual's judgment tended to be incomplete by itself thus had an important bearing upon the second of Keynes's two departures from Moore's *Principia*. Keynes had understood Moore's ideals as states of mind, thereby inadvertently giving Moore's theory of the good a highly subjectivistic interpretation. However, Keynes's later theory of intuition and judgment as interdependent undermined this early conception, and had the effect of opening up his list of intrinsic goods to that collection of heterogeneous intrinsic goods different individuals in society were willing to contemplate. Many of these, quite obviously, did not amount to states of mind, but were rather better described as states of affairs operating across social relationships. For example, in 1936 Keynes lauded "shows and entertainments in which the common man can take his delight and recreation after work is done, and which can make him feel, as nothing else can, that he is one with, and part of, a community, finer, more gifted, more splendid, more care-free than he can be by himself" (XXVIII, p. 344). This, certainly, was something good in itself as a general state of affairs. But more importantly, were one still inclined to characterize things of intrinsic value as good states of mind which were thought to "fit" the things that produced them – because that judgment of intrinsic value was now a characteristically intersubjective one – Keynes's new thinking was accordingly freed of that subjectivistic cast his early view of intuition had implied.

Parallel, perhaps not surprisingly then, to Keynes's expansion of the list of intrinsic goods was a comparable expansion of the list of social rules and conventions. Whereas the items that had been candidates for general rules in Moore's system included rules that might be thought appropriate to personal codes of conduct, such as that one told the truth, did not steal, and so forth, Keynes reconceptualized these rules as social rules and conventions to include all those maxims, norms, standards, and principles that might conceivably sustain society as a dynamic system of interdependent individual judgment. Some of these principles, admittedly, might well be quite nebulous, and it is also not difficult to fault Keynes at times for his defense of conservative traditions. What is especially valuable in this later emphasis, however, is Keynes's recognition of the pervasiveness of social rules and conventions throughout the fabric of society and economy. Keynes gives expression to this in his references to the "pattern of life" in "My Early Beliefs" and "business as a way of life" in *The General Theory*. He also, it should be emphasized, suggests that society's rules and conventions solidify in institutions that themselves merit our special attention. Below, we will focus on one such set of institutions that Keynes made the subject of his most important long-term policy proposals. Before doing so, the connection between Keynes's ethics and economic policy orientation needs brief examination.

Keynes's ethical thinking and his economic policy orientation

The philosophical thinking behind Keynes's orientation on policy recommendation has been the subject of much recent scholarly investigation (e.g., Hamouda and Smithin, 1988). One thing that can be inferred from much of this work is that, contrary to what many have believed, Keynes was not so much interested in expanding the role of the State as traditionally conceived, and was perhaps more interested in fostering the development of a pervasive public-spiritedness in economic life (Skidelsky, 1989). Put differently, Keynes replaced the traditional view of the State with one distinguishing its nuclear and extended spheres, where the latter included public-spirited activities beyond the domain of the State proper (Jensen, 1991, 1994). Here, this theme will be supported and developed in an argument that relates Keynes's interest in long-term policy proposals to his underlying social philosophy and ethics. The argument is that this latter foundation, especially in regard to Keynes's theme of the integration of being good and doing good, reveals Keynes to have had a consistent interest in policy that would likely promote structural economic change and social development. An implication of this is that what is customarily referred to as Keynesian economic policy, and generally associated with short-term demand management strategies, really has very little foundation in Keynes's deeper philosophical thinking about society and ethics.[4]

There is no little evidence in Keynes's writing, in fact, that Keynes had a strong interest in structural social-economic reform. His social justice concerns were an important element in his thinking about the overall functioning of capitalist economies (Elliott and Clark, 1987), and he had expressed his commitment to the realization of deeper ethical principles in economic life in insisting in his 1930 "Economic Possibilities for Our Grandchildren" that people should ultimately "value ends above means and prefer the good to the useful" (Keynes, IX, p. 331). Indeed, he held out for the possibility that economic policy might be so designed as to ultimately remove the economic problem itself from society's primary consideration, allowing "for the first time since his creation [that] man be faced with his real, his permanent problem – how to use his freedom from pressing economic cares, how to occupy [his] leisure . . . to live wisely and agreeably well" (p. 328). From this deeper perspective, economic policy for Keynes was in an important respect social policy in the sense that it was best aimed at transforming economic institutions themselves, rather than changing economic outcomes within the framework of existing institutions.

What, then, were Keynes's essential convictions concerning the character of economic policy in the long run? Recently there has been renewed interest in Keynes's long-term policy proposals among Keynes scholars themselves (Jensen, 1991, 1994; Kregel, 1985; Pressman, 1987; Smithin, 1989; Bateman, 1994). For these writers, Keynes's interest in the composition of government expenditure and opportunities for government investment and capital spending were part of a larger interest Keynes developed in the topic of the social control of investment. Since in *The General Theory* the major defect of capitalism was an inadequate volume of private investment expenditure due to recurring uncertainty on the part of investors about future economic performance, Keynes recommended structural changes in the organization of the economy that he hoped would improve the average performance of the economy by raising the level of investment expenditure.

Of course Keynes also advanced other long-term policy proposals in *The General Theory*, most notably, recommendations for a more equitable distribution of income. He argued that the "State will have to exercise a guiding influence on the propensity to consume," in order to promote high levels of effective demand and the growth of wealth, and that the primary means by which this might be accomplished was through a redistribution of income from the rich, whose "abstinence" from consumption dampened economic growth, to wage-earners, for whom increases in purchasing power would generally mean increases in consumption (VII, pp. 378, 373). This recommendation was emphasized after the completion of *The General Theory* in three articles contributed to *The Times* in 1937 entitled "How to Avoid a Slump."

The maintenance of prosperity and of a stable economic life only depends on increased investment if we take as unalterable the existing distribution of purchasing power and the willingness of those who enjoy purchasing power to use it for consumption. The wealthier we get and the smaller, therefore, the profit to be gained from adding to our capital goods, the more it is incumbent on us to see that those who would benefit from increasing their consumption . . . have the power and opportunity to do so . . . (XXI, p. 393)

A redistribution of income, then, was needed both to help reduce the likelihood of continued sub-normal economic activity, and to redress the inequities of past economic development. Indeed Keynes's assertion in the last chapter of *The General Theory*, that "The outstanding faults of the economic society in which we live are its failure to provide for full employment and its arbitrary and inequitable distribution of wealth and incomes" (VII, p. 372), led one prominent early commentator to conclude that "in the *General Theory* inequality is in a very fundamental sense the root cause of unemployment and the greatest barrier to economic progress . . ." (Dillard, 1948, p. 316).

Nonetheless, Keynes thought such redistributional measures unlikely to fully remove the chronic tendency to underemployment output levels exhibited by capitalism, and accordingly he went on to emphasize the central importance of "a somewhat comprehensive socialisation of investment" that would, he believed, ultimately "prove the only means of securing an approximation to full employment" (VII, p. 378). By the "socialisation of investment" Keynes did not mean the adoption of a "State Socialism which would embrace most of the economic life of the community," nor indeed even a governmental "ownership of the instruments of production" in the manner of the socialist states of Eastern Europe (*Ibid.*). In his view, though there was a "necessity of central controls to bring about an adjustment between the propensity to consume and the inducement to invest, there is no more reason to socialise economic life than there was before" (p. 379). Indeed, there still remained for him "a wide field for the exercise of private initiative and responsibility" (p. 380), and it was thus important to avoid the mistakes of those "authoritarian state systems of to-day [which] seem to solve the problem of unemployment at the expense of efficiency and freedom" (p. 381).

What, then, did Keynes actually mean by "a somewhat comprehensive socialisation of investment"? Though *The General Theory* emphasizes the desirablility of the policy, it provides little explanation of what Keynes meant by the idea. The book does provide an understanding of what Keynes thought was problematic about the investment process, especially in its important twelfth chapter on long-term expectations, where, as we saw above, Keynes emphasizes the role of convention in the determination of investors' calculation of future yields from capital assets. There, in stressing the precariousness of conventional determinations of what constitutes a good investment, Keynes especially draws attention to the activity of professional speculators, whose understanding of the ruling conventions in the investment process differed in important respects from the understanding of investment exercised by those individuals whose business activity Keynes termed enterprise. This much discussed distinction, though suggesting deeper views on Keynes's part regarding conduct and social behavior, has in fact been little explored from a philosophical perspective, despite the fact that, in writing to Townshend in 1938, Keynes emphasized that "the economic problem is . . . only a particular department of the general principles of conduct" (XXIX, p. 289). Is there, then, some way to make sense of Keynes's thinking about investment, and his recommendation for its "somewhat comprehensive socialisation," that links his account of the rise of speculation to his views regarding "the general principles of conduct," particularly as we have understood them above? Closer consideration of Keynes's reasoning about speculation and enterprise shows that Keynes indeed thought the relationship between being good and doing good very much at issue in the modern development of the investment process.

For Keynes, we saw earlier, the fact that the determination of prospective returns in investment depended upon the maintenance of a convention represented a relatively recent historical development. "In former times, when enterprises were mainly owned by those who undertook them or by their friends and associates, investment depended on a sufficient supply of individuals of sanguine temperament and constructive impulses who embarked on business as a way of life, not really relying on a precise calculation of prospective profit" (p. 150). In terms of the categories of Keynes's general principles of conduct, this meant that individuals in the era of enterprise essentially conducted themselves as had those Keynes described as rational egoists in "My Early Beliefs" in that their being good was generally consistent with their doing good. Specifically, in regard to the future consequences of investment for possible future earnings, these "individuals of sanguine temperament" simply asked themselves which investments in their enterprises were intuitively likely to produce a maximum of good consequences for future enterprise earnings, confident in the belief that this was best for the enterprise and the economy as a whole. And indeed, the era of enterprise in Keynes's estimation was a time when being good and doing good in the economic world did appear to be in natural harmony with one another (just as they had very briefly appeared to be in ethical life for Keynes when he first read *Principia Ethica* and before encountering his "favorite dilemma"). A verdict very much to this effect was rendered in *The Economic Consequences of the Peace* where, acknowledging the admittedly objectionable social inequalities of the period, Keynes portrayed this former age as a time when each entrepreneur's judgment of what was good for the enterprise turned out to be right for the economy as a whole, since the saving and investment practices of individual firms led to "immense accumulations of fixed capital which [were] to the great benefit of mankind" (II, p. 11).

However, with the historic separation of ownership and management, the era of enterprise gave way to a world in which a larger share of investment was carried out in speculative fashion on Stock Exchanges. In this world, new investment was lower, and, as investment was now no longer likely to produce full employment and growing income levels, the past, happy relation between being good and doing good that enterprise investment had produced before Versailles also was no longer in evidence. Keynes explained the nature and origins of this change as follows:

With the separation between ownership and management which prevails to-day and with the development of organised investment markets, a new factor of great importance has entered in, which sometimes facilitates investment but sometimes adds greatly to the instability of the system. In the absence of security markets, there is no object in frequently attempting to revalue an investment to which we are committed . . . But the daily revaluations of the Stock Exchange . . . inevitably exert a decisive influence on the rate of current investment. For there is no sense in building up a new enterprise at a cost greater than that at which a similar existing enterprise can be purchased . . . Thus certain classes of investment are governed by the average expectation of those who deal on the Stock Exchange as revealed in the price of shares, rather than by the genuine expectations of the professional entrepreneur. (VII, p. 151)

With this daily revaluation of investments possible on the Stock Exchange, the long-term commitment of the professional entrepreneur to the slow building up of new investments was shaken. At the same time, speculators put aside any serious concern with the operations of those enterprises in which they invested to attend instead to the "mass psychology" of "the general public."

It might have been supposed that competition between expert professionals, possessing judgment and knowledge beyond that of the average private investor, would correct the vagaries of the ignorant individual left to himself. It happens, however, that the energies and skill of the professional investor and speculator are mainly occupied otherwise. For most of these persons are, in fact, largely concerned, not with making superior long-term forecasts of the probable yield of an investment over its whole life, but with foreseeing changes in the conventional basis of valuation a short time ahead of the general public. They are concerned, not with what an investment is really worth to a man who buys it "for keeps", but with what the market will value it at, under the influence of mass psychology, three months or a year hence. (pp. 154-5)

For speculators, right conduct regarding investment bore almost no relation to either the good of the enterprise or to the good of the economy as a whole. For traditional entrepreneurs, right conduct regarding enterprise investment was less clear than it had been when "business was a way of life." What was really at bottom in the historic separation of ownership and management, then, was an equally historic and monumental change in the general principles of conduct that governed the investment process.

For Keynes, that is, a new dilemma over the relationship between being good and doing good, one that drew on the logic of his old "favorite dilemma" in ethics, now confronted the economic world in regard to which principles of conduct ought to govern investment decisions. On the one hand, though professional entrepreneurs were still largely attached to the ideal of making long-term commitments to their investments, the fact that the economy with a smaller share of new investment was no longer a steadily growing one made many of these investments questionable. As a result it often made sense for enterprises to adopt a more cautious policy toward expansion and investment, and this new view of the enterprise's good meant a less robust economy in general. We might term this the problem of making long-term commitments. In the language of Keynes's principles of conduct, it meant that being good now no longer implied doing good. On the other hand, professional speculators, in pursuit of quick money gains on the Stock Exchange, operated according to principles of conduct derived from a view of being good basically unrelated to any notion of the good of the enterprise. Their approach to investment rivaled the entrepreneurial view of "business as a way of life," which, in stark contrast, had never really relied upon "precise calculation of prospective profit" from an investment. We might term this the problem of the desired returns on investment. In Keynes's language of conduct, the speculator's being good produced principles of right conduct highly remote from the historic nexus of being good and doing good.

Thus, Keynes's new dilemma was a two-sided one. The old entrepreneurial practices of traditional enterprises were no longer sufficient to generate a coincidence of being good and doing good, and the new practices of speculators on Stock Exchanges threw up new principles of conduct that threatened to undermine the historic connection between being good and doing good. To be sure, a notable difference did distinguish Keynes's two linked dilemmas. When Keynes in his 1906 "Egoism" paper first contemplated his ethical dilemma over being good and doing good, where what seemed intuitively good to the individual might conflict with what generally seemed right, he did not conceive of what generally seemed right in terms of the rules and conventions he later drew attention to in "My Early Beliefs" which were discussed immediately above. Thus, that Keynes later embraced a society's rules and conventions in "My Early Beliefs," while also criticizing his own early attachment to intuition, might well suggest that just as Keynes resolved his early ethical dilemma by attending to the normative importance of society's rules and conventions, so he also came to believe that the reign of average expectation, convention, and the rules of the Stock Exchange, with all its attendant speculative practices, somehow resolved the dilemma over whether the professional entrepreneur or professional speculator understood investment properly. But this, of course, was hardly Keynes's conclusion in the twelfth chapter of *The General Theory* where he asserted plainly in regard to speculation that "There is no clear evidence from experience that the investment policy which is socially advantageous coincides with that which is most profitable" (VII, p. 157). Speculation might be profitable, and it might be good for the speculator, but it was not socially advantageous, that is, it was not a new way of melding doing good and being good.

In contrast to the situation in ethics, then, in the economic world convention and conventional practices not only did not offer a solution to Keynes's new dilemma over right conduct in investment, but were indeed now an essential source of this new dilemma. The intractability of this new dilemma, moreover, was reinforced by the fact that the historic separation of ownership and management had also had certain beneficial effects on the investment process. That development which had produced the "daily revaluations of the Stock Exchange" also brought a liquidity to investment markets which encouraged investors to take risks that would have otherwise been avoided. One could not and should not thus attempt a return to the past when investors acted entrepreneurially through the institution of legal measures that would force individuals to make long-term commitments to their investments (for example, through the imposition of high transfer taxes on stock transactions).

The spectacle of modern investment markets has sometimes moved me towards the conclusion that to make the purchase of an investment permanent and indissoluble . . . might be a useful remedy for our contemporary evils. For this would force the investor to direct his mind to the long-term prospects and to those only. But a little consideration of this expedient brings us up against a dilemma, and shows us how the liquidity of investment markets often facilitates, though it sometimes impedes, the course of new investment. For the fact that each individual investor flatters himself that his commitment is 'liquid' . . . calms his nerves and makes him much more willing to run a risk. (p. 160)

Keynes's new dilemma, then, rooted as it was in recent historical development, was evidently less susceptible to solution than had been his earlier ethical dilemma. From the perspective of investor liquidity, the dilemma now was that, with many owners being detached from the management of enterprise operations, there was a real need for investors to feel that if they ran risks in certain investments, they might easily withdraw those investments. Investment liquidity, however, undermined long-term commitments to investments. Alternatively, the long-term commitment to an investment, which had been based upon close contact and knowledge of the operations and good of the enterprise, conflicted with the liquidity needs of investors. In the simple categories of Keynes's principles of conduct, being good and doing good did not coincide in the modern investment process as a whole.

This conclusion directs our attention to a further, more important difference between Keynes's new dilemma in economics and his old one in ethics. Though we have just seen that we may speak about the dilemma over right conduct regarding investment as a dilemma facing the investment process as a whole, Keynes's new dilemma, as we saw above, really exists between different sets of people – entrepreneurs and speculators – who find themselves attached to different theories of right conduct. This contrasts with the nature of Keynes's old ethical dilemma that can fairly be said to confront all individuals in much the same way. It is an important dimension of Keynes's new dilemma, because the attachment to different and competing theories of right conduct on the part of different groups of individuals had a disabling effect on investment and income. No wonder, then, that Keynes's new dilemma merited central treatment in *The General Theory*, and has long preoccupied numerous economists and social scientists (though very few have thought there was much to learn from what concerned Keynes in his philosophy and ethics).

The argument here, however, is that understanding Keynes's long-term policy recommendation regarding the socialization of investment depends in important ways upon understanding the development in Keynes's general principles of conduct. Keynes had a strong interest in policies of social-economic reform that would help bring about the good society, enable people to "value ends above means and prefer the good to the useful" (IX, p. 331), and perhaps ultimately even remove the economic problem from society's primary consideration. These visionary goals had roots in Keynes's ethical convictions, and it would be short-sighted not to expect some connection between Keynes's policy views and his ethics. To determine how, then, Keynes's diagnosis of the ills of the modern investment process, with its foundation in his understanding of the general principles of conduct, led to his recommendation for "a somewhat comprehensive socialisation of investment," we must see just what Keynes believed such a policy would entail.

"A somewhat comprehensive socialisation of investment"

At the end of his *General Theory* chapter on long-term expectations, Keynes concluded that "I am now somewhat sceptical of the success of a merely monetary policy directed towards influencing the rate of interest [and] I expect to see the State ... taking an ever greater responsibility for directly organising investment . . ." (VII, p. 164). Yet we saw above that Keynes did not intend this to imply that there should be an increase in the State ownership of industry, and that he also was quick to emphasize that his recommendation for "a somewhat comprehensive socialisation of investment" was consistent with the preservation of "a wide field for the exercise of private initiative and responsibility" (VII, p. 380). Skidelsky (1989) and Jensen (1994) have addressed this puzzling combination of ideas by arguing persuasively that in Keynes's mind the State was distinguished from the private sector not so much as a set of governmental institutions, but according to whether the public service motive or the private profit motive represented individuals' dominant orientation. By the State, then, Keynes intended all those institutions, public and private, in which individuals pursued characteristically public aims. Contemporary political theory of course generally represents the State far more narrowly than this, typically restricting the State to those institutions constitutionally defined as being part of government. Keynes, Skidelsky and Jensen suggest, inherited a Victorian view of public service as the preoccupation of those relatively altruistic individuals, who, whatever their location in society or the economy, took the general good as the primary object of their life work.[5] His policy recommendation that there be "a somewhat comprehensive socialisation of investment" thus reflected a conviction that such individuals might well increasingly find new institutional avenues along which to channel their public-spiritedness in the latter half of the twentieth century.[6]

Thus, rather than a call for State ownership of industry, Keynes's real interest was in the emergence of a new set of institutions that lay somewhere between the State and the traditional profit-oriented enterprise. This is evident in the concluding chapter of *The General Theory*, but also in remarks Keynes made in his less often noted wartime Treasury memoranda of 1943–4. There, in arguments in the Spring of 1943 concerning what he characterized as the eventual second phase of postwar economic adjustment, Keynes stressed the possibility of avoiding the sharp fluctuations in investment that were likely to ensue after the War through a policy of placing a greater share of total investment under new forms of public control in "public or semi-public bodies."

If two-thirds or three-quarters of total investment is carried out or can be influenced by public or semi-public bodies, a long-term programme of a stable character should be capable of reducing the potential range of fluctuation to much narrower limits than formerly, when a smaller volume of investment was under public control and when even this part tended to follow, rather than correct, fluctuations of investment in the strictly private sector of the economy. (XXVII, p. 322)

A coherent postwar investment policy was thus first and foremost a matter of a change in the nature of the institutions principally responsible for investment. Keynes had in fact hinted at the much same idea ten years before the publication of *The General Theory* in his 1926 "The End of Laissez-Faire." There he linked this to the issue of individualism in the economy that he had described in *The Economic Consequences of the Peace*, and asserted that, as this individualism was no longer likely to have the same beneficial effect on material progress in the modern world as it had had in the last century, a greater role in the investment process should now be sought for a variety of new "semi-autonomous bodies within the State."

I believe that in many cases the ideal size for the unit of control and organisation lies somewhere between the individual and the modern State. I suggest, therefore, that progress lies in the growth and recognition of semi-autonomous bodies within the State – bodies whose criterion of action within their own field is solely the public good as they understand it, and from whose deliberations motives of private advantage are excluded . . . (IX, p. 288)

These "semi-autonomous bodies" or "semi-public bodies" were neither private firms nor agencies of a government that was regularly reconstituted through the electoral process. In fact, Keynes originally imagined them as a type of institution having roots in an ancient English tradition that regarded the corporation as "a mode of government," listing such entities as "the universities, the Bank of England, the Port of London Authority, even perhaps the railway companies" as examples of what he had in mind (IX, p. 289).

Most important here, however, is Keynes's notion of an organization whose members' object was "the public good as they understand it, and from whose deliberations motives of private advantage are excluded." Such organizations would clearly differ from the traditional profit-oriented enterprise in their pursuit of the public good, but they would also differ from government in their pursuit of the public good "as they understand it." Given his suggested examples, by this latter expression Keynes can be taken to have been thinking of organizations which would combine a public service motive with responsibility for economic action within a limited, functionally defined jurisdiction. Should, for example, the universities and railways carry out programs of investment, these programs would naturally be motivated by their respective conceptions of "the public good as they [would] understand it" in their particular areas of concern. Such conceptions, moreover, would reflect the status of these organizations as relatively permanent economic concerns, whose corresponding conceptions of the public good were not likely to change significantly with changes in political power in government. Indeed, since organizations of this sort would maintain relatively constant (or steadily growing) levels of investment expenditure, an increase in their number would be likely to lead to both higher levels of investment expenditure generally and a dampening of the business cycle. This, almost certainly, would also have further beneficial effects upon traditional enterprises' private investment.

Keynes's policy recommendation for a socialization of investment, however, possessed an even deeper rationale, since in the final analysis his proposal really amounted to a call to replace the existing system of investment, with its disabling conflict between two competing theories of right conduct, with a new set of social institutions predicated upon a single, new, self-consistent view of right conduct. Two related problems, we have seen, beset the existing system. First, there was the problem of the long-term commitment to investment. In the past when the good of the enterprise had coincided with the good of the economy as a whole, entrepreneurs had sustained long-term commitments to expansion and investment. However, when speculators began to argue that there was "no sense in building up a new enterprise at a cost greater than that at which a similar existing enterprise can be purchased," new investment and economic growth slowed, and this tended to undermine entrepreneurs' confidence in long-term commitments to enterprise expansion. Second, there was the problem of the desired returns on investment. Entrepreneurs had never made "a very precise calculation of prospective profit," because for much of the nineteenth century "business had been a way of life." Speculators, however, pursued a way of life that turned on the realization of quick money gains from Stock Exchange investments, and this in turn raised questions about the nature and magnitude of returns to enterprise. Both of these problems, then, had to be addressed by Keynes's semi-autonomous or semi-public bodies to resolve the modern economic dilemma.

Addressing the problem of long-term commitment to investment was a matter of drawing upon these organizations' public side, as manifested through their public service objective. As organizations that concerned themselves with the public good, and on the assumption that opportunities to serve the public were abundant, these organizations were likely to pursue their programs of investment and expansion in spite of slower rates of economic growth attendant upon slower rates of new investment by traditional enterprises. Their long-term commitment to investment, therefore, would in considerable degree be independent of the forces that dampened traditional investment. At the same time, with sustained programs of investment and expansion, these organizations would clearly be doing good, both in their addition to new investment (Keynes's chief concern), but also of course in the beneficial effects of their activities on the public. This doing good, it should be emphasized, would flow directly from these organizations' view of their own good as public service organizations, so that for them being good would identically be a matter of doing good. Keynes's semi-public or semi-autonomous bodies, then, successfully addressed the problem of long-term commitment to investment by means of their institutional reconciliation of being good and doing good.

Addressing the problem of desired returns on investment, on the other hand, meant drawing upon the private side of these organizations, as was manifest in the private character of their members' activity. These organizations, recall, were to address "the public good as they understand it." Given Keynes's examples, this was to say that these organizations would not be responsible in their choice of activities to such extra-organizational authorities as government or shareholder boards, and that their programs of expansion and investment would be judged by internally generated criteria. On the assumption that such organizations would generally be independent of one another as well, their programs of investment and expansion would only reflect their respective private perspectives on the public good. Each such organization would possess, in effect, "a way of life" of its own, and this ultimately would mean that, for these organizations, investment, and its return, would be explained in terms of the rationales of this "way of life" dedicated to public service. In contrast to the existing system, therefore, in which speculation offered principles of right conduct distant from any conception of the relationship between being good and doing good, these organizations would solve the problem of desired returns on investment by offering their principles of right conduct that depended upon a new linkage between being good and doing good.

Thus, Keynes's policy recommendation concerning "a somewhat comprehensive socialisation of investment" was tantamount to a call for structural social-economic reform aimed at resolving a fundamental dilemma in the principles of conduct in the modern system of investment. This recommendation can be yet better understood if we recall the development that Keynes's general principles of conduct themselves underwent in his reversal in thinking about the importance of rules. Social rules and conventions, we saw above in connection with Keynes's conclusions in "My Early Beliefs," were normatively valuable, because they were the means by which being good and doing good were reconciled in ethical terms. These social rules and conventions deserved our respect, moreover, because of their having been "skilfully put across and guilefully preserved," and because they represented "the extraordinary accomplishment of our predecessors in the ordering of life" (X, pp. 447,

448). From this perspective, Keynes's structural social-economic policy recommendation was a recommendation to establish a set of semi-public, semi-autonomous institutions whose practices would embody new intrinsically valuable rules and conventions. Alternatively, Keynes's reconciliation of his "favorite" dilemma in ethics was ultimately a matter of the establishment of institutions that would effect a practical reconciliation of being good and doing good.

Ethics and economic policy, then, interconnectedly aimed at the same goal for Keynes. The first implication of this is that social rules and conventions possess concrete institutions as their framework. While this is not to say that all of society's normatively valuable rules and conventions are institutionally embedded, it seems fair to conclude (especially in light of Keynes's preoccupation with institutions at the international level during the last years of his career) that Keynes's social-economic reform thinking was principally aimed at the creation of normatively valuable institutions whose practices reflected intrinsically valuable rules and conventions. The second implication of this, then, is that these institutions and their practices were not (at least in the first instance) valuable in virtue of the good consequences their activities might produce. Rather, Keynes's later intuitionist moral thinking about social rules and conventions carried over to his view of the good of institutions. Just as society's rules and conventions were to be defended as the painstaking accomplishment of past generations that were ever more successful in reconciling being good and doing good, so also society's good institutions were to be defended for their contribution to making being good and doing good harmonious.

Finally, it should also be noted that Keynes's long-term policy recommendation concerning the socialization of investment found some support in his conviction that there was already afoot in many larger, traditional enterprises a socializing trend that bore considerable resemblance to much of what he was proposing for his new, semi-public institutions. Thus, in "The End of Laissez-Faire," immediately after his discussion of semi-autonomous institutions, Keynes went on to assert that the increasing separation of ownership and management in many traditional enterprises had reduced shareholder influence over the direction of the enterprise, and enabled the management of these enterprises to focus upon "the general stability and reputation of the institution."

One of the most interesting and unnoticed developments of recent decades has been the tendency of big enterprise to socialise itself. A point arrives in the growth of a big institution – particularly a big railway or big public utility enterprise, but also a big bank or a big insurance company – at which the owners of the capital, i.e. the shareholders, are almost entirely dissociated from the management, with the result that the direct personal interest of the latter in the making of great profit becomes quite secondary. When this stage is reached, the general stability and reputation of the institution are the more considered by the management than the maximum of profit for the shareholders. (IX, p. 289)

In its effects on investment, this trend was likely to accomplish much the same thing Keynes expected of semi-public institutions. Investment would likely be higher on account of greater long-term commitments and reduced concern over short-term money returns. At the same time, a development of this sort was unlikely to offer the same reconciliation of being good and doing good as might Keynes's semi-public institutions, since even the newly evolved traditional institution still looked principally to its own private advantage, though that might be more and more determined by a relatively independent management. Indeed, this difference highlights the importance of Keynes's desired reconciliation of being good and doing good in his overall thinking, since if it had merely been higher, more stable investment that Keynes had been seeking, the evolution of traditional enterprise might well have been sufficient.

Individuality and sociality

In conclusion, it is important to note the connections between Keynes's ethics and policy thinking and his underlying philosophical thinking about individuality and sociality. In Chapter 4, it was argued that the relation between being good and doing good that frames Keynes's general principles of conduct also makes Keynes's fundamental philosophical concerns the nature of individuality and sociality. Here, we have also seen that rather than a growth of the institutions of the State, Keynes was interested in seeing an extension of the attitude of public-spiritedness consistent with his own Victorian notions of individual commitment to the public good. This extension, moreover, was to occur through an institutional change that would embody intrinsically valuable social rules and conventions in semi-autonomous, semi-public bodies. Two sets of philosophical issues naturally arise in such an analysis: first, how this institutional development would affect the nature of individuality, and second, how it would result in the further manifestation of individuals' social side in individual experience.

In regard to the first issue, the implication of Keynes's ethics and policy thinking is that individuality would itself be transformed in important respects as individuals increasingly occupied positions in economic organizations that sought the public good rather than private advantage. In the analysis of Chapter 4, individual identity was a matter of the particular individual's organic organization of common or shared social ideas and feelings. On this understanding, any greater preoccupation on the part of the individual with characteristically public aims would naturally tend to reconstitute the individual's self-identity in more public-spirited terms. In effect, the mix of concepts and convictions that each person individually integrated would contain a greater share of matters that concerned the public, and this would transform each individual's personal orientation. Keynes's theory of individual identity, it is now clear, was an especially flexible one since, in explaining individual nature according to a formal, non-substantive principle of self-organization, it allows a considerable role for effects of social influences on individuals, and thus for social policy that changes the conceptual and conative materials on which individuals operate.

In regard to the second issue, the implication of Keynes's ethics and policy thinking is that individuals' social side is manifest in the manner in which they are likely to respond to society's rules and conventions. For Keynes, we have seen, a society's rules and conventions possessed an intrinsic normative significance. This meant that they carried a moral obligatoriness, and that a society's rules and conventions act upon individuals with the particular force that moral obligation imposes. Specifically, a society's rules and conventions are compelling, yet are also sufficiently flexible to admit individual interpretation. We have seen that this combination reflects the status of convention as the relatively settled product of a system of interdependent judgment. Conventions both have a command over individuals to the extent that past judgments carry an elementary plausibility, and also evolve with the continuing play of individual judgment. In contrast, Keynes's early candidate for explaining individuals' social side, namely, the commonality of human nature, lacks this conceptual flexibility, since reference to a common nature fails to explain how individuals differ in judgment.

Keynes's philosophical convictions regarding the nature of individuality and sociality, then, underwent change and development as he re-evaluated the importance of society's rules and conventions and their role in social-economic reform. In this development, it is fair to say, there persisted an element of utopian thinking on Keynes's part. Clearly, the social-economic reform Keynes imagined was fundamental, both in its impact upon society's institutions and in the further effects of this on the nature of individuality and sociality. But beyond this, what was truly utopian in Keynes's thinking regarding social-economic reform was the notion that such reform needed to aim at a harmonization of being good and doing good. In this, Keynes continually demonstrated himself committed to the notion of an ideal existence removed from the world of ordinary experience. Such utopianianism, it is worth noting, cannot be captured by consequentialist interpretations of Keynes's thinking, because they must ultimately frame Keynes's chief normative aim as the greatest happiness possible, and such a notion represents only a best improvement on this world, not the characterization of an ideal world. Whether, however, Keynes had any real hopes for the millennium must be left to speculation. Though his ideal remained constant through his career, as his recent biographers have so well demonstrated (Skidelsky, 1983, 1992; Moggridge, 1992), the battles of this world were disillusioning and all-absorbing.

Conclusion: Keynes's philosophical development

The issue of whether there is significant development in Keynes's philosophical thinking has been associated with the question of the continuity or discontinuity of that thinking (Bateman, 1991a; Skidelsky, 1992). But it must seem to many readers that though these alternative positions are clear in outline – that either Keynes's philosophical thinking in *The General Theory* remained essentially as it was in the *Treatise*, or that important elements of the earlier work were abandoned and new themes were introduced in the later work – ultimately whether one adopts the continuity or discontinuity view appears to be chiefly a matter of the emphasis one would like to put upon one's exposition of Keynes's philosophical views. Certainly proponents of both views admit elements of the opposite interpretation. Continuity theorists allow there are changes in Keynes's views, simply regarding them as comparatively minor modifications on major themes, and discontinuity theorists recognize continuities, allowing there to be a relatively constant backdrop against which Keynes made changes. Accordingly, since there seems to be really no way of establishing a definitive measure of the balance between change and permanence in Keynes's views, it seems that one interpreter's selection of themes for discussion sets one balance on the subject while another's selection simply sets another. From this point of view, all interpretations investigate the development of Keynes's philosophical thinking, continuity theorists arguing for a deepening of views and discontinuity theorists arguing for redirection of views, but the notion of development itself in the final analysis adds little to the topic.

The position taken in this work is that this interpretation of Keynes's philosophical development is mistaken. Because Keynes left one discipline and discourse for another, and because he then radically restructured his theoretical concerns in that latter discipline and discourse, development in his thinking involved an unmistakable and not insignificant transition in the manner of his philosophical conceptualizing. That is, real development occurred in Keynes's philosophical thinking when he ceased attempting to work out philosophers' solutions to philosophical questions, and came to regard economic reasoning as the site upon which philosophical issues were to be delineated and investigated. It is not suggested here that this was necessarily a clear, conscious decision on Keynes's part (though there is nothing in his writings and papers to indicate that it was not). Rather, it is presumed here that any author's self-understanding is of limited value for the analysis of that author's work. Indeed no philosopher has ever anticipated the full range of interpretations of his or her thinking, and all philosophers have been evaluated according to the coherence of their ideas, not their author's own appraisal of those ideas. What is claimed here, then, is that understanding the real development in Keynes's philosophical thinking requires that one take stock of the change in Keynes's material concerns that necessarily changed his very approach to philosophical questions. It is these data that should then be used to evaluate Keynes's own hints and claims about the significance of his work.

These issues may be illustrated in connection with an homology of concerns between Keynes's unknown probabilities of the *Treatise* and fundamental uncertainty of *The General Theory* and the weight of argument in the former and the state of confidence in the latter. The puzzle is why, among all Keynes's early notions, were unknown probabilities and the weight of argument upgraded in significance in *The General Theory*, and how do uncertainty and confidence then actually correspond to their kindred notions used in the *Treatise*? On the assumption that no real development occurred in Keynes's philosophical thinking, or the view that all Keynes's subsequent philosophical ideas appeared in some form or another in his early work, somehow a mere re-ordering of philosophical themes or perhaps a restructuring of philosophical concerns must account for all Keynes's later conceptions. Uncertainty and confidence, that is, just are those original *Treatise* notions, despite their re-naming, and their significance and meaning in *The General Theory* are precisely their meaning and significance in the *Treatise*. But of course the change in Keynes's thinking in this regard to these notions did not arise from Keynes's reflecting upon the internal adequacy of the *Treatise*, nor from an intention to re-apply simply those original philosophical ideas to new political and economic issues of the 1920s and thirties. What brought on Keynes's preoccupation with uncertainty and confidence was his effort to sort out theoretical problems in the domain of economics. These were notions one used if conversant in the debates among economists in the inter-war period (cf. Clarke, 1989), and no special philosophical background was needed to understand them in that domain. Thus, while interpreters of Keynes's philosophy can indeed construct readings of *The General Theory* in terms of the categories of the *Treatise*, they thereby miss Keynes's own effort at genuine development of his early thinking from a system of reference beyond it.

Keynes's philosophical development was thus truly discontinuous. This means that the philosophical questions relevant to Keynes's later thought have their own distinct framework of significance, and that the adequacy of that later thought – its theoretical credentials, it might be said – must be established upon the conceptual terrain on which Keynes's later philosophical views were elaborated. Much has been written about the focus of the *Treatise* on how judgment is objective. Gillies and Ieto-Gillies (1991), however, have suggested that this concept of objectivity is replaced in Keynes's later thinking by a concept of an intersubjectively objective judgment, a notion resembling in a number of respects the idea of interdependent belief expectations advanced here. But in the domain of pure philosophy, it might be said that the concept of intersubjective judgment is neither fish nor fowl, neither an obviously successful new way of describing objective judgment, nor one that successfully incorporates the subjective dimensions of individual judgment. That individual behavior and judgment are interactive does not necessarily make them objective, and that individuals interact does not clearly explain more about the subjective elements of judgment. Moving beyond the domain of traditional philosophy to the philosophical concerns of economics, however, puts the concept of intersubjective judgment in an altogether different light.

While traditional philosophy tends to investigate judgment from the perspective of its epistemological and logical credentials, economics explains judgment as a choice behavior in which autonomous individuals are related to one another through the concept of equilibrium exchange. In effect, economics since Adam Smith uses the equilibrium concept to invest choice behavior with a derived objectivity, in that through the play of the invisible hand seemingly unrelated, subjective decision-making produces an overall coherence in the form of the market system. Yet in its modern Marshallian and Walrasian forms, economics relies on the questionable assumption that individuals are uninfluenced by one another, despite the fact that casual evidence indicates that the contrary is more likely true, and this throws into question the very adequacy of the market equilibrium explanation. In this connection, the idea of judgment as interdependent or intersubjective, with its account of response to error and revision of individual judgment, offers an alternative explanation of the integrating function of the market that potentially accomplishes some of the goals of a classical equilibrium of atomistic individuals. This is not the place to enter further into this explanation, but it may be said that this, as it were, reflected objectivity, which judgment acquires through individuals' interaction with one another, produces an added dimension to individual subjective judgment, which is meaningful in economics in light of the specific abstract philosophical concern in that subject with the philosophical idea of systemic coherence. Thus, while the idea of an interdependent judgment may in principle seem to contain minimal insights for epistemologists and logicians, for economists the notion seems full of potential insights that demand a specifically philosophical kind of speculation (as attested to by economists' continued fascination with the range of permutations of game theory).

The standards, then, by which Keynes's later philosophical thinking should be evaluated are in important respects internal to the philosophy of economics. Keynes wanted first and foremost to explain equilibrium unemployment. He thus accepted Smith's philosophical vision of the social-economic world as a collection of independent but related individuals, but employed the concept of convention to account for how the economic system might become locked into less than full employment levels of activity. His concept of convention, as based in the idea of interdependent belief expectations, thus extended the Smithian vision by giving an explanation of how the market system could get into a certain configuration of individual activities on the part of relatively independent individuals. But it adopted in the process a richer view of individual decision-making and interaction that permitted an understanding of previously unexplained phenomena. As philosophical explanation in economics this represented arguably a progressive advance on past views, because it went further in describing the systemic effects of relatively autonomous individuals, and accomplished this in a manner more adequate to our intuitions concerning individuals' influence upon one another.

The argument advanced in this work has attempted to chart the path of Keynes's philosophical development through tracing a logic of development of a series of concepts and principles from his early to his later philosophy. Seeing the end-points of the process, but having limited and not always straightforward evidence for how Keynes himself reconceptualized his most basic theoretical commitments, the strategy here has been to set out a number of conceptual steps by which Keynes might have progressively freed himself from certain early views about judgment and intuition. The discussion began essentially with an investigation of the problems that attach to explaining the complex notion of intuitive judgment. The topic of judgment was then seen to raise questions about the nature of language and communication in view of emotivist renderings of ethical judgment as non-cognitive. Language and communication themselves signal the centrality of rules and conventions in human interaction, and rules and conventions in Keynes's later economic thinking required formulation in terms of expectations. From his earliest view of judgment as pure intuitive insight, then, Keynes thus enlarged his conception of judgment to include what roughly may be termed a social component, from which vantage point he was then ultimately able to explain the patterns of the economy and recommend appropriate policy. For him, I have concluded, this resolved the twin responsibilities of being good and doing good that he early saw as a fundamental personal dilemma. This was, perhaps, the final step in a philosophical development to which he most fervently aspired.

Notes

INTRODUCTION

1 In this respect, the view here differs from the less restrictive view of Gerrard (1991).

1 Keynes's early intuitionism

1 There is a controversy over the dating of "Ethics in Relation to Conduct." Skidelsky (1983, 1992) and O'Donnell (1989) favor 1904 and Moggridge (1992) favors a much later date. I have retained the 1904 dating on the grounds that the record of questions addressed that was kept by the Cambridge Conversazione Society, or the Apostles, the then-secret society for which Keynes wrote the paper, puts the question Keynes discussed on January 23, 1904 as "Is there an objective probability?" The paper itself, however, is untitled, having since come to be referred to as "Ethics in relation to conduct."

Keynes's unpublished Apostles papers are identified according to their date and the system of classification adopted in the King's College Library catalogue of the papers of John Maynard Keynes. For a chronology and brief explanation of Keynes's Apostles papers deposited in the King's College Modern Archive, see Moggridge. For a history of the Apostles, see Levy.

2 References to *The Collected Works of John Maynard Keynes* are by volume number and page.

3 "Miscellanea Ethica" was dated by Keynes July–September 1905. It is not clear whether it was read to the Apostles. "A Theory of Beauty", which uses much of the same language and argument, was dated August–October 1905. According to a letter of Keynes's to G.L. Strachey of November 12, 1905, "A Theory of Beauty" was read to G.L. Dickinson's Discussion Society on November 8, 1905. It was re-read to the Apostles Society on May 25, 1912 with Moore present.

4 Popper puts the matter especially well:

Science does not rest upon solid bedrock. The bold structure of its theories rises, as it were, above a swamp. It is like a building erected on piles. The piles are driven down from above into the swamp, but not down to any natural or 'given' base; and if we stop driving the piles deeper, it is not because we have reached firm ground. We simply stop when we are satisfied that the piles are firm enough to carry the structure, at least for the time

being. (1934, p. 111)
For more recent statements of anti-foundationalist thinking in epistemology, see Quinton, 1966; Will, 1974; Evans, 1978; Rorty, 1979.

5 For the history of the Vienna Circle's influential development of the idea of an observation statement, see Gillies (1993).

6 This reading was more popular in the early Vienna Circle. As Gillies argues, Rudolph Carnap and Otto Neurath later moved towards views more associated with the later Wittgenstein by emphasizing the intersubjective nature of language (1993, pp. 120–4). The early Vienna Circle reading has more recently been contested by Anscombe (1959) and Janik and Toulmin (1973).

7 The passage appears in slightly different form and without the reference to Duhem in the widely used translation of Neurath's influential paper on protocol sentences (1932–3) by George Schick in Ayer (1959). Will translates the passage from its original appearance in Neurath's monograph *Anti-Spengler* (1921).

2   The dilemmas of Moore's *Principia* for ethics and economics

1 MacIntyre in his influential analysis of the rise of a contemporary emotivist culture, in which moral judgments are nothing but expressions of preference, feeling, and attitude, not only linked the rise of emotivism to Moore's views, but also attributed to the later Keynes of "My Early Beliefs" a recognition of this connection (1984, pp. 14–17) Drakopoulos (1991) has addressed the relationship between emotivist thinking and Robbins's views. Skidelsky (1992) also recognizes these linkages. My own research on the subject appears in Davis (1990) in regard to emotivism and in Davis (1994a) in regard to Robbins.

2 Though see Gibbard (1990).

3 Ramsey, importantly, was also an emotivist in ethics.

4 For more on the emotivists, see Urmson (1968).

5 Ordinalist utility theory, of course, had important origins in Robbins's thinking and the work that it immediately influenced, especially Hicks and Allen's paper (1934) and Hicks's subsequent book (1939).

6 Though see Kirzner (1960) for a critical view of Robbins's methodological commitments from an Austrian perspective.

7 Samuelson was representative of most economists when in discussion Robbins's view that "ethical value judgments have no place in scientific analysis" concluded that Robbins was "undoubtedly correct" (Samuelson, 1947, pp. 219–20).

8 Though empirical economists are rarely familiar with the economic methodology literature, virtually all econometric work implicitly recognizes the significance of the Duhem–Quine thesis concerning the relationship between auxiliary assumptions and testing. On the Duhem–Quine principle in economics see Cross (1982).

9 Here, among the many accounts of Wittgenstein's reasoning about private language, I rely principally on Kripke (1982). However, the general outline of the argument goes back to Winch's application of Wittgenstein's thinking to social science (1958).

10 See Parfit (1984) for an extended discussion of the question of agent self-identity. The issue is parallel to the question of whether an equilibrium exists and is unique. Indeed, without some confidence regarding agent self-identity, it is not clear that the latter issue can be discussed coherently.

3 Keynes's self-critique

1 The importance of the papers was brought to the attention of scholars by Skidelsky in the first volume of his biography of Keynes (1983). Moggridge (1992) also surveys a number of these papers, some of which are of a serious nature and some of which are written on lighter topics. An earlier version of my argument appeared in Davis (1991). See Fitzgibbons (1988) for a different view.

2 I thus take O'Donnell's (1989) assertion that "My Early Beliefs" is not an important document to reflect a misappreciation of Keynes's intellectual development. Keynes seems to have rendered just such a verdict himself in requesting in his will that "My Early Beliefs" (and but one other unpublished writing) be published after his death.

3 Keynes later repeated the substance of his arguments in the paper in his *Treatise on Probability* (Keynes, VIII, pp. 341ff). The paper's title comes from the name of the chapter in Moore's *Principia* that Keynes critiqued (Chapter 5).

4 This, of course, was later one of Keynes's key positions in the *Treatise on Probability*.

I maintain . . . that there are some pairs of probabilities between the members of which *no* comparison of magnitude is possible; that we can say, nevertheless, of some pairs . . . that the one is greater and the other less, although it is not possible to measure the difference between them; and that in a very special type of case . . . a meaning can be given to a *numerical* comparison of magnitude. (Keynes, VIII, pp. 36–7)

5 Rather than the view that when we judge we are acquainted with a single entity, Russell and Moore moved to the view that judgment is a many-termed relation, whose terms include the individual judger and those entities, universal and particular, with which one is acquainted.

6 Keynes returned to this doctrine after the *Treatise* in 1926 in his oft-quoted comment on Edgeworth's system that the mind's contents could not be treated atomistically:

The atomic hypothesis which has worked so splendidly in Physics breaks down in Psychics. We are faced at every turn with the problems of Organic Unity, of Discreteness, of Discontinuity – the whole is not equal to the sum of the parts, comparisons of quantity fail us, small changes produce large effects, the assumptions of uniform and homogeneous continuum are not satisfied. (X, p. 262)

Rather, the mind had to be understood to be an organic whole.

7 Similarly, in Russell's *Principles of Mathematics* (1903) a concept was an objective entity not belonging to any particular mind.

8 The *Treatise* was essentially complete by 1914, but not published until 1921 on account of interruptions from Keynes's other activities, particularly the

Versailles negotiations. Russell introduced his distinction between knowledge by acquaintance and description in his 1910–11 paper. One can be acquainted with universal entities, such as when we know the meaning of a general term which signifies such an entity, and one can be acquainted with particular entities, such as one's own psychical states and one's sense-data. All other particular entities, such as material objects and other people, are known only by description. Moore had advanced, less influentially and less sharply, similar arguments in his 1910–11 London Lectures (Moore, 1953). Nothing resembling these notions appears in Keynes's second fellowship dissertation which is dated December 12, 1908.

4   Keynes's later philosophy

1 Both resulted from doctoral dissertations at Cambridge University.

2 Ramsey, recall, had defended emotivist views in ethics also.

3 Ramsey, it seems, gave special emphasis to his charge by mimicking David Hume's famous assertion that upon looking into himself he found nothing one might term the self, merely his perceptions (1739, pp. 251–2). Hume's skepticism regarding enduring, self-subsistent entities was entirely familiar to Keynes, who had indeed referred to it in "Miscellanea Ethica."

4 For the origins of the twentieth-century view of economics as a moral science at Cambridge, see Groenewegen (1988).

5 Though the purpose was different, Adam Smith's *Theory of Moral Sentiments* (1759) account of an impartial spectator bears comparison with Keynes's reasoning. Each sought a comparison of own behavior with that of others, in order to establish a linkage between behavior and intention. A more recent but again somewhat different analysis also bearing affinities to this method of reasoning is John Rawls's (1971) use of a veil of ignorance. Rawls also asks us to put ourselves in the place of others, though for the purpose of establishing principles of justice. In comparison with the normative investigations of Smith and Rawls, Keynes was interested in accounting only for behavior dependent upon "motives, expectations, psychological uncertainties."

6 For a review of Keynes on uncertainty in both the *Treatise* and in *The General Theory*, see Runde (1990, 1991).

7 For opposing views, see Brown–Collier (1985) and Rotheim (1989–90).

8 Though see Runde (1994a) for a somewhat more charitable view of Ramsey's thinking, and Gillies and Ietto-Gillies (1987) for a broader view of De Finetti.

9 Wittgenstein's assertion, "An intention is embedded in its situation, in human customs and institutions" (para. 337), suggests a thinking not unlike Keynes's.

10 Referring to Sraffa's criticisms of his early ideas in the Preface to the *Philosophical Investigations*, Wittgenstein asserts: "I am indebted to *this* stimulus for the most consequential ideas of this book' (1953, p. x; also see Malcolm, 1958, p. 69). For an interpretation of Sraffa's influence on Wittgenstein, see Davis (1988). For an interpretation of Marxist influences on Sraffa, see Davis (1993). It should be added that the other individual to whom Wittgenstein gave special credit was Ramsey: "I was helped to realize these

[grave] mistakes . . . by the criticism which my ideas encountered from Frank Ramsey" (*ibid.*). For the influence of Ramsey, see Monk (1990).

5 The philosophical thinking of *The General Theory*

1 The 1970s breakdown of the postwar consensus regarding Keynesian thinking was an important stimulus for much of this work. Scholars also recognized that Keynes's own thinking differed in many respects from its conventional interpretation – an appreciation assisted by the appearance of the first volumes of Keynes's *Collected Writings* in 1971. A selection of these later accounts of Keynes's economics upon which I have relied includes Kregel (1976), Patinkin (1990), Davidson (1978), Chick (1983), Kahn (1984), Harcourt (1987), Dimand (1988), Amadeo (1989), Clarke (1989), Meltzer (1989), Rogers (1989), Sardoni (1989–90), Asimakopulos (1991), Cottrell and Lawlor (1991), Moggridge (1992), Bateman (1994), Elliott (1994), Harcourt and Sardoni (1994), Jensen (1994), Lawlor (1994), and Runde (1994b). Shackle (1967) was a pioneer in insisting on the distinction between Keynes and Keynesianism. Young (1987) and Patinkin (1990) survey different interpretations of Keynes's economics. Two compendiums of papers on Keynes are Wood (1983) and Blaug (1991). Keynesian thinking, as distinct from Keynes's own thinking, is now loosely differentiated as old and new Keynesianism. See Romer (1993), Greenwald and Stiglitz (1993), and Tobin (1993) for a symposium on these later differences.

2 Here she echoes Harrod's summing-up of *The General Theory*:

The theory of interest is, I think, the central point in his scheme. He departs from old orthodoxy in holding that the failure of the system to move to a position of full activity is not primarily due to friction, rigidity, immobility or to phenomena essentially connected with the trade cycle. If a certain level of interest is established which is inconsistent with full activity, no flexibility or mobility in the other parts of the system will get the system to move to full activity. But this wrong rate of interest, as we may call it, is not itself a rigidity or inflexibility. It is natural, durable, and in a certain sense, in the free system inevitable. That is why he lays what may seem an undue emphasis on the doctrine that interest is essentially the reward for not saving but for parting with liquidity. Given the complex forces affecting liquidity preference, such and such is the rate of interest that will naturally and necessarily and, so long as underlying forces remain unchanged, permanently obtain. Yet that rate of interest may be inconsistent with the full activity of the system. (1947, pp. 69–70)

3 To this might be added the influence of the Neoclassical Keynesian synthesis with its emphasis on the market-clearing concept of equilibrium and models producing determinate results. Perhaps the most prominent and successful critic of this way of thinking is Shackle (esp. 1972).

4 For more on Keynes and different conventions, see Littleboy (1990).

5 It should also be recognized that the analysis in the chapter is in many respects autobiographical in nature (see Keynes, XII, Chapter 1).

6 Strictly speaking, the market clears continuously, and average expectation is continuously registered as quoted price.

7 For a full discussion of the meaning and import of this term in Keynes's thinking, see Dow and Dow (1985) and Matthews (1991).

8 Keynes's most famous comment regarding uncertainty is the following:
> By 'uncertain' knowledge, let me explain, I do not mean merely to distinguish what is known for certain from what is only probable. The game of roulette is not subject, in this sense, to uncertainty; nor is the prospect of a Victory bond being drawn. Or, again, the expectation of life is only slightly uncertain. Even the weather is only moderately uncertain. The sense in which I am using the term is that in which the prospect of a European war is uncertain, or the price of copper and the rate of interest twenty years hence, or the obsolescence of a new invention, or the position of private wealth owners in the social system in 1970. About these matters there is no scientific basis on which to form any calculable probability whatever. We simply do not know. (XIV, pp. 113–14).

9 On this understanding, buyers would seek out other buyers and sellers seek out other sellers to confirm their respective views about the hoped-for direction of the market. A, say, persistently rising market, then, would reflect a dominant bullish psychology, or a shared confidence among bulls that dominated the shared confidence among bears.

10 For an interesting application of this sort of thinking to Keynes and the topic of speculation, see Orlean (1989). Orlean characterizes the state of affairs in which individuals attempt to predict average opinion as a self-referential system. Speculative behavior is then interpreted as a type of intersubjectivity within a self-referential system.

11 Here my interpretation of the role played by animal spirits in Keynes's thinking differs from Dow and Dow (1985) and Matthews (1991) in the emphasis it places on social determination of the level of animal spirits. Just as uncertainty is in important respects a social relation, so also the role played by animal spirits is very much a matter of the form taken by the system of interdependent belief affecting investment.

12 It needs to be emphasized that the interpretation here does not pretend that investors explicitly coordinate their investment plans. Rather, an implicit coordination occurs when any group of investors develops a shared confidence about some investment.

13 And it seems Keynes still adhered to much of the analysis of the probability calculus that had made up the bulk of his *Treatise*.

14 Wittgenstein, in fact, explicitly criticizes Platonism in mathematics (where it is perhaps most plausible) in his *Remarks on the Foundations of Mathematics*. This was brought to my attention by Donald Gillies.

6 Ethics and policy

1 Ayer and Stevenson, of course, reacted to Moore's work, not Keynes's. That Keynes, a follower of Moore in ethics, interpreted Moore in this way demonstrated an important tendency in the latter's ideas (and of course in Keynes's own ideas). Moore, however, apparently did not appreciate the significance of Keynes's sort of reading until he found himself under attack by the emotivists.

2 Similarly, in the *Treatise on Probability* Keynes had treated probability and weight as separate intuitions.

3 Keynes had begun his paper with a critique of Moore's rejection of egoism. Moore had developed his own view in response to Sidgwick's (Moore's teacher) defense of a rational egoism. Thus, Keynes's difficulties with the notion in many respects replicate those Sidgwick encountered in his *Methods of Ethics* (1922). Ironically, Keynes disparaged Sidgwick's moral dilemmas, which arguably were not significantly different from his own. See Helburn (1992) for a discussion of these issues, and an interpretation of Keynes's ethics emphasizing duty and virtue not unrelated to the being good and doing good framework here.

4 For an analysis of Keynes's theory of state power based on his early interest in Edmund Burke's ideas, see Helburn (1991).

5 This line of reasoning also reflects Harrod's emphasis on the "presuppositions of 6 Harvey Road" (1951, p. 4).

6 On Keynes and the "socialisation of investment," also see Bateman (1994), Jensen (1994), and Skidelsky (1992).

References

Alston, W. (1964), *Philosophy of Language*. Englewood Cliffs: Prentice-Hall.
Amadeo, E. (1989), *Keynes's Principle of Effective Demand*. Aldershot: Edward Elgar.
Ambrose, A., ed. (1979), *Wittgenstein's Lectures, Cambridge, 1932–1935*. Oxford: Blackwell.
Anscombe, G. (1959), *An Introduction to Wittgenstein's Tractatus*, 2nd edn., revised. New York: Harper & Row, 1963.
Archibald, G. (1959), "Welfare Economics, Ethics, and Essentialism." *Economica* 26, 316–27.
Asimakopulos, A. (1991), *Keynes's General Theory and Accumulation*. Cambridge: Cambridge University Press.
Austin, J. (1962), *How to Do Things with Words*. Oxford: Oxford University Press.
Ayer, A. (1936), *Language, Truth and Logic*, 2nd edn. New York: Dover, 1946.
    ed. (1959), *Logical Positivism*. New York: Free Press.
Bateman, B. (1987), "Keynes's Changing Conception of Probability." *Economics and Philosophy* 3, 97–120.
    (1990), "Keynes, Induction, and Econometrics." *History of Political Economy* 22, 359–79.
    (1991a), "*Das Maynard Keynes Problem*." *Cambridge Journal of Economics* 15, 101–11.
    (1991b), "Hutchison, Keynes, and Empiricism." *Review of Social Economy* 49, 20–36.
    (1994), "Rethinking the Keynesian Revolution." In *The State of Interpretation of Keynes*, ed. J. Davis. Dordrecht: Kluwer.
Blaug, M., ed. (1991), *John Maynard Keynes (1883–1946)*, 2 vols. Aldershot: Edward Elgar.
Braithwaite, R. (1975), "Keynes as a Philosopher." In *Essays on John Maynard Keynes*, ed. M. Keynes. Cambridge: Cambridge University Press.
Brandt, R. (1950), "The Emotive Theory of Ethics." *Philosophical Review* 59, 305–18.
Broad, C. (1934), "Is 'Goodness' a Name of a Simple Non-natural Quality?" *Proceedings of the Aristotelian Society*, pp. 249–68.
Brown-Collier, E. (1985), "Keynes' View of an Organic Economic Universe." *Review of Social Economy* 43, 14–23.
Carabelli, A. (1988), *On Keynes's Method*. London: Macmillan.
Carvalho, F. (1988), "Keynes on Probability, Uncertainty, and Decision-making." *Journal of Post Keynesian Economics* 11, 66–81.

Chick, V. (1983), *Macroeconomics After Keynes*. Cambridge, MA: MIT.

Clarke, P. (1989), *The Keynesian Revolution in the Making: 1924–1936*. Oxford: Oxford University Press.

Coates, J. (1990), "Ordinary Language Economics: Keynes and the Cambridge Philosophers." Ph.D. dissertation, Cambridge University.

Cottrell, A. (1993), "Keynes's Theory of Probability and Its Relevance to His Economics: Three Theses." *Economics and Philosophy* 9, 25–51.

Cottrell, A. and M. Lawlor (1991), "'Natural Rate' Mutations: Keynes, Leijonhufvud and the Wicksell Connection." *History of Political Economy* 23, 625–44.

Cross, R. (1982), "The Duhem–Quine Thesis, Lakatos and the Appraisal of Theories in Macroeconomics." *Economic Journal* 92, 320–40.

Davidson, P. (1978), *Money and the Real World*, 2nd edn., revised. London: Macmillan.

Davis, J. (1988), "Sraffa, Wittgenstein and Neoclassical Economics." *Cambridge Journal of Economics* 12, 29–36.

(1989), "Keynes on Atomism and Organicism." *Economic Journal* 99, 1159–72.

(1989–90), "Keynes and Organicism." *Journal of Post Keynesian Economics* 12, 308–15.

(1990), "Cooter and Rappoport on the Normative." *Economics and Philosophy* 6, 139–46.

(1991), "Keynes's Critiques of Moore: Philosophical Foundations of Keynes's Economics." *Cambridge Journal of Economics* 15, 61–77.

(1993), "Sraffa, Demand, and Interdependence." *Review of Political Economy* 5, 22–39.

(1994a), "Is Emotive Theory the Philosopher's Stone of the Ordinalist Revolution?" In *Measurement, Quantification, and the Development of Modern Economic Analysis*, ed. I. Rima. London: Routledge.

(1994b), "The Locus of Keynes's Philosophical Thinking in *The General Theory*: the Concept of Convention." In *Perspectives on the History of Economic Thought*, vol. X, ed. K. Vaughn. Aldershot: Edward Elgar.

(1995a) "Keynes's Later Philosophy." Forthcoming in *History of Policical Economy*.

(1995b), "On Interpreting Keynes's Philosophical Thinking." Forthcoming in *Research in the History of Economic Thought and Methodology*.

De Finetti, B. (1937), "Foresight: Its Logical Laws, Its Subjective Sources." In *Studies in Subjective Probability*, ed. H. Kyburg and H. Smokler. New York: Wiley, 1964.

Dillard, D. (1948), *The Economics of John Maynard Keynes*. New York: Prentice-Hall.

Dimand, R. (1988), *The Origins of the Keynesian Revolution*. Stanford: Stanford University Press.

Dow, A. and S. Dow (1985), "Animal Spirits and Rationality." In *Keynes's Economics: Methodological Issues*, ed. T. Lawson and H. Pesaran. London: Croom Helm.

Drakopoulos, S. (1991), *Values and Economic Theory*. Aldershot: Avebury.

Duhem, P. (1906), *La Théorie physique, son objet et sa structure*. Paris: Chevalier et Rivière.

Elliott, J. (1994), "The Two Perspectives of Keynes in the General Theory and After." In *Perspectives on the History of Economic Thought*, vol. X, ed. K. Vaughn. Aldershot: Edward Elgar.

Elliott, J. and B. Clark (1987), "Keynes's *General Theory* and Social Justice." *Journal of Post Keynesian Economics* 9, 381–94.

Evans, J. (1978), *Knowledge and Infallibility*. London: Macmillan.

Fitzgibbons, A. (1988), *Keynes's Vision: A New Political Economy*. Oxford: Clarendon Press.

Geach, P. (1957), *Mental Acts*. London: Routledge & Kegan Paul.

Gerrard, B. (1991), "Keynes's *General Theory*: Interpreting the Interpretations." *Economic Journal* 101, 276–87.

Gibbard, A. (1990), *Wise Choices, Apt Feelings: A Theory of Normative Judgment*. Cambridge, MA: Harvard University Press.

Gillies, D. (1988), "Keynes as a Methodologist." *British Journal for the Philosophy of Science* 39, 117–29.

(1993), *Philosophy of Science in the Twentieth Century*. Oxford: Blackwell.

Gillies, D. and G. Ieto-Gillies (1987), "Probability and Economics in the Works of Bruno De Finetti." *Economia Internazionale* 40, 3–20.

(1991), "Intersubjective probability and economics." *Review of Political Economy* 3, 393–417.

Greenwald, B. and J. Stiglitz (1993), "New and Old Keynesians." *Journal of Economic Perspectives* 7, 23–44.

Groenewegen, P. (1988), "Alfred Marshall and the Establishment of the Cambridge Economic Tripos." *History of Political Economy* 20, 627–67.

Hamouda, O. and J. Smithin, eds. (1988), *Keynes and Public Policy After Fifty Years*. Aldershot: Edward Elgar.

Harcourt, G. (1987), "Theoretical Methods and Unfinished Business." In *The Legacy of Keynes. Nobel Conference XXII*, ed. D. Reese. San Francisco: Harper and Row.

Harcourt, G. and C. Sardoni (1994), "Keynes's Vision: Method, Analysis and 'Tactics.'" In *The State of Interpretation of Keynes*, ed. J. Davis. Dordrecht: Kluwer.

Hare, R. (1981), *Moral Thinking*. Oxford: Oxford University Press.

Harrod, R. (1938), "Scope and Method of Economics." *Economic Journal* 48, 383–412.

(1947), "Keynes, the Economist." In *The New Economics: Keynes' Influence on Theory and Policy*, ed. S. Harris. New York: Alfred E. Knopf.

(1951), *The Life of John Maynard Keynes*. London: Macmillan.

Helburn, S. (1991), "Burke and Keynes." In *Keynes and Philosophy*, ed. B. Bateman and J. Davis. Aldershot: Edward Elgar.

(1992), "On Keynes's Ethics." In *Recent Developments in Post-Keynesian Economics*, ed. P. Arestis and V. Chick. Aldershot: Edward Elgar.

Hicks, J. (1939), *Value and Capital*. Oxford: Clarendon Press.

Hicks, J. and R. Allen (1934), "A Reconsideration of the Theory of Value." *Economica*, N.S., vol. 1, 52–76, 196–219.

Hudson, W. (1970), *Modern Moral Philosophy*. New York: St. Martin's, 1983.

Hume, D. (1739), *A Treatise of Human Nature*, ed. L. Selby-Bigge. Oxford: Clarendon, 1888.

Hutchison, T. (1938), *The Significance of the Basic Postulates of Economic Theory*. New York: Augustus M. Kelley, 1950.

Hylton, P. (1992), *Russell, Idealism, and the Emergence of Analytic Philosophy*. Oxford: Oxford University Press.

Janik, A. and S. Toulmin (1973), *Wittgenstein's Vienna*. New York: Simon and Schuster.

Jensen, H. (1991), "J.M. Keynes's Theory of the State as a Path to His Social Economics of Reform in *The General Theory*." *Review of Social Economy* 49, 292–316.

(1994), "Aspects of J.M. Keynes's Vision and Conceptualized Reality." In *The State of Interpretation of Keynes*, ed. J. Davis. Dordrecht: Kluwer.

Kahn, R. (1984), *The Making of Keynes' General Theory*. Cambridge: Cambridge University Press.

Keynes, J. (1904), "Ethics in Relation to Conduct." Unpublished paper, King's College, Cambridge University.

(1905a), "A Theory of Beauty." Unpublished paper, King's College, Cambridge University.

(1905b), "Miscellanea Ethica." Unpublished paper, King's College, Cambridge University.

(1906), "Egoism." Unpublished paper, King's College, Cambridge University.

(1928), Unpublished letter to F.L. Lucas, February 1928, King's College, Cambridge University.

(1971–89), *The Collected Writings of John Maynard Keynes*, vols. I–XXX. Edited by D. Moggridge for the Royal Economic Society. London: Macmillan.

Kirzner, I. (1960), *The Economic Point of View*. Kansas City: Sheed and Ward.

Klant, J. (1985), "The Slippery Transition." In *Keynes' Economics*, ed. T. Lawson and H. Pesaran. London: Croom Helm.

Kneale, W. (1949), *Probability and Induction*. Oxford: Oxford University Press.

Kregel, J. (1976), "Economic Methodology in the Face of Uncertainty." *Economic Journal* 86, 209–25.

(1985), "Budget Deficits, Stabilisation Policy and Liquidity Preference: Keynes's Post-war Policy Proposals." In *Keynes's Relevance Today*, ed. F. Vicarelli. London: Macmillan.

Kripke, S. (1982), *Wittgenstein on Rules and Private Language*. Cambridge, MA: Harvard University Press.

Lakatos, I. and A. Musgrave, eds. (1970), *Criticism and the Growth of Knowledge*. Cambridge: Cambridge University Press.

Lawlor, M. (1994). "The Own-Rates Framework as an Interpretation of the *General Theory*: A Suggestion for Complicating the Keynesian Theory of Money." In *The State of Interpretation of Keynes*, ed. J. Davis. Dordrecht: Kluwer.

Lawson, T. (1985), "Uncertainty and Economic Analysis." *Economic Journal* 95, 909–27.

(1988), "Probability and Uncertainty in Economic Analysis." *Journal of Post Keynesian Economics* 11, 38–65.

(1993), "Keynes and Convention." *Review of Social Economy*, 51, 174–200.

Levy, P. (1979), *Moore*. Oxford: Oxford University Press.

Lewis, D. (1969), *Convention: A Philosophical Study*. Cambridge, MA: Harvard University Press.

Littleboy, B. (1990). *On Interpreting Keynes: A Study in Reconciliation*. London: Routledge.

MacIntyre, A. (1984), *After Virtue, A Study in Moral Theory*. Notre Dame, IN: University of Notre Dame Press.

Mackenzie, J. (1906), "The New Realism and the Old Idealism." *Mind* 15, 308–28.

Malcolm, N. (1958), *Ludwig Wittgenstein: A Memoir*. Oxford: Oxford University Press.

Matthews, R. (1991), "Animal Spirits." In *Thoughtful Economic Man*, ed. J. Meeks. Cambridge: Cambridge University Press.

Mayo, B. (1986), *The Philosophy of Right and Wrong*. London: Routledge & Kegan Paul.

Meltzer, A. (1989), *Keynes's Monetary Thought*. Cambridge: Cambridge University Press.

Moggridge, D. (1992), *Maynard Keynes, An Economist's Biography*. London: Routledge.

Monk, R. (1990), *Wittgenstein. The Duty of Genius*. London: Cape.

Moore, G. (1903a), *Principia Ethica*. Cambridge: Cambridge University Press.

(1903b), "Refutation of Idealism." In *Philosophical Studies*. London: Routledge & Kegan Paul, 1922.

(1912), *Ethics*. New York: Holt.

(1925), "A Defence of Common Sense." In *Contemporary British Philosophy*, second series, ed. J. Muirhead. London: Allen and Unwin.

(1939), "Proof of an External World." In *Philosophical Papers*. London: Allen and Unwin, 1959.

(1942), "A Reply to My Critics." In *The Philosophy of G.E. Moore*, ed. P. Schilpp. Evanston: Northwestern University Press.

(1953), *Some Main Problems of Philosophy*. New York: Macmillan.

Neurath, O. (1921), *Anti-Spengler*. Munich: G.D.W. Callwey.

(1932–3), "Protokollsätze." *Erkenntnis* 3, 204–14.

(1959), "Protocol Sentences," trans. G. Schick. In *Logical Positivism*, ed. A. Ayer. New York: Free Press.

O'Donnell, R. (1989), *Keynes: Philosophy, Economics and Politics*. London: Macmillan.

Ogden, C. and I. Richards (1923), *The Meaning of Meaning*. London: Kegan Paul.

Orlean, A. (1989), "Mimetic Contagion and Speculative Bubbles." *Theory and Decision* 27, 63–92.

Parfit, D. (1984), *Reasons and Persons*. Oxford: Oxford University Press.

Passmore, J. (1966), *A Hundred Years of Philosophy*. Middlesex: Penguin.

(1985), *Recent Philosophers*. LaSalle, IL: Open Court.

Patinkin, D. (1990), "On Different Interpretations of the *General Theory*." *Journal of Monetary Economics* 24, 205–43.

Popper, K. (1934), *The Logic of Scientific Discovery*. New York: Basic, 1959.
  (1963), *Conjectures and Refutations*. New York: Harper & Row.
Pressman, S. (1987). "The Policy Relevance of the *General Theory*." *Journal of Economic Studies* 14, 13–23.
Prichard, H. (1929), *Duty and Interest*. Oxford: Clarendon Press.
Quine, W. (1961), *From a Logical Point of View*. Cambridge, MA: Harvard University Press.
  (1969), *Ontological Relativity and Other Essays*. New York: Columbia University Press.
Quinton, A. (1966), "The Foundations of Knowledge." In *British Analytic Philosophy*, eds. B. Williams and A. Montifiore. London: Routledge & Kegan Paul.
Ramsey, F. 1978. *Foundations of Mathematics*. London: Routledge & Kegan Paul.
Rawls, J. (1971), *A Theory of Justice*. Cambridge, MA: Harvard University Press.
Robbins, L. (1935), *An Essay on the Nature and Significance of Economic Science*, 2nd edn. London: Macmillan, 1938.
  (1938), "Interpersonal Comparisons of Utility: A Comment." *Economic Journal* 48, 635–41.
Rogers, C. (1989), *Money, Interest and Capital*. Cambridge: Cambridge University Press.
Romer, D. (1993), "The New Keynesian Synthesis." *Journal of Economic Perspectives* 7, 5–22.
Rorty, R. (1979), *Philosophy and the Mirror of Nature*. Princeton: Princeton University Press.
Ross, W. (1930), *The Right and the Good*. Oxford: Clarendon Press.
Rotheim, R. (1989–90), "Organicism and the Role of the Individual in Keynes' Thought." *Journal of Post Keynesian Economics* 12, 316–26.
Runde, J. (1990), "Keynesian Uncertainty and the Weight of Arguments." *Economics and Philosophy* 6, 275–92.
  (1991), "Keynesian Uncertainty and the Instability of Beliefs." *Review of Political Economy* 3, 125–45.
  (1994a), "Keynes after Ramsey." Forthcoming in *Studies in the History and Philosophy of Science* 25, 97–121.
  (1994b), "Keynesian Uncertainty and Liquidity Preference." Forthcoming in *Cambridge Journal of Economics* 18, 129–44.
Russell, B. (1903), *The Principles of Mathematics*. Cambridge: Cambridge University Press.
  (1910–11), "Knowledge by Acquaintance and Knowledge by Description." In *Mysticism and Logic*. London: Longmans, Green and Co., 1925.
  (1912), *The Problems of Philosophy*. New York: Henry Holt.
Russell, B. and A. Whitehead (1910), *Principia Mathematica*. Cambridge: Cambridge University Press.
Samuelson, P. (1947), *Foundations of Economic Analysis*. Cambridge, MA: Harvard University Press.
Sardoni, C. (1989–90), "Chapter 18 of the *General Theory*: its Methodological Importance." *Journal of Post Keynesian Economics* 12, 293–307.

Schelling, T. (1960), *The Strategy of Conflict*. Cambridge, MA: Harvard University Press.

Schwartz, S., ed. (1977), *Naming, Necessity, and Natural Kinds*. Ithaca: Cornell University Press.

Shackle, G. (1967), *The Years of High Theory*. Cambridge: Cambridge University Press.

(1972), *Epistemics and Economics*. Cambridge: Cambridge University Press.

Shionoya, Y. (1991), "Sidgwick, Moore and Keynes: A Philosophical Analysis of Keynes's 'My Early Beliefs'." In *Keynes and Philosophy*, ed. B. Bateman and J. Davis. Aldershot: Edward Elgar.

Sidgwick, H. (1922), *The Methods of Ethics*. London: Macmillan.

Skidelsky, R. (1983), *John Maynard Keynes*, vol. I, *Hopes Betrayed 1883–1920*. London: Macmillan.

(1989), "Keynes and the State." In *The Economic Borders of the State*, ed. D. Helm. Oxford: Oxford University Press.

(1992), *John Maynard Keynes*, vol. II, *The Economist as Saviour*. London: Macmillan.

Smith, A. (1759), *Theory of Moral Sentiments*, ed. D. Raphael and A. Macfie. Oxford: Oxford University Press, 1976.

Smithin, J. (1989), "The Composition of Government Expenditures and the Effectiveness of Fiscal Policy." In *New Directions in Post-Keynesian Economics*, ed. J. Pheby. Aldershot: Edward Elgar.

Stalnaker, R. (1968), "A Theory of Conditionals." In *Studies in Logical Theory*, ed. N. Rescher. Oxford: Blackwell.

(1987), *Enquiry*. Cambridge, MA: MIT Press.

Stevenson, C. (1937), "The Emotive Meaning of Ethical Terms." *Mind* 46, 10–31.

Strong, C. (1905), "Has Mr. Moore Refuted Idealism?" *Mind* 14, 174–89.

Tinbergen, J. (1939), *A Method and Its Application to Investment Activity*. Geneva: League of Nations.

Tobin, J. (1993), "Price Flexibility and Output Stability: An Old Keynesian View." *Journal of Economic Perspectives* 7, 45–65.

Urmson, J. (1956), *Philosophical Analysis*. Oxford: Clarendon Press.

(1968), *The Emotive Theory*. London: Hutchinson.

Waismann, F. (1965), *The Principles of Linguistic Philosophy*. London: Macmillan.

Warnock, M. (1960), *Ethics since 1900*. London: Oxford University Press.

Weitz, M. (1967), "Philosophical Analysis." In *Encyclopedia of Philosophy*, ed. P. Edwards. London: Macmillan.

Will, F. (1974), *Induction and Justification*. Ithaca, NY: Cornell University Press.

Winch, P. (1958), *The Idea of A Social Science*. London: Routledge & Kegan Paul.

Wittgenstein, L. (1921), *Tractatus Logico-Philosophicus*, trans. D. Pears and B. McGuinness. New York: Routledge & Kegan Paul, 1961.

(1953), *Philosophical Investigations*, 2nd edn., revised. Oxford: Blackwell, 1958.

(1958), *The Blue and Brown Books*. Oxford: Blackwell.

Wood, J., ed. (1983), *John Maynard Keynes, Critical Assessments*, 4 vols. London: Routledge.

Young, W. (1987), *Interpreting Mr. Keynes: The IS–LM Enigma*. London: Polity.

Index